WITHDRAWN
UTSA LIBRARIES

WITHDRAWN
UTSA LIBRARIES

CONFLICT-RELATED SEXUAL VIOLENCE

D0195190

CONFLICT-RELATED SEXUAL VIOLENCE
INTERNATIONAL LAW, LOCAL RESPONSES

EDITED BY TONIA ST. GERMAIN AND SUSAN DEWEY

Kumarian Press
An Imprint of Stylus Publishing
Sterling, Virginia

Published by Stylus Publishing, LLC
22883 Quicksilver Drive
Sterling, Virginia 20166-2102

Copyright © 2012 by Kumarian Press, an imprint of Stylus Publishing, LLC.

All rights reserved. No part of this book may be reprinted or reproduced in any form or by any electronic, mechanical or other means, now known or hereafter invented, including photocopying, recording and information storage and retrieval, without permission in writing from the publisher.

Design by Pro Production Graphic Services
Copyedit by Mary Bearden
Proofread by Beth Richards
Index by Jennifer Cheddar
The text of this book is set in 11/13 Adobe Garamond

Printed in the United States of America

∞ All first editions printed on acid-free paper that meets the American National Standards Institute Z39-48 Standard.

Library of Congress Cataloging-in-Publication Data
Conflict-related sexual violence : international law, local responses /
  Tonia St. Germain and Susan Dewey, editors.
   p. cm.
  Includes bibliographical references and index.
  ISBN 978-1-56549-503-6 (cloth : alk. paper) — ISBN 978-1-56549-504-3
  (pbk. : alk. paper) — ISBN 978-1-56549-505-0 (library networkable e-edition) —
  ISBN 978-1-56549-506-7 (consumer e-edition)
   1. Rape as a weapon of war. 2. Sex crimes. 3. Women—Violence against. 4. Women—
Crimes against. 5. Women (International law) I. St. Germain, Tonia (Tonia Prisca), 1960.
II. Dewey, Susan (Susan Catherine), 1976–
  KZ7162.C67 2012
  341.6'7—dc23
                                                                              2012002084

13-digit ISBN: 978-1-56549-503-6 (cloth)
13-digit ISBN: 978-1-56549-504-3 (paper)
13-digit ISBN: 978-1-56549-505-0 (library networkable e-edition)
13-digit ISBN: 978-1-56549-506-7 (consumer e-edition)

Bulk Purchases

Quantity discounts are available for use in workshops and for staff development.

Call 1-800-232-0223

First Edition, 2012

   10 9 8 7 6 5 4 3 2 1

**Library
University of Texas
at San Antonio**

Contents

Acknowledgments

THIS VOLUME IS THE RESULT OF THE COLLECTIVE ENERGIES AND ENTHUSIASM OF A NUMBER of committed feminist activists and scholars whose work is featured here. It has been a true honor to collaborate with individuals of such caliber, and we remain humbled by their willingness to share their work with us. Members of the editorial and production staff at Kumarian Press/Stylus Publishing poured a tremendous amount of energy and enthusiasm into the manuscript, for which we remain grateful. Editor and Associate Publisher James Lance believed in this project from its inception, and gently guided it along into production, where it was greatly assisted by Managing Production Editor Alexandra Hartnett and copyeditor Mary Bearden.

We owe Jenny Venn tremendous thanks for her vision in producing an extraordinarily evocative cover, and no lesser thanks are due to Jennifer Cheddar for her excellent work in indexing the book.

On an individual level, Susan is grateful to her wonderful colleagues in Gender & Women's Studies and International Studies at the University of Wyoming for the supportive and collegial environment they provide.

Tonia wishes to thank the Five College Women's Studies Research Center at Mount Holyoke College for supporting her research without which this project would not have originated, and Susan Dewey for sharing her passion for the work and sisterhood in the process of taking it to completion.

1

Introduction

Tonia St. Germain and *Susan Dewey*

THE IMAGES ARE HAUNTING. ONE CLOSE-UP PHOTOGRAPH FEATURES A HOLLOW-EYED young woman holding an infant swaddled in brightly colored printed cloth, staring straight through the camera as if it were not there. The photograph's caption, which could feature in any major newspaper, informs the reader that she is one of the thousands of Central African women who have been raped as part of ongoing conflict-related instability (Nylind 2006). An alternate image shows an elderly Congolese woman shielding her face from the camera, her cheeks clearly contorted in an expression of acute suffering. "Sometimes," the caption quotes Lieutenant Colonel R.D. Sharma as saying, "the women here are ashamed to tell a soldier, especially a male soldier, that they've been raped. And we don't have any female soldiers" (Kamber 2010). In another image, taken from the other side of the world almost two decades previously, two middle-aged Bosnian women avert their eyes from the camera. One is seated on a comfortable sofa, her face obscured by a tissue she is using to wipe away her tears. Behind her hangs an enormous map of her fractured country, its borders thickly outlined in black (Kratochivil 2010).

Such images have become standard fodder in most major North American and Western European newspapers in the past two decades. Whether it takes place in Rwanda, Kosovo, Afghanistan, or any number of other war zones, conflict-related sexual violence has increasingly captured international attention. Yet these are far more than what sociologist Patricia Hill Collins might call "controlling images" (2000, 69), as they constitute the only means

1

by which most North Americans and Western Europeans come to understand the pervasive and enduring nature of rape in wartime. Yet the greatest and perhaps most painful irony lies in the reality that conflict-related sexual violence is, as one of our volume's contributors notes, "nothing new."

Indeed, conflict-related sexual violence permeates human cultural consciousness even in the earliest accounts of war: in the *Odyssey*, the kidnap of Cassandra proves a pivotal moment in the sacking of Troy, while the Hindu epic *Ramayana* revolves around the rescue of the goddess Sita by her husband from behind enemy lines. The implication of rape serves as a powerful subtext in both tales, which have myriad variations throughout the world. Yet despite this centrality of sexual violence against women in war narratives, both ancient and contemporary, it is only relatively recently that states have begun to regard conflict-related sexual violence as an offense against individual women rather than the family honor of her male relatives.

The chapters in this volume follow the World Health Organization in defining *sexual violence* as "any sexual act, attempt to obtain a sexual act, unwanted sexual comments or advances, or acts to traffic, or otherwise directed, against a person's sexuality using coercion, by any person regardless of their relationship to the victim, in any setting" (WHO 2002, 149). We acknowledge the unique circumstances of conflict that combine to render consent a murky proposition at best due to widespread socioeconomic disruption. This is compounded by the fact that, as psychiatrist Ruth Seifert has noted, rape serves a function in conflict zones through its power to destroy families and communities. As "the final symbolic expression of the humiliation of the male opponent," conflict-related sexual violence features "an additional aspect of cultural destruction in the fact that the female body functions as a symbolic representation of the body politic" (Seifert 1994, 59, 63). Indeed, women's bodies and the varieties of nationalism that so frequently accompany war are inexorably tied in the perpetuation of conflict-related sexual violence.

Although a growing literature documents the use of rape as a tool of war, there is a glaring lack of accessible work on the initiatives and institutions currently tackling sexual violence as a grave issue in conflict and postconflict situations throughout the world. In order to address this gap, this book employs case studies drawn from research on global and local responses to the problem, thereby arriving at a deeper understanding of the various ways in which communities approach this issue cross-culturally. Chapters that follow employ a variety of methodological, theoretical, and disciplinary standpoints to examine three key areas of analysis: (1) rhetoric and discourses; (2) international criminal justice; and (3) conflict-related sexual violence and its aftermath. This organizational scheme was intended to make connections across disciplines and between theory and application to better explicate the varied and nuanced responses to wartime rape.

Regardless of their disciplinary orientation, all of the chapters in this volume draw on a long history of feminist interrogation that seeks to examine the social and structural elements that facilitate the pervasive and enduring nature of conflict-related sexual violence. The integral feminist practice of interdisciplinarity informs discussions throughout the book, with perspectives drawn from anthropologists, health practitioners and therapists, legal theorists, and political scientists. All are deeply embedded within decades-old debates regarding the need to incorporate feminist perspectives into international humanitarian law and initiatives designed to end conflict-related sexual violence. With this in mind, we now turn to a brief introduction to (and critique of) international efforts to address this global problem.

Perspectives on Violence Against Women: From the Geneva Conventions to Contemporary International Humanitarian Law

A number of post–World War II international gatherings and initiatives formed the basis for what is now known as international humanitarian law, the body of law that seeks to reduce and redress the human suffering caused by armed conflict. International humanitarian law governs relations between states in times of war and protects individuals from enemy powers and is thus distinguished from human rights law, which applies principally in times of peace as a way to protect individuals from their own governments. International humanitarian law also safeguards persons who are not (or who are no longer) participating in hostilities and restricts the means and methods of warfare. Violations of human rights law result principally in state responsibility, while violations of humanitarian law could lead not only to state responsibility and armed reprisals, but also to individual criminal liability for perpetrators.

Irrespective of the conflicts that preceded it, the sheer scale of destruction wrought by World War II was truly instrumental in the expansion of humanitarian law and the international organizations charged with developing it. Contemporary understandings of international humanitarian law were shaped by both the Nuremburg War Crimes Tribunal and the Tokyo Tribunal, both of which addressed, albeit obliquely, the issue of conflict-related sexual violence, including the use of comfort women (Soh 2009) and the mass rape of Chinese women by Japanese troops at Nanking (Yoshida 2009). The Nuremberg War Crimes Tribunal did not prosecute rape, although testimony about sexual violence was presented (Askin 1997, 31). These historical events paved the way for the International Criminal Tribunal for Rwanda (ICTR) and the International Criminal Tribunal for the former Yugoslavia (ICTY), the latter of which was the first to successfully prosecute rape as a war crime.

The United Nations Universal Declaration of Human Rights (1948), another post–World War II development, was a critical step toward what we now know as international humanitarian law. Although it does not specifically address gender, this important document laid the foundation for future, more gender-sensitive initiatives. The fourth Geneva convention, which dealt with the treatment of civilians in wartime, was particularly path breaking in that it specifically notes that "women shall be especially protected against any attack on their honor, in particular against rape, enforced prostitution, or any form of indecent assault" (Geneva Convention 1949, Art. 27). In 1979, the United Nations General Assembly adopted the Convention on the Elimination of All Forms of Discrimination against Women (CEDAW), which stated a clear commitment to fight what became known as "gender-based violence," defined as any act or threat that targets an individual or group upon the basis of their gender (United Nations 1979). These critical initiatives laid the foundation for the subsequent "women's rights are human rights" movement that emerged in the wake of the 1994 International Conference on Population and Development in Cairo and the 1995 Fourth World Women's Conference in Beijing, which, in turn, drew on decades of feminist organizing.

With this focus on women's rights as human rights, these international gatherings at Cairo and Beijing condemned all forms of violence against women, including those rooted in religion and custom, and upheld sexual self-determination, particularly in the form of reproductive rights. In recent years, the experience of women both during and after conflict has been increasingly incorporated into the political agenda of international law and national governments. A number of patterns have developed that reflect this "add women" approach, such as a dramatic increase in the number of adult female soldiers (Stiehm 1996; Weinstein and White 1997; Ziegler and Gunderson 2005) and gender-mainstreaming efforts at incorporating women into the postconflict peace-building process (Cockburn 2007; Mazurana, Raven-Roberts, and Parpart 2005; Meintjes, Turshen, and Pillay 2002).

As the feminist campaign against conflict-related sexual violence grew, a powerful narrative describing women as victims in need of protection became integrated into state and international organizations, most notably in the form of UN Security Council Resolution 1325, which urges women's increased participation in peace and security efforts (United Nations Security Council 2000), and Resolution 1820, which makes specific reference to the need to protect women from sexual violence in conflict (United Nations 2008).

Despite such progress, the vast majority of international law and policy initiatives designed to address conflict-related sexual violence stem from the Western rape law reform movement of the late twentieth century (Halley 2008). Feminists of that era largely accepted the frame presented by liberal legal concepts of rights and liberties and called for criminal punishment as the ultimate solution to sexual violence. This approach remains deeply entrenched in the "end the culture of impunity" paradigm that drives UN policy and international criminal law (Del Ponti and Sudetic 2009). Prosecution-led initiatives continue to dominate international solutions to conflict-related sexual violence, resulting in an agenda that amounts to large-scale expansion of legal institutions such as the International Criminal Court (ICC), rather than solutions based on local understandings of the problem that focus holistically on counteracting other forms of domination in women's private and public lives.

The US rape law reform movement transformed legal procedures and substantive law designed to address sexual violence and then expanded the agenda into the international arena. The potentialities and limitations of this 40-year campaign are just now beginning to be analyzed in terms of the advancement of the interests of women. Feminist activist movements to aid victim-survivors of domestic violence in the United States resulted in the creation of shelters and counselor-advocates, who worked to help victim-survivors navigate the criminal justice system and the sometimes complex world of public assistance (Rothenberg 2003; Schmitt and Yancey Martin 1999). The passage of the 1994 Violence Against Women Act (VAWA), the first federal law to devote significant legal and monetary resources to the problem in the United States, transformed this activist movement into a bureaucratic marriage between federal and state funding and shelters for victim-survivors. This professionalization of social services and increased government involvement in and regulation of what was formerly an exclusively activist domain was deemed problematic by some who felt that the state did not necessarily incorporate feminist ideologies or goals (Wies 2006).

The situation was even more complex from a legal perspective. Critics of domestic violence and sexual assault service providers began to argue that women of color remained underserved by such organizations and reluctant to report abusive partners out of fear that they would experience police brutality (Richie 2000; West 2002). Yet regardless of race or ethnicity, the prosecutorial agenda was often relentless as part of a belief that convictions were the best way to address sexual violence. Sex crimes' prosecutors maintained very clear state policing functions, which caused somewhat of a conflict with service providers, many of whom were still reeling from the post-VAWA transition.

The evolution that occurred within the service provider sector during this period is also mirrored within the international aid organizations working to help victim-survivors of conflict-related sexual violence. Not surprisingly, several chapters in this volume explore the development of similar points of disjuncture in international efforts to address the problem. This is partly because feminist activists, scholars, and legal practitioners, which includes investigators, prosecutors, and jurists, actively participated in the development of the law and policy that resulted in the ICC's Rome Statute, which declared rape, sexual slavery, and forced forms of prostitution, pregnancy, and sterilization as crimes against humanity (Rome Statute 1998). In fact, many legal practitioners were selected to serve in the ICTR and ICTY because they had been part of the legal rape reform movement in the United States and Western Europe that valued using criminal law as the primary vehicle to address sexualized violence. It was through these practitioners that such solutions were exported to the ICC (Halley 2008).

Such North American and Western European solutions are now securely in place throughout the case law, procedural law, and the administrative structures that surround the treatment of victim-witnesses in cases of conflict-related sexual violence. These have now become "best practices" that are used to train prosecutors, judges, UN peacekeepers, and aid workers. Interestingly, North American and Western European feminist perceptions regarding the efficacy of criminalizing sexual violence via prosecution have shifted into a lively debate (Bumiller 2008). This is due to the fact that efforts that adopt prevailing views of criminality and victimhood have produced mixed results yet remain popular among legal practitioners and the general public.

Since the 1970s, feminist scholarship has clearly acknowledged how the criminal justice system can conduct a "second rape" of the victim-witness, thus resulting in retraumatization. Yet international criminal lawyers involved in prosecuting sexual violence during conflict have some very powerful perceptions of the law's boundaries in using them to achieve their ultimate goal: the conviction. From this perspective, the victim-witness is little more than a means to an end. Victim-witnesses may share the same faith in prosecution as the best possible solution, but more often than not, they must be groomed for months (or even years) to take the stand and provide testimony, often in cases that have been specifically selected for their ability to produce a conviction. Lead ICTY and ICTR prosecutor Carla del Ponte summarized this view quite concisely in noting, "victims feel we are picking and choosing perpetrators" (quoted in Purvis 2006). In the legal framework, the prosecution has jurisdiction over the crime and must often violate boundaries and disregard the agency of the victim-witness to achieve what the North American and Western European legal systems regard as "justice."

Accordingly, some feminist scholars have long challenged this pro-prosecution approach by arguing that these legal practices have failed with respect to rape in the United States. Political theorist Hannah Arendt (1970), for instance, believed that the protection of human rights could never come through formal legal means or institutional structures. Legal scholar Aya Gruber cautions us to carefully consider "any purported benefits of reform against the considerable philosophical and practical costs of criminalization strategies before considering making further investments of time, resources, and intellect in rape reform" (2009, 581). Feminist lawyer Catherine MacKinnon has characterized this problem as a situation in which "the liberal state coercively and authoritatively constitutes the social order in the interest of men as a gender" (1983, 635). MacKinnon has more recently noted that "criminal law treats violence against women unequally, with no constitutional controls" (2006, 33).

Critical race theorist Angela Davis has further recognized a tension between the basic tenets of feminism, democracy, and the philosophy that animates the US penal state (2005, 39). Although "ending the culture of impunity" by prosecuting conflict-related sexual violence is seen as a panacea by political leaders and their legal operatives, it has been challenged from the start by some of the most influential feminist theorists. The purported cultural and utilitarian benefits arising from criminalization are even more destructive in the international criminal prosecution arena when cultural beliefs about gender, sexuality, and violence are quite different from predominant North American and Western European social norms. This is particularly problematic in cases where sexual violence is not interpersonal but systemic and widespread among the civilian population.

Exporting flawed solutions from North American and Western European criminal justice systems that reflect a white supremacist patriarchy is even less likely to produce social justice in the cultures where they are imposed. This fact raises serious ethical and human rights concerns for scholars who study conflict-related sexual violence, a great deal of which takes place in communities outside the ideological purview of such powerful groups. Feminist scholars (Helms 2003; Puri 2008) have recently begun to document how such macrodiscourses are increasingly used by populations outside these geographic regions in ways that illuminate gendered points of tension in local communities. Anthropologist Sally Engle Merry (2006), for instance, argues that despite advances in international humanitarian law and the United Nations's best efforts, violence against women continues to be perpetrated throughout the world in the gap between legal principles and local practices.

There are many similarities between what happened in the US rape law reform movement of the 1980s and 1990s and the contemporary international response to conflict-related sexual violence. Political scientist Kristin Bumiller has sharply critiqued the liberal rape law reform movement of that period for its lack of feminist sensitivity, noting that programs and initiatives designed to address sexual violence "are implemented according to gender-neutral standards, both formally and in terms of the state's interest in the problem" (2008, 12). Put another way, even if rape law reform is good in theory, it fails in practice because its practitioners reify gender neutrality in ways that do not reflect reality. As we will see repeatedly throughout this volume, this approach can have dire consequences for survivors of conflict-related sexual violence and their families throughout the world. It remains to be seen, however, what the enduring impact of the internationalization of these policies will have on victim-survivors of conflict-related sexual violence.

Yet this volume's contributors remain hopeful that feminist legal analyses will continue to generate change by deriving "theoretical force from immediate experience of the role of the legal system in creating and perpetuating the unequal position of women" (Charlesworth, Chinkin, and Wright 1991, 613). Indeed, feminist principles of inclusivity encourage the problematization and questioning of categories (Nussbaum 2000; Ortega 2006) in ways that can help suggest new tools for examining exclusionary categories that can prove counterproductive in both legal and policy contexts. Each chapter addresses this dilemma while simultaneously underscoring the means by which feminist analysis provides an invaluable toolkit to help ascertain how law and public policy might better serve vulnerable populations.

There is clearly room for improvement in integrating feminist perspectives and practices into international responses to conflict-related sexual violence. As Bumiller notes, "human rights strategies should seek to empower women through forms of political action that support victims' individual sovereignty, rather than reliance on state powers of surveillance and pun-ishment" (2008, 135). Many contributors to this volume argue that inter-national legal systems need to be reconceived from the Western dogmatic monologue model into one of mutually respectful, cross-cultural dialogue. Accordingly, this volume forges new ground in its diverse contributors' suggestions for tailoring international humanitarian law and human rights standards to account for the particulars of each individual country, ethnic group, or regional situation.

Summary of Key Themes and Structure of the Book

Part One, "Rhetoric and Discourses," contains two chapters that tackle the complex disjuncture between international law and its practice. Chapter 2 features a comparative analysis by Bronwyn Winter focusing on profes-sional discourses that surround conflict-related sexual violence. It discusses the dilemma inherent in the framing language that developed from a lib-eral tradition meant to exclude women, and how the use of these terms today exposes a problematic alliance between feminist campaigns to stop sexual violence and the neoliberal state. Further it elucidates how employ-ing a transnational feminist frame could transform discussions of conflict and postconflict sexual violence to reveal (not conceal) the complex issues that confront feminist practitioners and scholars.

Chapter 3, by researcher Laura Sparling, explores the linkages between the international humanitarian rhetoric of protection and the violent tar-geting of women and girls in war. It argues that the exclusion of women from high-ranking military roles and the protective nature of international law, including the Geneva Conventions and Security Council Resolutions 1325 and 1820, effectively reduce the scope of female participation in war to that of second-class citizen or passive victim. She draws on the stereotypes regarding female weakness that undermine women's ability to self-protect and even encourage the targeting of women in conflict. The rape narrative has had far-reaching and often unforeseen effects that have allowed for the exercise of coercive administrative power over both men as perpetrators and the female victim-survivors.

All four of the chapters in Part Two, "International Criminal Justice," clearly emphasize the masculine nature of international initiatives to end conflict-related sexual violence. The authors point to a broken system that is fundamentally unable to recognize that the root of the problem lies in the system of international humanitarian law itself, which effectively renders perpetrators invisible by focusing on the protection of potential victim-survivors. As a consequence, the root of the true problem of women's oppression remains thoroughly obscured. Chapter 4, by lawyer Avory Faucette, accordingly argues that what is truly needed is more attention to victim-survivors' experiences rather than increased amounts of what she terms "the law on paper." Faucette argues that while the ICTR, the ICTY, and the ICC have made massive strides in addressing conflict-related sexual violence, the limited scope of indictments and convictions, conflicts of interest in working with witnesses and investigating rape in wartime, and a lack of culturally appropriate interventions present significant challenges.

Chapter 5, by international human rights lawyer Kiran Grewal, contends that the United Nations Special Court for Sierra Leone has done little to facilitate the development of a new gender paradigm in postconflict Sierra Leone. Rather, through the selective prosecution of crimes of sexual and gender-based violence, the implementation of insufficient gender competency measures, and the adoption of conservative legal definitions, the Special Court has reinforced existing gender norms. Echoing Faucette, Grewal notes that rather than additional prosecutions, what is desperately needed is more "critical reflection on what is being prosecuted and why."

International relations scholar Peace A. Medie provides a complement to Faucette's and Grewal's arguments in chapter 6, which first illustrates the postconflict Liberian and Sierra Leonean governments' efforts to reduce sexual violence in these tense zones. These include increasing the numbers of female police officers, implementing programs aimed at educating women on their rights, strengthening the justice system, and reforming existing domestic violence laws. Despite such initiatives, Medie reports that rates of violence against women remain high, and rape is the most commonly reported crime in Liberia. Drawing on interviews with Liberian women's groups and institutional reports from both countries, this chapter details the challenges such reforms face and offers suggestions for more efficiently addressing the problem in the face of very limited resources and weak institutions.

Chapter 7 draws on law professor Benedetta Faedi Duramy's research in Haiti, where sexual violence perpetrated by rival armed groups is both widespread and vastly underreported. Faedi Duramy explores the reasons why rape victim-survivors sought justice so infrequently and, in the very few cases in which rape was prosecuted, with so little success. This chapter explores the inadequacies of the Haitian security and judicial systems as well as their impact on the victim-survivor's decision-making process in help seeking and resistance.

The three chapters in Part Three, "Conflict-Related Sexual Violence and Its Aftermath," focus on the complex roles men play in conflict-related sexual violence. Chapter 8, by researcher and activist Carol Mann, illustrates the disjuncture between constitutional rights enjoyed by all women in Afghanistan and the demands of Sunni Islamic law and tribal practice. This chapter documents how, despite the US-backed Karzai government's attempt to advance human rights for women, everyday life for women has worsened in almost every respect. In Afghanistan, the sole definition of sexual violence involves a sexual act that takes place without the consent of the woman's male kin, even if she has consented to the act, thus positioning the woman's male relatives as the real "victims" of the act. It directly challenges the Western victim narrative (the innocent female victim) that dominates international criminal law discourses surrounding sexual violence precisely because of the cultural and social disconnect between liberal human rights discourse and Islamic legal/religious ideologies. Chapter 9, by mental health nurse Evalina van Wijk, documents the painful psychological journey of South African men whose intimate partners have been raped. Unique in this volume due to its focus on men, van Wijk situates sexual assault within the context of its impact on families and communities in Cape Town, a city forever scarred by apartheid's violent legacy. For these men, their partner's rape developed into the defining moment that symbolized their lives in terms of past, present, and future. This chapter is particularly striking in its focus on how sexual violence is an act that deliberately tears, sometimes irrevocably, the social fabric of families and communities.

Chapter 10, by anthropologist José Miguel Nieto Olivar and physician Carlos Iván Pacheco Sánchez, employs ethnographic findings from their joint research on the devastating socioeconomic impacts paramilitary groups have had on women's everyday lives in Colombia. This chapter analyzes what the authors term the "paramilitary development model," whereby guerrilla groups become pivotal actors in civilian lives. Nieto Olivar and Pacheco Sánchez skillfully unfold the story of Lady, an impoverished teenage mother who, like many of her compatriots in this violence-plagued region, engages in survival sex with paramilitary soldiers. Analysis that follows demonstrates the entrenched nature of sexual aggression in an environment of constant violence, poverty, and instability, thereby unpacking the otherwise muted connections between cultural constructions of masculinity and militarism.

Our ultimate goal is that these chapters, drawn from worlds of scholarly research and everyday practice, will help others to see the photographs of hopelessness that regularly appear on the covers of newspapers throughout North America and Western Europe in a more diverse and multifaceted light. Through the analyses presented in this volume, we hope that the haunted faces and hollow eyes of women in these photographs, whether they be Congolese or Bosnian, Colombian or Somali, will reveal not just the world of violence and lack that structures their existence, but the desperate need for the incorporation of transnational feminist practices into international humanitarian law.

Part One

Rhetoric and Discourses

2

International Versus Transnational?

The Politics of Prefixes in Feminist International Relations

Bronwyn Winter

IN CONSIDERING INTERNATIONAL EFFORTS TO ADDRESS SEXUAL VIOLENCE DURING AND AFTER armed conflict, one almost immediately thinks of third-millennium land-mark developments in international law and international criminal law, whether "hard" (conventions, treaties, or tribunal rulings) or "soft" (decla-rations and resolutions). The first of these, adopted just before the end of the millennium in October 2000, is UN Security Council Resolution 1325 urging member states "to ensure increased representation of women at all de-cision-making levels in national, regional, and international institutions and mechanisms for the prevention, management, and resolution of conflict" (UN 2000, Art. 1). The second is the International Criminal Tribunal for the former Yugoslavia in The Hague, which in February 2001 found three members of the Serbian military guilty of mass rape, torture, and enslave-ment of Bosnian women during the 1992–1995 war. This ruling established mass rape and sexual enslavement during war as crimes against humanity for the first time in world history. The third is the Rome Statute of the In-ternational Criminal Court (ICC), signed in 1998 and in force since July 1, 2002, setting up a permanent international tribunal to try crimes of geno-cide and other serious crimes against humanity; it contains, among other things, important provisions concerning the participatory rights of victims (Cohen 2009). The fourth and most recent at the time of this writing is UN Security Council Resolution 1820 (2008), which formally establishes rape as a war crime, albeit in rather temperate language. Its Article 4 "*notes* that rape and other forms of sexual violence *can* constitute a war crime, a crime

I am indebted, in preparing this chapter, to the research assistance and valuable insights of Shirlita Espinosa.

against humanity, or a constitutive act with respect to genocide" (emphasis added). The article also

> *stresses the need for* the exclusion of sexual violence crimes from amnesty provisions in the context of conflict resolution processes, and *calls upon* Member States to comply with their obligations for prosecuting persons responsible for such acts, to ensure that all victims of sexual violence, particularly women and girls, have equal protection under the law and equal access to justice, and *stresses* the importance of ending impunity for such acts as part of a comprehensive approach to seeking sustainable peace, justice, truth, and national reconciliation. (Emphasis added)

On the face of it, these are laudable developments. They appear to constitute a feminist victory in making international institutions take notice of violence against women and its particular expressions during conflict situations, similarly taking notice of women's voices in peace building and conflict prevention.

Yet they are not without their problems. First, most international provisions remain enforceable due to the preeminence of national sovereignty in international law, which means that national inaction, and indeed national actions that undermine the impact of international provisions, are not easy to sanction. Second, institutions set up under these provisions are not always effective: they often disempower victims within war tribunals in ways that are sometimes reminiscent of peacetime rape trials at the national level. Third, they create a conceptual and practical separation between wartime victims and those of "ordinary" sexual violence during peacetime. Fourth, they do not directly address sexual violence by the very UN peacekeeping forces and interim administrative structures that are supposed to be protecting women. Fifth, the very civil society feminist organizations that lobbied for these laws and structures to be adopted often find themselves, paradoxically, marginalized by or coopted within them.

My intent in this chapter is less to canvass these issues in detail via case studies than to discuss what they reveal about dilemmas of framing (and disciplinarity) in feminist international relations and transnational feminist politics and scholarship. What does a focus on the *inter*national and the institutional reveal or hide in discussions of conflict and postconflict sexual violence? How does it help or hinder us? How would a consideration of conceptual and political distinctions between the *inter*national and the *trans*national—as well as of their links and overlaps—assist us in teasing out the complex issues briefly outlined? And what of the global? Does it have any place in such conversations? This chapter, then, will reexamine these terms with a view toward helping our feminist thinking about what is becoming, to use a painfully apt metaphor, a political and strategic minefield for feminists investigating issues of sexual violence in conflict and postconflict contexts.

I will first briefly discuss the differences between the national, the transnational, the international, and the global. I will follow this with a little background on the appearance of the term *transnational,* followed by feminists' discussion on the term's implications for feminist analysis and action. Finally, I will suggest some ways in which understanding the parameters and politics of the international and transnational might help us sort out some of the previously mentioned third-millennium dilemmas.

The Implications of Etymology

The prefix *trans-* means "beyond," as opposed to *inter-,* which means "between." *Global* means both "pertaining to the whole world" (from the association of *globe* or sphere with the world) and, by extension, "all-encompassing." These distinctions have some epistemological and political implications, which I describe in the following section. Like all discussions, mine will not say it all, and it will not account for all those blurrings and contradictions with which we are invariably faced. But in order not to descend into an incomprehensibility reminiscent of what Marilyn Frye (1990) has called the "relativistic apolitical bog" of postmodernism at its worst, we need a framework. We can argue about the criteria for its construction, debate its parameters, or obsess about its inclusiveness—and we surely will. We can explore its paradoxes, contradictions, and questions left unanswered— and I intend to, at least in part. But for debate to be meaningful, we need some common understanding of the framework within which that debate is being carried on. So, I will start with a brief point-form comparison of the terms *national, international, global,* and *transnational,* with reference to actors, space and sovereignty, relationships between entities, degrees of equality and reciprocity, and how relationships are regulated.

National: Within Borders

- The actors are citizens, presumed to be rallied around a common identity or common will to coexist according to agreed principles (Anderson 1983).
- Citizens are presumed to occupy the same space, understand its borders, and subscribe to the national entity as sovereign.

- The relationship is one of subject to a sovereign entity and fellow to cocitizens and is directly or tacitly mediated by the institutions of the state.
- Full citizenship is presumed to guarantee equality of status, rights, and obligations; reciprocity is between the state and the citizen.
- Exchanges among citizens are constitutionally, legally, and politically regulated.

International: Between Nations

- The actors are states or identified with them, presumed to be discrete, incommensurable, clearly demarcated, and internally homogenous.
- The nation-states are presumed to occupy different spaces and borders, and sovereignty remains intact.
- Their relationship is one of exchange and is direct or overtly mediated by the states.
- Actors are presumed to be equal in status, and reciprocity is implied.
- Exchanges are legally and politically regulated.

Global: Around the World

- The actors are multiple, networked, and not clearly distinguished, and incommensurability otherwise becomes irrelevant.
- Space becomes largely irrelevant; borders and sovereignty are either inoperable or serve the network.
- The relationship is one of homogenization, usually indirectly.
- Reciprocity and equity are irrelevant.
- The context is largely unregulated.

Transnational: Beyond Nations

- The actors are not nation-states, are not always clearly demarcated or internally homogenous, nor seamlessly networked; incommensurability is not assumed.
- Space remains relevant but borders become blurred, and sovereignty may be undermined or challenged.
- The relationship is one of movement and is often indirect and unstable.
- Inequities are acknowledged; exchange and reciprocity may or may not exist.

- The context is multilayered, and formal regulation is only one component.

There is an encyclopedic literature on the idea of the nation, and I will not revisit that literature here. Suffice it to say that much of it refers to a modern world structured by the idea of the nation as a fundamental political, economic, and sociocultural organizing principle. The emergence of the nation-state is typically associated with the Peace of Westphalia in 1648, which ended two major European wars and encoded, for the first time, the idea of national sovereignty. Along with subsequently developed ideologies of nationalism in the nineteenth century, the nation-state has profoundly informed not only the laws that regulate women's lives but also our understandings of what it means to be human and to be free. Without a nation one has neither location, identity, nor community; without a state one has neither location, identity, nor mobility. National sovereignty has been at the heart of anticolonial struggles; it is at the heart of many feminist peace and antiglobalization struggles. It is at the heart of what oppresses and what protects. National sovereignty and nationalism are also at the heart of the conflicts that are the subject of this book.

Nations have always been a problem for women. They are a problem, first and foremost, because the citizen is a public being. This being has, historically, been presumed to be an adult male (and usually of a particular ethnic group as well); in a few cases, that is still formally so (Saudi women, for example, do not have the right to vote). Whatever belongs to a man's household, his private domain, is not the province of the laws of the nation: it is the fiefdom of the individual citizen. Feminists politicized this introduction of the public–private divide in the post-Enlightenment modern nation-state as a tool to ensure the preservation of male supremacy in supposedly egalitarian democracies (Pateman 1988). Yet the public is the terrain on which we fight the battles of the private (Winter 2012). The private is the terrain we claim for our right to love whom we wish, have children or not as we wish, and so on. This public–private distinction also informs current understandings of sexual violence as a weapon of war in international politics and criminal law. It is a *public* crime perpetrated by warring groups of strangers that has come to be regarded as distinct from the *private* crime perpetrated in peacetime by individuals who are more often than not known to the victim. The former is associated with crimes by *states* or communities with claims to statehood, the latter with crimes by civil society actors. And so too, the state has always been a problem for women.

Little wonder, then, that the *inter*national has not resolved the dilemma of the national, but simply rendered it more complex. To be participants in the international conversation, women first have to be part of the national one. The women who joined forces in The Hague in 1915 to found the Women's International League for Peace and Freedom knew this. The women in nongovernmental organizations (NGOs) who try to negotiate the labyrinthine institutions and politics of the United Nations know this. The main conversations still happen between nation-states. Even if women get to play bit parts on occasion, the main act is still played out between the sovereign masculinist nation-states, in a relationship of presumed equality, clarity, simplicity, and reciprocity. Moreover, the realities and complexities of women's lives do not fit easily within the boundaries of international law, which, like national law, still conceptualizes the human as male and thus establishes categories based on male experience (Charlesworth and Chinkin 2000, 17).

Yet the international, through its institutions and laws, is where feminist attention has been largely directed to address the types of problems that are the subject of this book. This is not as senselessly foolhardy a measure as my previous comments might lead one to think, but a strategic and self-interested one. The international has come to be the public domain in which the nation's right to its own national privacy is restricted. Even if the principle of national sovereignty continues to underpin international law, the latter, notably with the post–World War II advent of human rights treaties and the legal regime based on them, has become the public watchdog. International institutions represent the community of nations to which the nation becomes accountable, if not always legally, then morally. As such, they become the mediator, and increasingly, police force and judge, to which those whose welfare is not ensured within the nation have recourse. Unfortunately, the law, the police, and the judiciary are no less problematic for women internationally than they are nationally.

The global realm does not, of course, solve these problems, but rather evacuates them. It does so because it sidesteps the public sphere, to which women have, paradoxically, had recourse to try to change the concepts, structures, and rules that determine what being human and being free mean. Although it is demonstrably true that, far from being powerless in the face of globalization, governments have actively regulated in favor of it, it is also demonstrably true that globalization, because of the diversification of actors within a network, is, like some sort of invisible yet omnipresent alien, devilishly hard to combat. Of the many networks that constitute systems of oppression (Frye 1983), capitalist globalization is surely one of the most complex. Even oppositional framings of the global do not always help. The idea of global sisterhood, popularized in particular by Robin Morgan's anthology *Sisterhood Is Global* (1984), inspiring as it is, has also been criticized as doing within feminism what globalization has done within capitalism: fading the particular into the general, homogenizing the discrete and diverse, and masking hegemony behind a veneer of participation.

The idea of the transnational is of a qualitatively different order to both the international and the global. Taking us beyond the national, as the prefix implies, it introduces complexity, destabilizes certainty and fixity, and ruffles the neatness of edges implied in the concept of the international. At the same time, it does not share the "all-encompassing" homogenizing—and disappearance of clearly identifiable actors—that is suggested by the global. But in liberating us from these inadequacies, does the transnational simply cast us adrift in conceptual limbo, not really any closer to new understandings or methods for grappling with our third-millennium dilemmas?

Many different claims have been made as to the meaning and origin of the term transnational, which has served as much to increase ambiguity as to provide clarification (Guarnizo and Smith 1998; Vertovec 1999). The first uses of the term have been in relation to the "melting-pot" immigrant culture of the United States (Bourne 1916) and international law (Prélot circa 1920 then 1961, cited in Huss 1962; Jessup 1956). Aided by post–World War II and postcolonial developments in the global economy, legal systems and movements of people, capital, and ideas, the transnational quickly developed into what are today some of its better known connotations, whether we are speaking of corporations (Keohane and Nye 1972), migrations (Tyrrell 2007), or civil society networks (Iriye 2002; Kaldor 2003). The term is now variously understood "as a social morphology, as a type of consciousness, as a mode of cultural reproduction, as an avenue of capital, as a site of political engagement, and as a reconstruction of 'place' or locality" (Vertovec 1999, 447).

What emerges from this extremely brief overview is that the transnational is at once distinct from the national, international, and global and inextricably related to them. Clearly, before one can go between or beyond nations, one has to live in a world articulated around them; before one can posit a form of civil society activity beyond national borders that is distinct from institutional activity, that *inter*national institutional activity must exist; before one can discuss a reconceptualization of globalization-enabled "migrations" in the world that are at once physical and symbolic, concrete, and ideational, globalization must exist. As concerns the topic of this book, then, "transnational communities" of women, however conceptualized, operate within both the possibilities and the constraints provided by national and international laws, economies, and politics and are subject to the pressures and configurations of globalization.

Transnational Feminist Understandings
of an Internationalized World

The first articulation of the term *transnational feminism* appears to be by Gayatri Spivak in 1993, although the idea of global feminism or "global sisterhood" dates back to the 1980s. For Spivak, the principal contribution of transnational feminism was to "complicate" socioeconomic theories and political philosophies with the introduction of "cultural material" (cited in Kaplan and Grewal 1994, 430). It was, however, Caren Kaplan and Inderpal Grewal who then proceeded to elaborate a "theory of transnational feminist practices" (Kaplan and Grewal 1994, 430). Using Spivak's comment as a starting point and positioning themselves within poststructuralist cultural studies rather than sociology, political science, or feminist international law, they argued that transnational feminism was a way to problematize the divides between Marxism, poststructuralism, and feminism as well as the political and historical fixities of the national (Grewal and Kaplan 1994, 1999, 2000).

The exact nature of demarcations between the global, international, and transnational—and their practical implications—nonetheless continues to be a matter for feminist debate. In an interdisciplinary roundtable on the topic held at the University of California, Los Angeles in 2005, historian Leila Rupp and political scientist Spike Peterson stressed that the disciplines in which they were trained are largely configured around the nation-state and relations between them and rarely move outside the northern transatlantic (US-EU) axis in doing so (see DuBois et al. 2005). I would add that when they do move outside this axis, they focus either on sites configured as military, political, or economic power centers (such as the Soviet bloc, China, or Japan), constructed as threatening yet equal (sort of) in the international relations game; or on locations of crisis, locations *defined by* crisis, threatening yet definitely *not* equal (such as Afghanistan post-2001, Haiti after various coups or the 2010 earthquake, Bosnia-Herzegovina in 1992–1995, Rwanda in 1994, Israel/Palestine just about any time since 1947–1948, but particularly since the six-day war of 1967, and so on). "Crisis" as a defining concept is important to the discussion in this book. As one of its contributors, Kiran Grewal, has pointed out, conflict sites, especially when constructed conceptually in "ethnic" terms, become constructed as *inherently* conflictual, through some ethnic attribute of warring groups.[1] International intervention, which is largely driven by the previously mentioned US-EU axis, then becomes a rescue operation, not simply to save ethnically essentialized women victims from ethnically essentialized violent men (be they brown or otherwise—with another nod to Spivak [1988][2]), but to save *all* those involved *from themselves*. Women's experience of so many conflict situations is complicated by this framing of ethnicity, by the construction of some ethnic groups as inherently more violent or racist or woman-hating, and the women as thus inherently more hegemonic or alternatively inherently more victimized, depending on which group they come from.

This even applies outside conflict zones. "What is a white woman anyway?" asked Catharine MacKinnon (1996). What is a "Western" woman? Are northern and western Europeans whiter than southern and eastern Europeans? What if you are Jewish? Or live in Northern Ireland—a rare Western "conflict or postconflict zone"? Moreover, the connotations of ethnonational labeling will shift according to which country, or which part of that country, one is in, and at which moment. Consider, for example, the multiple understandings of the label "Chinese," which are shaped by history, geopolitics, and ethnolinguistic diversity.

Ethnonational naming is a political exercise, nowhere more so than in "conflict and postconflict zones." This observation is all the more crucial to our discussion in that *feminization* itself, of any issue, will almost systematically mean one of two outcomes (and often, perversely, both together). The first is that the issue itself is downgraded as less important or urgent, as we have seen time and again when women's issues are removed from international and national institutional agendas or deprioritized in an exercise of anticolonial political blackmail:

> During wars of liberation women are not to protest about women's rights. Nor are they allowed to before and after. It is never the right moment. Defending women's rights "now"—this now being any historical moment—is always a betrayal of the people, the nation, the revolution, religion, national identity, cultural roots. . . . We are caught between two legitimacies: belonging to our people and identifying with other oppressed women. (Hélie-Lucas 1990, 108)

This is as true today for Palestinian or East Timorese or Ouigir women as it has been—and continues to be—for the Algerian women of whom Hélie-Lucas was writing. Women are still required to choose between the interests of "the people" (men) and themselves (apparently *not* "the people"). Which returns us to the question asked by Spike Peterson and Laura Parisi in the title of their 1998 article: "Are women human? It's not an academic question" (Peterson and Parisi 1998; see also MacKinnon 2006). Clearly, this question still needs to be asked, even in our times of UN Resolutions 1325 and 1820.

The other outcome is that the women's issue makes it onto the agenda, but only symbolically: women's rights or welfare or safety is used in a flag-waving or muscle-flexing exercise between men, but women's *voices* are rarely heard and their participation is carefully controlled, if allowed at all. We have seen this happen many times: during colonial and anticolonial battles for power; during the 1990s Bosnian crisis, among others; but perhaps most cynically, at the time of George W. Bush's war on Afghanistan (Eisenstein 2007; Hawthorne and Winter 2002; Winter 2006). Not only do "women's rights" become a manipulable symbol put to the service of various hegemonic or nationalist interests, but the targeting of women *as women* in conflict or postconflict situations disappears within masculinist conversations about ethnic conflict, terrorism, or just or unjust wars. Women are perceived to be collateral damage, or instrumentalized *in the service of,* but never as targeted simply because they are women, and as such *not* human in masculinist terms. Much has been written about the racial dehumanization process informing the logic of torture, in which the objects of torture become just that: objects, not subjects; things, not people. This insight, however, is not always readily transferred to an examination of the treatment of women in war. Given the plethora of foundational twentieth-century feminist literature about the sexual objectification of women and the dynamics of woman hating, this is more than a little surprising.

When one considers the political and conceptual foundation of the post–World War II human rights regime in the aftermath of the Shoah (Holocaust), the location of rights and their violations within ethnonational framings appears less surprising. The 1948 UN Convention on the Prevention and Punishment of Genocide, which has informed judgments of international war tribunals ever since, defines genocide as a range of acts of violence committed "with intent to destroy, in whole or in part, a national, ethnical, racial or religious group" (UN 1948, Art. II). "Women" are not constituted as a group under the terms of this convention, which leaves us in a bind with respect to international criminal proceedings concerning conflict-related sexual violence. For example, the 1998 International Criminal Tribunal for Rwanda was only able to determine that the mass rape of Tutsi women constituted genocide because it targeted an ethnic group, not because it targeted women en masse:

The Trial Chamber held that rape, which it defined as "a physical invasion of a sexual nature committed on a person under circumstances which
are coercive," and sexual assault constitute acts of genocide insofar as they
were committed with the intent to destroy, in whole or in part, a targeted
group, as such. It found that sexual assault formed an integral part of the
process of destroying the Tutsi ethnic group and that the rape was systematic and had been perpetrated against Tutsi women only, manifesting the
specific intent required for those acts to constitute genocide. (UN 1999, 6)

Even this inclusion of rape among the crimes considered by the tribunal
would not have occurred had it not been for the persistence of the only female judge on the tribunal, Navi Pillay (Charlesworth and Chinkin 2002,
312). In 2008 Pillay became UN high commissioner for human rights for
a four-year term.

Transnational Feminist Connections

Faced with these masculinist legal and political agendas, Maylei Blackwell
points out that feminist social movement actors constantly engage in

> complex navigations of multiple scales of power, so when indigenous
> women feel blocked at the local level, they work at the national level.
> When they are getting blocked at the national level of their organizing
> they move to the transnational network that they're building. When they
> get blocked in the UN Permanent Forum on Indigenous Issues, they move
> back to the transnational. So they weave in and out of those different,
> multiple scales of power to try to leverage new spaces, new discourses, new
> identities, and new solidarities. (quoted in DuBois et al. 2005)

It is these navigations that point to the core of what one might consider to be the transnational feminist practices of which Kaplan and Grewal
had written a decade earlier. Migration and mobility (physical or virtual)
are central to these understandings, as are the shifting role of the state and
the reemergence of both nationalisms and transnational political formations based on cultural and religious identities (Moghadam 2005). It may
seem odd to speak of mobility when we are considering populations whose
mobility is at best forced: women who have become members of internally
displaced populations, or are forced into exile, becoming diasporic rather
than cosmopolitan (the former term implying a lack of choice or at least a
limited one, the latter implying an economic, political, and cultural liberty

that women in conflict and postconflict situations rarely have outside the
metaphorically gated communities of elites). Yet the metaphorical activist
mobility described by Blackwell is precisely what characterizes the dynamics of a feminism working in areas such as the one of concern to us here.

It is even important, conceptually and politically, to consider this mobility as not always the privilege of a cosmopolitan activist community that
has the wherewithal, in terms of economic status, cultural capital, and freedom of movement, to work the system effectively, but rather as a discursive
and political tool of communities of women who are on other levels facing
situations of extreme violence or constraint. It is easy for the US-(Anglo)-
European critique of the transatlantic feminist axis to become, oddly, another way of focusing on that axis as the only site of feminist power. From
there, it is a very simple step to a rescue mentality, a return to the "mater-
nalistic" exercise of cross-cultural feminist charity in evidence during the
colonial era, which, often despite good intentions, served to reinforce hegemonic practices. Such good intentions have continued to plague us: Tripp
(2008) reminds of the damaging effects of some misplaced feminist international solidarity actions following the 2002 Nigerian condemnation to
death by stoning of Amina Lawal Kurami for adultery or in relation to the
Bosnian genocide. This is not to imply that the other stance suggested by
the US-(Anglo)-European obsession with the wrongs of its own power is
preferable, namely, inaction because "we" cannot speak "for" "them," the
conclusion then being that "we" should not speak at all.

The problem with both of these positions when expressed within the
West (or indeed from any site of presumed greater power or privilege) is that
they assume a nation-like, clearly demarcated incommensurability between
"us" (mobile, transnational holders of the power to speak or remain silent,
to intervene or refrain from intervening) and "them" (located within an in-
escapable cultural and geographic specificity from which "they" speak with
one voice, and from one place—once we let them). These positionings do
not question hegemony, even though they may purport to. Reconceptualizing the dynamics of transnational feminist mobility, voice, and power is
core to transnational feminist practice, not because it creates "equality"—
there is clearly not equality of status or power or opportunity between displaced populations in conflict zones and cosmopolitan feminists of whatever
national origin who have at their disposal the tools of hegemony—but because it creates the possibility of *reciprocity*. Transnational feminism is necessarily based on the understanding that feminist exchanges happen within
contexts that are complex and shaped by unevenness and heterogeneities

of location, experience, analysis, and even goals, but it is also based on the understanding that *exchanges do, and must, happen.*

Cynthia Cockburn suggests that "having different knowledges in play need not mean incoherence," but that achieving coherent dialogue among diversely located (and diversely mobile) feminists working against war and violence needs particular "relational skills" (2007, 11). This is all the more the case because "anti-militarist and anti-war feminism is by definition multi-dimensional" (228), although I would argue that this multidimensionality necessarily informs feminism of any kind. Developing such "relational skills," and reconceptualizing the locations of feminist "migrations and mobilities," arguably underpins successful transnational feminist practices, although Valentine Moghadam has pointed out that successful transnational feminist networks will tend to emphasize commonality of experience rather than difference (Moghadam 2005, 196).

If transnational feminism allows both multidimensionality and commonality, then what is the link? What informs the understanding that even though Emma's war is a very different one from Nimo's war (to paraphrase Enloe's [2010] study of the Iraq war), Emma's war also *is* Nimo's war? Some years ago, I despairingly remarked to an acquaintance, an antioccupation Ashkenazi woman born in Australia and living in Sydney, that I feared the "situation" in the Middle East would never be fixed. The polarization, the vested interests on both sides of the divide in keeping the "Middle East" unstable, seemed insurmountable. She replied, without hesitation: "But it has to be fixed. So it will be." Other options are unthinkable because "the Middle East" is not "over there." It is here. It is us. Silence and inaction are not options. Avoidance of difficult conversations is thus also not an option—assuming we really want "the Middle East" or indeed any one of a number of other places to be "fixed."

The experience of women in Iraq or Israel/Palestine is connected to that of women in the United States or Australia in layered ways. Whether the women articulate a commonality or not, it is there. It is even painfully obvious. It is core to the question addressed by this book. Violence, or rather, *male* violence, is the link. This is where the transformative potential of transnational feminist analyses and practices resides: the here-not-here, the us-not-us. It resides in the recognition of the fundamental violence that links us as women and informs our analysis as feminists, accompanied by the simultaneous recognition that in order to have intelligible conversations, we need to understand many languages. We need to understand that trust among feminists is not automatic or essential.

Transnational Feminists
Working the International System

The many third-millennium international institutional measures relating to violence against women in conflict situations and the involvement of women in peace building had at least two important precursors (which themselves built on others such as the 1979 Convention on the Elimination of All Forms of Discrimination Against Women). In 1993, the UN General Assembly adopted the Declaration on the Elimination of Violence Against Women (UN 1993), and the following year Radhika Coomaraswamy, first UN special rapporteur on violence against women, handed in her report (UN 1994). Both documents, and Coomaraswamy's (1994) report in particular, clearly draw on decades of feminist analysis. The UN declaration recognized that violence against women encompassed both physical and psychological violence and occurred both within the family and the community and was also perpetrated or condoned by the state (Art. 2). The Declaration even recognized the role of NGOs in combating violence against women (Art. 4[e]). Coomaraswamy's report recognized both the universality of violence against women, its root in "historically unequal power relations," and the desire to control female sexuality (UN 1994, Section II). The use of "doctrines of privacy" in the perpetuation of violence against women is condemned, as are patterns of battering and sexual abuse of women within "patterns of conflict resolution" (Sections E and F).

Who desires the control, uses privacy as a justification, or uses women in conflict resolution, however, is never specified.

This is one of the reasons the violence remains so hard to eradicate. As is the case in many UN treaties and declarations, the *acts* and *victims* of oppression are spelled out but the *agents* of that oppression are not directly mentioned. These documents abound with sentences constructed in the passive voice. Violence is "directed against women," but it is never clearly stated by *whom;* it happens "within the family," but which family members perpetrate the violence is never stated. It is clearly structural, systemic, and systematic, as Coomaraswamy explains at length, but the structures and systems become the agents and are thus largely faceless and dehumanized. Only the state is named, since 1993 in particular, as an agent of violence against women. But the state is an apparatus, not a person or group of people.

The second reason the violence remains so hard to eradicate is, once again, the question of national sovereignty. Even if these declarations call upon states, as perpetrators or accomplices of violence against women, to act to eradicate it, states can, and do, take refuge in their sovereignty and do nothing. No UN soldiers in purple (rather than blue) berets would be there to stop them. And would we want them to? In 1992 women mobilized massively, and transnationally, around the militarized male violence against Bosnian women. They called for intervention to stop the violence. But did they for a moment imagine that such intervention would happen without the use of military force? Surely we were not that naïve.

A third reason it is so hard to eradicate the violence is that the policing of violence against women in conflict situations divides the world's military into "good" and "bad" soldiers, just as the logic of agentless sexual violence creates distinctions between "good" and "bad" men (and by extension, "good" and "bad" states or ethnonational groups): those who do not bash and rape and exploit women and those who do. But if the problem is structural and systemic, informed by an ideology in which only men count as fully human, are such distinctions ultimately going to serve women? Do they not return us to class- and nation- and ethnicity-based constructions of perpetrators and victims?

This is the root of our dilemma in looking at international efforts to address violence in conflict and postconflict situations. Because the answer, for women, to Catharine MacKinnon's (2002) question "When is a war?" is "Most of the time."

Such observations may not appear to take us very far, but their continued articulation in the face of consistent denial by so many others is in itself a revolutionary act. Consider the lone voice of Judge Pillay, which helped alter, ever so slightly, the framing of the Rwanda genocide. Even such small changes are a step toward challenging the *concepts* that inform international (criminal) law. Seen in that light, removal of male agency notwithstanding, Coomaraswamy's (1994) report is cause for jubilation. Finally, someone in the United Nations was embracing what many feminists had been repeatedly saying for a very long time.

Indeed, these UN advances did not happen because the male-dominated United Nations and some of its male-dominated member states suddenly decided, all on their own, that women may just be a little bit human after all. These men were lobbied. They encountered, in every aspect of their lives, women who labored to get onto their political radar. And much of that labor took the form of transnational feminist navigations of that complex network of the local, national, and international of which Blackwell spoke. For example, "without TFN [transnational feminist network] activity the world would hardly have known about the atrocities facing Algerian and Afghan women in the 1990s" (Moghadam 2005, 195). Similarly, Resolutions 1325 and 1820 did not just happen (Hill, Aboitiz, and Poehlman-Doumbouya 2003; Porter 2007), just as Judge Pillay did not just happen to become a judge.

At the same time, notwithstanding enormous feminist lobbying, Resolutions 1325 and 1820 and the ICC are not getting us where they should as fast or completely as they should. This is partly because the international institutional frameworks set up remain controlled by men (Spees 2003). It is also because, even though the changes in international law that have led to the creation of human rights treaties and the international criminal court are ostensibly part of a shift away from a Westphalian world order toward a "charter" order where national sovereignty is less absolute (Charlesworth and Chinkin 2002; Cooper 2009), nothing can happen without the willing participation of nation-states and particularly the most powerful among them. The fact that the United States is not a party to the Rome Statute has, for example, been considered to weaken the ICC's authority and effectiveness. A related concern is that feminists do not trust the international or national masculinist institutions that have carriage of the women's rights agenda for which they themselves have fought. Khulud Khamis, resource development coordinator with Isha L'Isha ("woman to woman"), Haifa Feminist Center, underlined this contradiction. She pointed out that she could probably give the Israeli government the names of 200 feminists tomorrow, were the government seriously interested in applying Resolution 1325; unfortunately, however, it is unlikely that many of them—if any at all—would trust any peace process brokered by the current Israeli regime and so would probably decline to participate anyway.[3] Similarly, some feminists are skeptical of the "gender mainstreaming" and "Millennium Development Goaling" of women's rights and NGO-ization of feminist activism that coopt women into particular institutional interactions and neutralize feminist radicalism (Falquet 2008; Khan 2000; Wichterich 2000). They argue that allowing some women a few more bit parts in the play still does not fundamentally change the script (Cohn 2008).

These reservations notwithstanding, the past decade, even as it has seen the exacerbation of conflicts and ever more complicated and drawn-out "postconflict" scenarios, has also seen a renewed feminist hope in our own potential, through transnational action, to change the way international politics is done. Even if on-the-ground impacts of international instruments such as Resolution 1325 are slow to be felt, they signal, for some, a "new norm in the making" (Tryggestad 2009, 552), which "has the potential to have tremendously important effects on the lives of women who are already being ripped apart in the clutches of war" (Cohn 2008, 203). Even if mass conflict-related sexual violence against women remains framed in ways that are nationally or ethnically essentializing, it is nonetheless on the international agenda. Even if we need to understand that all nation-state and international institutions are masculinist and, as such, not completely trustworthy, they also happen to be, for the moment, the system that we are stuck with. So we need to learn to work it as effectively as we can. The scholarship cited here argues time and again that the best way to work this system without it working us is to do so at many levels. A certain level of participation in the logic of international and national laws and institutions is required if one wishes to push their boundaries. But most of all, radical and subversive transnational feminist networks that strive, multiskilled and multilingual, to *mobilize* women (in every sense of the word) collectively across the difficult terrains of our often contradictory experiences, are required if we ever wish to arrive at the types of analyses and practices that have the potential not just to work the system but also transform it.

Notes

1. Comment during the conference "Transcultural Mappings."
2. The phrase was used in the context of discussion of colonial British opposition to sati burning.
3. Khulud Khamis, personal communication, September 12, 2010.

3

Creating Second-Class Citizens at Home and Targets Abroad

A Feminist Analysis of Protection in the Use of Force

Laura Sparling

In 2008, THE FORMER COMMANDER TO THE UN PEACEKEEPING MISSION IN THE DEMO-cratic Republic of the Congo, Major General Patrick Cammaert, shocked much of the West with his declaration that "it has probably become more dangerous to be a woman than a soldier in an armed conflict" (Cammaert, 2008). Indeed, over the course of the past century, the targeting of women and girls in armed conflict has become widespread. Whether this is due to an increase in actual incidents or because reporting has improved is unclear. What is certain is that the number of incidents is not decreasing. According to current estimates, women and children represent an overwhelming 90 percent of casualties in recent conflicts (Avery 2005, 103). This increase has occurred despite numerous and significant political initiatives over the past 100 years to tighten rules of engagement regarding the treatment of civilians and the expansion of punishable crimes of war. However, if women and girls are specially protected under international humanitarian law (IHL), why has gender-discriminate violence reached such epidemic proportions? Where has IHL failed?

This chapter questions popular conceptions of protection and illustrates how the politics of protection have shaped and determined women's involvement in conflict. I examine this idea by juxtaposing two frameworks of analysis. By first analyzing domestic military policies, followed by a critique of state-supported international norms in conflict, I suggest that within the use-of-force realm, both the domestic and international actions of individual Western states exacerbate discrimination of women domestically and in conflicted states and relegate them to the inferior categories of

33

second-class citizens nationally and civilian victims in conflicts abroad. For instance, on the domestic front, the majority of national militaries worldwide continue to exclude women from prestigious ground combat positions and, thereby, subsequently perpetuate gendered power-structures by restricting women's access to the coveted status of "first-class citizen." Similarly, within the wider international community, the promises of protection declared within the covenants of IHL, in UN Security Council Resolutions 1325 and 1820, and in the agendas of various pro-women world conferences have effectively, though perhaps unintentionally, designated women as discriminate targets and passive victims of conflict.

Thus, by advocating protectionist rhetoric in the place of more profound social reconstruction, the exploited woman "remain[s] a victim regardless of the amount of attention directed [her] way, whereas the pitier [or protector] . . . markedly increase[s] their satisfaction and superiority" (Hannah Arendt in Nyers 2006, 89). Although the discriminate targeting of women is widely condemned, the message transmitted through these domestic and international paternalistic practices, laws, and policies suggests that the only role reserved for women in conflicts is that of subaltern soldier and the dehumanized target of violence.

It is not my intention to undermine the realities of women in conflict, for these atrocities are indeed real and merit genuine attention. Nor do I advocate a complete upheaval of existing protectionist measures. Instead, this chapter insists that effective and constructive responses to gender-discriminate abuses cannot remain centered on infantilizing initiatives of protection. The offer of protection fails to recognize the root of the problem—the lack of value placed on women and girls in all societies—and offers only dependency in the place of broad social reconstruction, emphasizing respect of women as equals and the punishment of abusers. Initiatives like protection direct massive amounts of energy at the wrong element of the problem; that is to say, women and girls are perceived as the problem to be remedied and not the misogynistic actions of the abusers and societies at large.

Building on feminist critiques, the first part of this chapter provides an analysis of the widely promulgated rhetoric of protection, which, while appearing benevolent, may actually incur harmful consequences by perpetuating the dangerous subaltern status of women. By challenging the myths of female inferiority and weakness, the second part of this chapter examines the *inward* national defense policies and practices of Western states, particularly the United States and Israel. This section concludes that the patriarchal and protective beliefs that shape these policies have led to the active exclusion of women from participation in the "legitimate" use of force while simultaneously preserving their incomplete and unequal citizenship status. Finally, building further on protectionist critiques, the third section of the chapter examines the way in which familiar narratives of female vulnerability influence *outward* global policies and practices, chiefly those legal norms that address sexual violence in conflict.

When juxtaposed, it becomes evident that these patriarchal politics form a comprehensive barrier to women's fair participation in the conflict, erode the (symbolic and actual) status of women as citizens, perpetuate dangerous images of female weakness, undermine a woman's ability to self-protect, and effectively relegate women to the perpetual roles of the subaltern and target of violence. In other terms, the continued emphasis on protectionist solutions actually does a disservice to women with respect to addressing sexual violence in war.

The Illusions and Perversion of Protection

By critically examining familiar and socialized knowledge, feminist scholars like Iris Marion Young (2003) and Judith Hicks Stiehm (1982) have challenged our commonly accepted practices of protection. Their resulting argument is that through society's uncontested internalization of the myth of women as the weaker sex, unequal power structures between men and women have endured and the inferior status of women has been conveniently maintained. While the first part of this chapter bolsters Young and Stiehm's arguments on the perpetuated inferiority of women through "masculinist protection," the latter parts propose an extension of this argument to hypothesize that within the context of war, this artificial subaltern and dependent status ultimately fuels the discriminate targeting of women and girls as subjects of gender-based violence. Protective practices directed disproportionately at females leave unchallenged the patriarchal depiction of women as weak and bearers of male and societal honor. It is precisely these reinforced and perpetuated stereotypes that make women ideal prey for violation by warring parties.

Portrayed as benign, benevolent, and altruistic, protection functions as a control mechanism that creates and sustains a social divide whereby one party is superior and retains power over another. Protection is a powerful instrument that, while capable of good, maintains unequal power structures and has the underlying potential for abuse and destruction; it grants the protector the ability to elect who is protected, when protection will be provided, and in what form.

This social hierarchy between protector and protected is dangerous and can be easily manipulated. For instance, as Stiehm suggests, "the division of society into protected and protectors offers the occasion for an immorality which would not exist in a society composed entirely of [equals]" (1982, 370). When applied to international conflicts, where protectors are often at a great distance from the actual violence, this potential for immorality is further heightened and may consequently increase its occurrence, as in the case of the 1994 Rwandan genocide where the decision-making bodies in their New York–based offices failed to see the urgent need for their assistance.

Perhaps there was more than distance that prevented the international community from intervening in Rwanda. In fact, contemporary conflicts and humanitarian disasters have demonstrated an uncomfortable truth: the protector cannot always provide protection. Nor is there necessarily always a strong desire to do so. In 1994, a pusillanimous response from the international community permitted the brutal massacre of nearly a million people in under 100 days in Rwanda. Likewise, since 2007, the ongoing peacekeeping mission in Darfur has been subjected to intense scrutiny over its inability to sufficiently protect the displaced Sudanese populations from the Sudanese government's proxies.

In contrast to the concerted international response in Kosovo in 1999, the weak international attention to these humanitarian crises ignited a "selective protection" discussion among many scholars (Barnett 2002; Power 2002). This conversation revealed that not only is the protector sometimes unable to provide protection, but protection is even further perverted when it is only provided to certain kinds of people or problems. Although Kosovo represented a strategic and security interest for the United States, involvement in Africa was and is perceived as politically risky and irrelevant to American security interests (Barnett 2002; Power 2002). There simply was no discernible benefit to protecting. Protection—or the lack thereof— has everything to do with the self-interests of the protector. As illustrated through the genocides and massacres in Rwanda, the Balkans, and Darfur, protection is an inconsistent and unreliable prospect. In fact, the power dynamics inherent in any protectionist relationship make it far from benign, benevolent, and altruistic.

Gender Construction and Protection

Isolating gender within this matrix reveals an intricate and carefully masked relationship between constructions of gender, protection, and state interests. State-endorsed gender construction has served to advance state interests from the time of the Roman Empire, through colonialism and the Cold War, to contemporary politics. As with decisions to protect or not, state interests are seminal in shaping popular perceptions of masculinity and femininity. In turn, these constructions are used by state officials to create opportunities for the manipulation of protection.

Western and European constructions of femininity and masculinity have evolved over time and circled the world while constantly serving the interests of the patriarchal and imperialist state. In an interview with Cynthia Enloe (2001), she interpreted the relationship between gender and state behavior as manifesting in two principal ways. First, state officials will deliberately manipulate perceptions of femininity and masculinity in ways to serve national security interests. This approach is particularly evident in American responses to security threats. For instance, because there was no political or popular will to intervene in the unraveling genocide, images of Rwandan women never entered mainstream American political discourse. However, in the immediate aftermath of the attacks of September 11, vivid images of the Afghan woman as "confined, mutilated, and sometimes murdered in the name of culture" suddenly intensified the threat of the "uncivilized" Afghan man and bolstered plans to invade for *her* protection (Razack 2008, 107).

Enloe's second example of states' use of gender constructions occurs when states introduce policies if they perceived that the "proper ordering of relationships between men and women" threatens masculine privilege (Enloe 2001, 656). This is more evident in domestic initiatives like the return of American women to domesticity immediately following World War II after years of performing jobs that were considered masculine and requiring masculine talent. Today, this type of regulation of gendered spaces is particularly inherent in the policies and practices used to exclude women from achievement in the military.

Constructions of femininity and masculinity are by no means static, nor are they universally applicable. Under patriarchal and colonial society a dual notion of "femininity" has been established where the white Western woman is sexually pure, passive, and responsible for the reproduction of the nation, whereas "racialized" women, women of color, and indigenous women are understood as impure, highly sexualized, and available for the exploitation of their physical and sexual labor (Lugones 2007). Whether analyzed at the local, national, or the broader international level, gender constructions are manipulated and reconceptualized over time and space to serve the interests of patriarchal states and to maintain the gender hierarchy.

The illusion of protection is pervasive in the relations between citizens and their governments and also between men and women. Although the benefits of protection are frequently touted, it is far more rare for political actors and policymakers to recognize that protection also subordinates women and erodes their ability to self-protect. At its core, protection has long been used as a tool to maintain the subordination of the "inferior female." In turn, this subordination has facilitated the exclusion of women from some realms, such as the use of force, and their confinement to others, such as target of violence (Sharma and Gupta 1991).

Perpetuations of Inequality in Domestic Policies

The treatment of women nationally is a good indicator of how women will be perceived and treated internationally. In Western militaries, women's participation has typically reflected the gender roles ascribed by Western society. Rather than participating in leading roles, women have generally been sequestered to auxiliary positions or have existed in the fringes of military bases as mothers, wives, girlfriends, or "comfort women" (Enloe 2000b). The following section examines the numerous ways in which both formal and informal protectionist practices have served to restrict women's equal participation in Western militaries. Through their active exclusion from decidedly "prestigious" combat roles, women are denied the opportunity to act as first-class citizens and consequently remain socially perceived as inferior.

In the Western and European experiences, protectionist rhetoric has been a leading factor in the exclusion of women, as a group, from the so-called legitimate use of force. White women of Western origin have traditionally been excluded from the masculinized domain of war because of their designation as "symbolic vessels of femininity and motherhood" (Peach 1996, 162). This constructed fragility has long backed the argument that women need to be protected from "the horrors of capture and imprisonment," not to mention the dangers commonly associated with direct combat (Peach 1996, 170). Through her involuntary casting as the "protected"—and consequently the subordinate—the Western woman has long been constructed as "[adoring] her protector and happily [deferring] to his judgment in return for the promise of security" (Young 2003, 5; see also Enloe 2000a). Through this masculinized and widely accepted conceptualization of women as dependent and desiring of protection, the pernicious gender hierarchy of masculine superiority and female inferiority are perpetuated in a highly calculated manner.

Among other feminist scholars, Cynthia Enloe has questioned the variety of roles and positions occupied by women in and around modern militaries. One of Enloe's most valuable critiques is that of the patriarchal state's regulation and manipulation of ideas about femininity and masculinity to make the military a well-greased machine. In *Maneuvers* (2000a), she illustrates how ideas about femininity are reshaped through deliberate decisions made by authorities. Enloe reveals how these calculated decisions have militarized the lives of certain women to the benefit of the military, but never to the extent that they threaten masculine privilege. This interpretation serves well to bring meaning to women's only partial inclusion in many of the world's biggest militaries.

The Invisible Soldiers

Although Western societies have witnessed the gradual integration of women into national militaries over the course of the past century, this has not been entirely genuine. In fact, the incorporation of women into European and North American militaries was largely a means to meet the widescale and insatiable demand for personnel during the world wars of the early twentieth century. This deliberate inclusion, however, did not last, and women were quickly commended and discharged following the end of the war (Peach 1996). In 1948, the US Congress formally recognized the contribution of women to the military service through the institutionalization of the Women's Armed Services Integration Act, which enabled women to serve, for the first time, as permanent and regular members of the US military (Moore 1996). As groundbreaking as the act may have been at the time, it nevertheless severely restricted the number of women permitted in the services, the types of jobs they performed, and the upward mobility of their military careers (U.S. General Accounting Office 1987, 2). Women were excluded from the air force, navy, and combat positions, and mothers of dependent children were entirely barred from entry.

Currently, women are permitted in all positions "except those units whose primary mission is to engage in direct ground combat. Generally speaking, this means that Armor, Infantry, Ranger, Special Forces and Field Artillery Battalions remain closed in the Army" (Skaine 1999, 91). These designations are considered the most prestigious, and women's exclusion from them consequently represents exclusion from equal value and respect. For instance, in the aftermath of the Persian Gulf War, US Secretary of Defense Dick Cheney publicly applauded the "magnificent" performance of female soldiers, noting that the war would not have been won without them (Peach 1996, 159). Yet for many female soldiers, the significance of this recognition had little influence on their careers as women in the military; through their exclusion from the most prestigious positions, their inequality and substatus as soldiers remained piercingly palpable.

Debunking Arguments for Exclusion

In contemporary war zones, the recognized and valued participation of female soldiers is complicated by the fact that traditional "frontlines" cease to exist. In operational quagmires such as Iraq and Afghanistan, for instance, the frontline is everywhere and nowhere at once. Under these evolved circumstances, improved military technology, like long-range artillery, has exposed female soldiers in combat-support positions to the same dangers as male ground combatants. This reality proved true in the case of US soldier Jessica Lynch who, while serving in the 2003 American invasion of Iraq, was captured as a prisoner of war despite her secondary designation as "combat support." Although Lynch was awarded two medals for her service and bravery, this is a rare recognition among female soldiers. For the large majority of female soldiers, their systematic exclusion from prestigious combat designations eliminates the possibility of promotion or formal military recognition for the risks they bear (Peach 1996).

Over the years, feminist scholars have dedicated much energy to the demystification of popular patriarchal arguments used to restrict women's access to direct combat positions (Peach 1996). As illustrated in the previous example, technological advancements in weaponry and the evolution of the combat landscape have shown that the traditional notion of a frontline no longer exists in contemporary conflicts. Today, auxiliary support soldiers positioned far from the action may be equally exposed to attack as the direct combat troops. Therefore, with the exception of returning women to secretarial desk posts, the exclusion of women on grounds of protection from direct combat is no longer a logical argument. Additionally, in intensive warfare these technological improvements have also resulted in a significant reduction in the overall weight and size of weapons, therefore, refuting the argument that women are not strong enough to perform the duties required by combatants (Peach 1996). The deflation of these patriarchal assertions, however, begs the question: Why are women still excluded from participation in the most prestigious and well-regarded military roles? As Enloe has argued, exclusion has much more to do with maintaining "the patriarchal multilayered arrangement of masculinities and femininities" than with these commonly propagated arguments of female inadequacies (Enloe 2000b, 199).

Although arguments attacking the capacity of women are easily refuted, other arguments that draw from patriarchy's ideals of Western women's femininity and fragility are more stubbornly entrenched. Not surprisingly, it is precisely these constructed differences that fuel the reproduction of the national protector-protected binary. For example, a major exclusionary factor against women in Western militaries is the biological and ideological function of women as the nation's child bearers. Ironically, this argument is far less concerned for the well-being and safety of women than for the survival of the nation. Women in this sense are perceived more as symbols or property of the nation than as individuals. In opposition to this narrow argument, some feminists scholars have argued that research shows higher male absenteeism for "being AWOL and for desertion, drug and alcohol abuse, and confinement" than their female comrades show for maternity leaves (Peach 1996, 170). Moreover, the assumptive notion that all women can and will eventually bear children is a patriarchal myth that men are not subjected to as would-be fathers.

Military Participation and Citizenship

In addition to propelling the upward mobility of many male soldiers in the armed forces, participation in direct combat roles in hypermilitarized societies, like the United States and Israel, is often symbolically interpreted the sine qua non of full citizenship (Feinman 2000, 1; Sasson-Levy and Amram-Katz 2007, 106). This pairing is rooted in ancient histories where states and empires were established through the waging of wars and soldiers were among the highest valued and most respected members of society. In this context, the military became a means of "transforming ordinary citizens into members of a heroic society" (Krebs 2006, 1). Although this correlation is not as palpable in less militarized countries like Canada, it is particularly relevant to societies like Israel, where, due to the state's ongoing conflicts with neighboring countries, the military is the most revered state institution and military service is mandatory for all. Despite the reality that Israel and its defense forces were established on a philosophy of gender equality, sexist barriers nonetheless consistently discriminate against women and restrict their equal participation, both in the military and, consequently, as celebrated leaders in the state.

Some feminist scholars have argued that female soldiers, through their exclusion from certain military roles, are also effectively excluded from the category of first-class citizen (Rimalt 2007, 1103; Sasson-Levy and Amram-Katz 2007, 110). As Sasson-Levy and Amram-Katz elaborate, "participation in armed conflicts has been an integral aspect of the normative definition of citizenship. In the West, military service emerged as a hallmark of citizenship" (109). Despite the cited historical significance of the notion of first-class citizenship, the fact that it is defined by participation in a hypermasculinized and majority male institution should be seen as highly problematic. To accept this correlation as fundamentally true is to "[leave] unexamined the militarization of 'first-class citizenship' itself" (Enloe 2000b, 245). As such, these mechanisms of exclusion work to maintain the patriarchal gender hierarchy, which places the masculine male superior to other members of society.

Interpreting military service as the sine qua non of full citizenship is not only problematic symbolically but also tangibly. This is particularly true with regard to political participation (Enloe 2000b). In Israel, military status is an important mobilizing mechanism for political ascension into the upper echelons of Israel's government (Sasson-Levy and Amram-Katz 2007, 110). Through their exclusion from combat roles, Israeli women are virtually barred from opportunities to genuinely influence national politics. Although Golda Meir served as prime minister in Israel between 1969 and 1974, the country lags behind many Western countries in terms of its representation of female politicians in both parliament and government (OECD 2010). Whether the notion of first-class citizenship is interpreted in terms of real and tangible benefits or simply as a symbol of social status, patriarchy's exclusion of women from some spaces and militarization in others effectively relegates women to the dependent and less visible role of second-class citizens, despite illusions of inclusivity.

Based on these examples and the critical analyses of several feminist academics, it appears that the ostensible protection extended by national militaries to female citizens is much less their protection from the horrors of war than the protection of the military from the "negative" influences of femininity. These policies and practices are representative of the perversion of protection; a guise that while purporting to value women is truly interested in maintaining ideas of feminine inferiority and masculine privilege. These patriarchal practices in Western state institutions are a good indication of how these Western nations—and creators of international norms—will perceive and treat women in other nations.

The Hidden Danger of Protection in IHL

Much like at the national level, the politics of protection are indelibly engrained in international use of force spheres. Within the context of war, few people ever question the validity of protectionist policies; they simply seem indispensable. In the short term, this may be true. However, when it comes to analyzing the potential long-term effects of protectionist initiatives, a less desirable picture comes into view. Beginning with an analysis of explanations for sexual violence, the following section aims to push aside images of a purely benevolent protector to expose the disempowered and vulnerable "protected" subject that is trapped below.

Propelling Sexual Violence as an Instrument of Open Warfare

The danger described by Major General Cammaert at the beginning of this chapter does not strictly refer to women as casualties of war. Rather, in addition to mortality, this danger takes on a multitude of sexually violent forms, including mass and strategic rape, sexual mutilation, forced abortions, sexual slavery, and trafficking. The conflict that Major General Cammaert describes is that of the eastern Congo, which has been blazing for over a decade. In 2008 alone, thousands of women and girls reported experiences of gender-based violence, and the UN peacekeeping mission posted there still struggles to provide adequate protection (International Rescue Committee 2009).

Traditional explanations for sexual violence in conflict have often been couched in biological arguments suggesting that the behavior is a natural by-product of the hyperviolent context of war and is waged by men who are genetically wired to behave so (Gottschall 2004). Despite serving as the leading explanation for hundreds of years' worth of violations, such a narrow interpretation "breeds complacency" and "blots out intentionality" (Enloe 2000b, 135). In contrast, some feminists have refuted this explanation by arguing that gender-based violence in war is little more than an outlet for venting deep-seated misogynistic sentiments (Brownmiller 1975; Mezey 1994). According to Mezey, sexual violence—in both peacetime and in conflict—is more prevalent in societies "characterized by male dominance, segregation of the sexes, [and] generally negative attitudes towards women" (586). Other literature has defined modern conflict as a battleground between male factions where "they are all warriors on behalf of their gender, and the enemy is woman" (Gottschall 2004, 131). This profound and visceral hatred of women is apparent in the horrific forms of violence used to mutilate women's bodies in conflict. Breasts are severed off, pregnant bellies are slashed open, and genitals are impaled with weapons or other sharp objects. Although these feminist analyses are more sophisticated than the biological argument, they fail to incorporate the broader and multilayered conceptualization of woman beyond gender.

Fortunately, greater gender analysis has given way to a more complex and layered explanation. Feminist academics and conflict analysts are increasingly redefining sexual violence in war as an inherently political action. In the words of Nayanika Mookherjee (2008), "the gendered performativity of rape during collective violence ensures that the gendering of women's bodies as female constitutes them as political signs, territories on which the political programs that also affect the nation, community and family get inscribed" (40). Women are often portrayed as the bearers of national and male honor, the reproductive vessels of the nation, the property of males, major contributors to communities, and the critical fibers of the uniting social fabric (Enloe 2000b; Koo 2002; Snyder et al. 2006). Attacks against women are, therefore, more multidimensional than strictly biological or misogynistic. Rather, stemming from the intersectionality of women's actual and symbolic identities in communities, strategic rape in war is interpreted as a debilitating attack against the entire enemy population. It is through this more nuanced interpretation that rape has now been identified as a weapon of war.

Regardless of the variability between these positions, they share one common element: the patriarchal perception of women as lesser in contrast to the dominant and masculine male. As a feature that branches from traditional masculinized theories to contemporary feminist arguments, this perception merits serious attention.

Protection in IHL

In response to this increasingly visible use of women as political pawns, states have joined together to drive the establishment of international humanitarian laws and norms advocating the "special" protection of women and girls. For instance, the Geneva Convention of 1949, the Additional Protocols of 1977, and the UN Security Council's Resolutions 1325 of 2000 and 1820 of 2008 all call for the improved protection of women as a measure to reduce sexual violence in conflict. On account of their progressive tone, these norms have largely been shielded from criticism. Although existing literature questions the effectiveness and application of gender-specific protection laws, very few academics actually question or challenge the epistemological systems that shape our understanding of the discriminate victimization of women in conflict and that consequently lead to the adoption of potentially harmful practices (Avery 2005; Gardam and Charlesworth 2000). I fill this gap by highlighting some of the unexamined harm embedded in international protectionist rhetoric. These subtle forms of subjugation should be of critical importance to feminist analyses of sexual and gender-based violence in conflicts.

Although the goal of the "special" protection afforded to women in IHL is to establish concrete rules to eliminate the egregious assaults against civilian women in conflict, this strategy is misdirected. This is true not only because the mechanisms currently set in place to address war crimes—such as the International Criminal Tribunals for Yugoslavia and Rwanda—are not

sensitive to women's conflict and postconflict experiences, but more so because they satisfy the patriarchal agenda of maintaining illusions of female
weakness and inferiority. IHL, together with Security Council Resolutions
1325 and 1820, has contributed to the normalization of the need for the
"special" protection of women and girls in conflict. Taking into account
the litany of terrible abuses committed against women and girls in conflict,
these concerted efforts to protect seem essential and, in fact, commendable.

There exists, however, a terrible danger in accepting this understanding as fundamentally true and necessary. Instead, critical questions need to
be examined. For instance, what drives these discriminate crimes against
women? Why are women considered to need "special" protection that is
not seen as necessary for their male counterparts? Where does the root of
the problem lie? These questions are best answered by critically examining
the socially constructed and internationally propagated myths of women
as weak, dependent, and inferior. Just as national defense policies actively
maintain the gender hierarchy, states' international policies and practices
also replicate dangerous portrayals that make women and girls ideal targets
of gender-based violence.

Advocates of IHL frequently herald its fundamentally egalitarian nature. For instance, within the Geneva conventions and their accompany-
ing protocols, numerous provisions affirm that application of the law must
be "without adverse distinction found on sex" (Geneva Convention I, Art.
12; Geneva Convention II, Art. 12; Geneva Convention III, Art. 16; Geneva Convention IV, Art. 27; Additional Protocol I, Art. 74; and Additional
Protocol II, Art. 4, 1949). However, in recognizing that women represent a
large majority of war victims, special attention has been afforded to women
in an attempt to address and eliminate their disproportionate victimization.
In fact, 43 provisions within the Geneva Convention and its protocols specifically address women's experiences in conflict (Gardam and Charlesworth
2000). Yet, despite the special recognition given to women's decisively different war experiences, the actual benefits of these laws remain constrained
by the ubiquitous hold of patriarchy. Ultimately, the inability of lawmakers to conceive of women's needs beyond the dictates of patriarchy poses a
permanent barrier to reducing violence against them.

Although respect for the "honor" of all civilians in war is explicitly
stated in Article 27 of Geneva Convention IV, an intentional reiteration of
this protection is made with regard to the specific and differentiated "honor"
of women. Article 76 of the same convention also differentiates between
genders by urging that women "shall be the object of special respect and
shall be protected in particular against rape, forced prostitution and any

other form of indecent assault" (Geneva Convention IV, Art. 27, Art. 76, 1949). Lastly, Article 12 of both the first and second conventions states that "women must be treated with all consideration due to their sex" (Geneva Convention I and II, Art. 12 (4), 1949).

The vocabulary selected in the drafting of these laws is problematic for a variety of reasons. For instance, within this international legal text, what is the intended meaning of "honor" of women? How does it differentiate from the honor of male civilians? Furthermore, how does its conception of a woman's "honor" differ from that of the men who systematically rape women in conflict to tarnish their "honor"? The reality is that there is no difference. Where the honor of men reflects the body and the mind, the honor of women—in both IHL and in the causes of sexual violence in conflict—"is constituted solely on the basis of sexual attributes, the characterizing features of which are what is seen as important to men, namely the chastity and modesty of women" (Gardam and Charlesworth 2000, 159).

Beyond this inability of IHL to reject patriarchal narratives that objectify women, the problematic nature of the special and differential attention afforded to women in IHL can be narrowed down to two core characteristics. First, such forms of protectionist practices fail to scrape beyond the surface of the problem. The special protection of women is essentially a response to the disproportionate targeting of women in conflict. However, the analysis consistently seems to stops there; no effort is made by conflict analysts or governments to question or address the motives behind these discriminate and unbalanced attacks. Outside feminist discourses, very few academics and lawmakers seem to question why women are the primary targets of conflicts that are generally not of their own making. Instead, government energy is routinely expended on superficial initiatives of protection. The second reason to be concerned by our increasing emphasis on protection is that no matter how benevolent and benign these "special" provisions appear to be, in reality they discreetly function to legitimize a rhetoric that perpetuates the subordination of women and, as I suggest, their consequent targeting in violent gender-based attacks.

Contrary to popular explanations for the victimization of women in war, women are not vulnerable simply because of their child-bearing functions and depicted roles as sexual objects. Rather, they are vulnerable because of "the underlying systemic discrimination that exists against women in all societies" (Gardam 2005, 119). In other words, women are not born vulnerable, they are made vulnerable. This vulnerability is constructed and maintained by systems of patriarchy that are intricately embedded in our social conventions, our state policies, and our international norms. The inferior status of women across the globe is not only reflected in their disproportionate targeting in conflict, but more often in everyday unequal "treatment by the law" (Gardam 2005, 119). When carried to the extreme, this inferior status can have fatal consequences.

The range of violations committed against female civilians in armed conflict does not occur by chance; rather, the pervasiveness of these violations is dependent on the normalization of the inferiority of women. In other words, socially perceived devaluation and dehumanization of the female person are fundamental to the widespread and intentional attacks on female bystanders. In gaining an understanding of this connection, Giorgio Agamben's interpretation of the *homo sacer* is a helpful explanatory tool. According to Agamben (1998), the *homo sacer* is an individual so socially denied of human qualities and rights that she or he is effectively reduced to the debilitated state of "bare life." In this state of ultimate inferiority, Agamben argues, the *homo sacer* can be violated and even murdered without condemnation.

The *homo sacer*, therefore, exists beyond the limits of law and is not considered protectable. The *homo sacer's* nakedness and consequent susceptibility to assault are comparable to that of the discriminately targeted female civilian in conflict. Even where protection is provided—or promised—this does not change the fact that her existence is perceived as inferior and her body is violated with little to no consequences. As Sherene Razack has said, "violence is easily authorized against those who do not belong" (2008, 176). Consequently, increased protection fails to address the underlying social problems that deem women as "bare life."

With the lack of attention afforded to these deeper social problems, statements like that of Major General Cammaert should not shock us. As previously illustrated, protectionist rhetoric is not synonymous with security. Nor does it challenge the patriarchal gender hierarchy. Rather, protectionist rhetoric exacerbates and reproduces the already unequal power structures between men and women, even when protection itself is never guaranteed. As Jo Doezema (2001) aptly observes, "to be 'protected' by the same power whose violation one fears perpetuates the very modality of dependence and powerlessness" (31). Although the protection of Afghan women was among the justifications for the invasion of Afghanistan, it is impossible to say that Afghan women are safer today than they were a decade ago. In fact, with daily civilian casualties at the hands of the international "protectors," Afghan women today do not consider themselves as having become more independent or empowered (Revolutionary Association of the Women of Afghanistan [RAWA]).

Curbing violence and preventing war crimes cannot be weighted in protection but rather in combating perceptions that lead to the devaluation and dehumanization of women as equals. Advocating protectionist laws infantilizes women and treats their rights and experiences as secondary to those of men. Alternatively, framing laws of sexual violence in conflict around *prohibition* instead of protection would credit women's rights and experiences with the genuine attention they merit (Gardam and Charlesworth 2000). Patriarchal socialization has discouraged us from questioning the underlying problem—the inferior status of women established globally through patriarchy—which not only permits but, through reproduced images of weakness, also encourages their discriminate persecution in times of war. When examined through a critical feminist lens, it becomes visible that protectionist rhetoric, as explicit in IHL, has a hidden and unexamined role in the containment of women within the realm of victim.

If the international community is truly interested in the well-being of women in (and outside of) conflict, a genuine and critical questioning of the inferior status of women is imperative. Above all, this includes a critical reconceptualization of the power relations between men and women and a deconstruction of the epistemologies that normalize the dehumanization of women.

Conclusion

Against a backdrop of ostensible compassion for the well-being and security of women in conflict, the repercussions of patriarchal national military policies and international legal norms continue to subvert any genuine attempts at ending the intentional targeting of women in conflict. Amid a deeply exclusionary and patriarchal world system, attempts by the international community to move beyond the victimhood of women through commitments to "protect" are futile, even potentially harmful. As I have argued, international legal norms emphasizing the protection of women in conflict coupled with domestic military policies that exclude women from the legitimate use of force effectively reproduce the subaltern status of all women to a point that permits, excuses, and encourages violent inequalities. Moreover, in keeping with Agamben's illustration of the *homo sacer,* the defilement of large majorities of civilian females in armed conflicts necessarily requires an extreme and pervasive social devaluation and dehumanization of women.

It is by no means my intention to deny the actual harm that is disproportionately inflicted against women in hostilities. Neither am I sanctioning the elimination of existing protection mechanisms. Rather, this chapter is merely the beginning of a more lengthy and in-depth analysis. My intention has been to cast doubt on the underlying assumptions that encourage and reproduce the perception that the most appropriate solution to gender-based violence in conflict is increased protection. As argued throughout this chapter, protectionist rhetoric, disseminated both through nationally exclusive military practices and internationally promulgated laws, is not inherently benevolent. Rather, this disguised domination provides the illusion of protection and security while simultaneously eroding the status of women and confining them within the role of vulnerable and dependent victim.

Within this site of contradictions, where protection perpetuates vulnerability, there is an urgent need among feminists and policymakers to break away from the familiar discourse and find new alternatives for reducing the gender-biased abuses committed against women and girls in conflict. Efforts must be made to challenge and change the subaltern status of women before any progress can be made to eliminate violence against women. This initiative must occur both within international humanitarian law and national security discourses. For example, in the institutionalization of national and international norms, we must consistently ask ourselves: For whom do these policies work? And, is it possible that this policy will have unintended and harmful consequences? At first glance, it can be easily mistaken that norms encouraging the special and differentiated protection of women in armed conflict are necessarily beneficial. However, deeper analysis into the potentially harmful consequences of such narratives reveals that the benefits are largely generated and perpetuated by the "generous" and "benevolent" protector who ultimately retains superiority. Taking into account the endemic discrimination that women experience globally, it is essential that those in positions of power carefully evaluate their actions and consider whether the law effectively responds to this phenomenon or merely reproduces, and in some instances exacerbates, its effects.

Protectionist policies that are not coupled with equal efforts to share power and challenge constructed perceptions of women as subhumans have a strong potential for destruction. An analysis of the destructiveness of protection first requires a readjustment to the parameters of the discourse—a problematization of everyday understandings of protection. This shift in analysis provides a new angle on protectionist rhetoric wherein protection alone is comparable to Hannah Arendt's interpretation of "pity," which she perceives as "crueler than cruelty itself" (quoted in Nyers 2006, 89). Like pity, protectionism creates a palpable hierarchy wherein one party's superiority is manifested and sustained through the endured inferiority of another.

Unfortunately, while feminist critiques of the politics of protection are well developed, there remains an alarming absence of literature in conflict studies that problematizes the notion of protection as it exists in the two realms highlighted here. Instead, from the existing literature it appears that, with regard to the implications of IHL on the protection of women in war, the debate is largely centered on the effective application of protectionist policies rather than a general problematizing of the law. Essentially, a resolution to the problematic targeting of women in conflict will require a thorough investigation into the impact of existing legal and military policies of states and the international community as a whole.

Part Two

International Criminal Justice

4

Improvements in the Legal Treatment of Systematic Mass Rape in Wartime

Where Do We Go From Here?

Avory Faucette

MASS RAPE IN WARTIME IS NOTHING NEW. HOWEVER, WITH THE CREATION OF THE INTERnational Criminal Tribunals for Rwanda (ICTR) and the former Yugoslavia (ICTY), the international legal treatment of this crime has recently transitioned from ambivalence to a concrete legal order that clearly prohibits and punishes systematic rape of civilians. This chapter will explore the current legal framework and how it is used to prosecute perpetrators. The analysis focuses on the purposes of systematic mass rape of women during wartime and on the effects of the crime as experienced by its victims to determine whether this legal framework is sufficient and to ask how it might better address these purposes and effects. Ultimately, this chapter concludes that the current legal framework for the most part sufficiently defines the crime and addresses its purposes and effects, but that enforcement is insufficient. The most important next steps are not further codification or development of case law but rather further attention to survivors' experiences, measures to make the international criminal process more efficient so it can serve a legitimate deterrent function, and nonlegal steps such as education to dilute the purposes and make wartime rape unacceptable worldwide.

The first section of the chapter asks how the law "on paper" and its case law application address systematic mass rape in wartime, concluding that the law itself is sufficient to match the purposes and effects of the crime. The second section of the chapter considers enforcement, finding significant gaps in ensuring effective use of the law and support for victims. It also offers both legal and nonlegal recommendations for change.

How Does the Law on Paper and Its Application by the Tribunals Meet the Purposes and Effects of Systematic Mass Rape in Wartime?

Rape has been a systematic tool of war in conflicts from distant history to the present day. A few examples of mass rape during armed conflict include Liberia, Burma, and Peru (Engle 2005, 785). Other chapters in this book delve deeper into those and other examples. This chapter focuses on Yugoslavia and Rwanda due to the amount of information available, the rapid development of the law in the International Criminal Tribunals, and the complexity of issues presented.

The legal response to systematic mass rape in Yugoslavia and Rwanda marks a major shift from the historical approach of international law. Although rape in wartime has historically been prohibited, enforcement was inconsistent and prone to gender stereotypes. Rather than a war crime, wartime rape was seen as inevitable and a private issue concerning individual soldiers. International lawyers left the issue of rape up to national governments, and many countries in turn treat rape not as a harm to women's "mental and physical integrity," but as a moral crime (Wagner 2005, 210).

The international response to rape in wartime changed, however, in response to "[t]he appalling use of sexual violence as a policy of warfare" in Yugoslavia and Rwanda (Wagner 2005, 210). The focus moved from individual sexual gratification to power, from a crime against men's property to a crime against women, and from a private crime to a crime of a public nature that can be seen as an attack on a group, sparking consideration of the opposing force's motivations for using rape in a conflict (Engle 2005, 779; Wagner 2005, 210–11). With the creation of the ICTY and ICTR, international law began to recognize the extent of harms caused by mass rape and focus on the motivations for this serious systematic crime. The first UN Security Council resolution condemning wartime rape was a major impetus for the creation of the ICTY, and the case law coming out of that tribunal and the ICTR drastically shifted legal thinking about mass rape in a short period of time (Goldstone 2002, 278). There is a real possibility that strong international legal condemnation can shift public opinion of wartime rape away from acceptance (Wagner 2005, 194).

The Law on Paper: Conventions and Tribunal Statutes

This chapter focuses on the three legal approaches to systematic mass rape— rape as a crime against humanity, rape as torture, and rape as genocide—that most directly address systematic mass rape in wartime. This section considers the law on paper applicable to these three approaches, as well as the definition of rape to the extent that one exists "on paper." The main documents discussed in this section are the statutes for the ICTR and ICTY, which define the jurisdiction and procedures of those tribunals, and the Rome Statute or ICC Statute, which does the same for the International Criminal Court.

Definition of Rape

Although the ICTR and ICTY statutes both mention rape specifically—in both as a crime against humanity, and in the ICTR statute as a war crime— neither statute defines rape (ICTR Statute Art. 3(g), Art. 4(e); ICTY Statute Art. 5, 1993). Though the Rome Statute (1998) does not define rape, the ICC's "Elements of Crimes" guidelines do include a definition influenced by the jurisprudence of the ICTY and ICTR and common law definitions. This definition uses gender-neutral language and the term "physical invasion" derived from ICTR case law, as discussed in the following sections, but also requires penetration of some part of the victim or perpetrator's body with a sexual organ. There must be a showing of force, but force can be inferred from the circumstances, including fear of "violence, duress, detention, psychological oppression, [or] abuse of power" or taking advantage of a "coercive environment" (Wood 2004, 296–97).

Rape as a Crime Against Humanity

The ICTY statute was the first legal instrument to explicitly recognize rape as a crime against humanity (Engle 2005, 781). To qualify, the rape has to be either part of a "widespread or systematic attack" directed against a civilian population or constitute such an attack on its own (Engle 2005, 800). Due to this language, the type of systematic mass rape described in this chapter falls under the crime against humanity rubric, where isolated incidents of rape in wartime would not. The ICTY statute specifically says that the crime must be committed in an internal or international "armed conflict" (Art. 5) rather than using the widespread or systematic language. The ICTR statute uses the words "widespread or systematic attack" and also requires that the grounds for the crime be "national, political, ethnic, racial, or religious" (Art. 3). The Rome Statute also comprehensively lists sexual crimes as crimes against humanity, including "[r]ape, sexual slavery, enforced prostitution, forced pregnancy, enforced sterilization, or any other form of sexual violence of comparable gravity" (Art. 7, §1[g]). It is important to note for all three of these approaches—crime against humanity, torture, and genocide—that the tribunals allow for convictions based on command as well as individual responsibility (Askin 1999, 98).

Rape as Torture

Both the ICTR statute (Art. 5[g]) and ICTY statute (Art. 3[f]) include torture as a crime against humanity, as well as a war crime. To show torture, under the definition found in the Convention Against Torture (CAT), an individual has to prove that torture was "inflicted by or at the instigation of or with the consent or acquiescence of a public official or ,other person acting in an official capacity" (Art. 1, §1). There is also an intent requirement, but in the case of rape in wartime this is not a particularly difficult standard to meet—intent to intimidate or coerce can often be shown, or alternatively the intent to discriminate based on sex (Wagner 2005, 236). Bodies that have recognized rape as falling within the definition of torture in the CAT include the European Court of Human Rights, the Inter-American Commission on Human Rights, and the ICTY (Wagner 2005, 235). The Rome Statute also lists torture as a crime against humanity (Art. 7, §2[e]) and notably only requires that the victim is "in the custody or under the control of the accused," not that the accused have a connection to the state.

Rape as Genocide

One strategy for combatting heinous crimes such as those committed in Yugoslavia and Rwanda has been to try to charge rape as genocide. This requires a showing of genocidal intent, or "intent to destroy, in whole or in part, a national, ethnical, racial or religious group, as such" (Convention on the Prevention and Punishment of the Crime of Genocide 1948, Art. 2). This can be difficult to show—for example, a UN report found that there was no genocidal intent in Darfur because of additional motivations such as counterinsurgency and intent to drive the victims from the land. The best response is that the text of the Genocide Convention says nothing about a *sole* intent to destroy the group, and in the case of Darfur there were examples that did not in fact meet the other proffered intents (Wagner 2005, 230–32).

Once the showing of intent is made, it is clear that acts of sexual violence would frequently fall under the acts listed in the Genocide Convention, including "serious bodily or mental harm to members of the group" and in some cases "conditions of life calculated to bring about [the group's] physical destruction in whole or in part" (Art. 2[b], Art. 2[c]). Cases of rape where women are kept in detention until they can no longer abort or where perpetrators make comments about the ethnicity of the baby would also tend to show "measures intended to prevent births within the group" (Art. 2[d]), especially where unmarried women are targeted and there is a cultural norm that makes it difficult for a woman with a child to later marry. The same would be true of particularly brutal and reproductively destructive rapes. The purpose of the rapes themselves may not need to be destruction of the group if rape is one tool in a genocidal war, but the intent requirement for the overall conflict is elevated (Engle 2005, 791). The ICTR statute (Art. 2) and ICTY statute (Art. 4) both incorporate the Genocide Convention definition of genocide.

Application of the Law: Yugoslavia and Rwanda

Rwanda

According to a conservative estimate, between 250,000 and 500,000 women were raped in Rwanda in a three-month period as part of a genocidal campaign by the Rwandan government (Wagner 2005, 215; Wood 2004, 285). This estimate shows that rape was the rule and not the exception during these attacks. It does not take into account additional harm from rapes that were so brutal as to make future pregnancy impossible, multiple consecutive rapes of a single woman, or gang rapes. Nearly all the female survivors of the Rwandan genocide, including women and young girls, were "raped and sexually brutalized." Rwandan officials "sanctioned and encouraged" this violence, instructing men to rape women before killing them or to use rape in lieu of killing the women (Wood 2004, 275–88).

The aims of Rwandan officials in carrying out this mass campaign of sexual violence varied. Simple elimination of the Tutsi ethnic group was one clear purpose, whether through killing women or preventing future pregnancies within the group. The use of sexual violence rather than simple killing illustrates the purposes of terror and humiliation. Soldiers with HIV, for example, were systematically ordered to rape women as "part of the terror campaign," and 70 percent of the women raped in Rwanda contracted the infection (Wagner 2005, 212; Wood 2004, 286). Women who were not killed were sometimes kept alive specifically for the purpose of rape (Askin 1999, 107). The purposes of humiliation and terror apparently were achieved, based on survivor testimony. One woman testified that humiliation was the soldiers' explicit purpose, and another described the consequences of rape as a "living death" (Askin 1999, 107; Wood 2004, 286). Askin notes that, "The female displaced civilians lived in constant fear and their physical and psychological health deteriorated" as a result of sexual violence (1999, 106). Ethnic stereotypes were also used to perpetuate sexual violence, and pregnancy contributed to the effects on rape victims as some unmarried women either aborted their own babies or committed infanticide to avoid the social ostracism that would otherwise result (Wood 2004, 285–86).

The *Akayesu* case before the ICTR (1998) addressed a situation in which the mayor of a Rwandan town allowed a number of crimes to take place in his commune while he was present and failed to prevent the crimes from occurring. The portions of the indictment relevant here stated that "female displaced civilians" seeking refuge in the commune "were regularly taken by armed local militia and/or communal police and subjected to sexual violence" (*Prosecutor v. Akayesu*, §5.5, 1998). The indictment noted that:

> Many women were forced to endure multiple acts of sexual violence which were at times committed by more than one assailant. These acts of sexual violence were generally accompanied by explicit threats of death or bodily harm. The female displaced civilians lived in constant fear and their physical and psychological health deteriorated as a result of the sexual violence and beatings and killings. (*Prosecutor v. Akayesu*, §5.5)

Akayesu was charged with knowledge of these acts, presence at some points during their commission, and facilitation of the acts by allowing them to occur "on or near the bureau communal premises" (*Prosecutor v. Akayesu*, §5.5).

This case is groundbreaking for a number of reasons. Prior to it, rape and sexual violence had never been defined in international law (Askin 1999, 109). In this case, the tribunal defined rape broadly as "a physical invasion of a sexual nature, committed on a person under circumstances which are coercive" (Wood 2004, 294). It defined sexual violence as any sexual act committed under coercive circumstances without requiring penetration or physical contact, and noted that sexual assault does not require physical force. The tribunal also recognized that there are different ways to show coercion, that physical force is not necessarily required, and that certain circumstances such as armed conflict may be inherently coercive. Focusing on coercive circumstances, the tribunal did not require a showing of nonconsent. This definition is notable in that it goes beyond many domestic law definitions of rape and sexual violence, using the victim-centered language of "physical invasion" rather than the perpetrator-centered language of "penetration," and accounts for the actual types of sexual violence used in Rwanda (Wood 2004, 294–95).

This case also recognized the possibility of trying rape as genocide for the first time (Wagner 2005, 215). The tribunal noted that sexual violence is "an integral part of the process of destruction" because the aim was to destroy the spirit, will, and/or life of each woman (Wood 2004, 295). The testimony of victims showed that sexual violence was a "fundamental and integral part of the genocide," with the use of HIV-positive soldiers as evidence of intent to destroy (Askin 1999, 106; Wood 2004, 295). Both mental and physical violence were used, pairing routine sexual violence with threats of death or bodily harm. The tribunal focused on the systematic nature of rape, the equivalence between sexual violence and other recognized genocidal acts, the targeting of Tutsi women, and the degree of harm, combining physical and mental elements (Askin 1999, 106–8). The fact that the sexual violence was exclusive as well as widespread and systematic against the defined group—Tutsi women—and often carried out with intent to kill was particularly important (Engle 2005, 788).

Akayesu was also found guilty of crimes against humanity, including torture and rape. The tribunal compared rape with torture based on its purposes, including "intimidation, degradation, humiliation, discrimination, punishment, control, or destruction of a person" (Wagner 2005, 216). It recognized rape as an injury to personal dignity and focused on the aggressive nature of rape beyond the sum of its elements (Wood 2004, 294).

The approach of trying the defendant for rape as a crime against humanity and as genocide was unprecedented in international law (Wood 2004, 275). In fact, the original indictment, which only dealt with the massacre of Tutsis, was amended upon the urging of the judge when testimony of rape and other sexual violence came out at trial (Askin 1999, 105; Wagner 2005, 215). Rather than treating rape as a private crime, it was recognized in this case to be a public tool of war (Wagner 2005, 215). Akayesu was not tried for direct participation in the acts, but for his official sanction as mayor of the town based on presence, knowledge, and failure to prevent the acts (Askin 1999, 106; Wagner 2005, 216).

Yugoslavia

In the words of Theodor Meron, "Indescribable abuse of thousands of women in the territory of former Yugoslavia . . . shock[ed] the international community into rethinking the prohibition of rape as a crime under the laws of war" (Engle 2005, 779). An estimated 20,000 women were raped in the former Yugoslavia in the 1992–1994 period (Wagner 2005, 216). About 80 percent of these rapes occurred in Serbian detention camps, where the victims were principally Bosnian Muslims, but rape was used on all sides. Tactics also varied greatly, which in some cases makes it difficult to determine the perpetrators' purposes for using this tool of war (Engle 2005, 779–90).

One clear purpose was humiliation, tied up in the desire to take over territory by making women's lives so miserable that they would leave. Rape in this conflict occurred within the context of a policy of ethnic cleansing that aimed to rid territory of Bosnian Muslims in order to free that land for ethnic Serbians. Seen in this context, there is a link between the use of rape to humiliate, "emotionally destroy," and terrorize Bosnian women and the policy of ethnic cleansing or forced removal (Engle 2005, 789). The Serbian military could not effectively hold territory with limited resources, so terror and destruction through sexual violence were more effective means of clearing certain areas of the civilian population than legal military means. An intent to rape "whole cultures" and "social relationships" rather than individuals is tied up in an additional purpose to prove an ethnic group subordinate (Schwartz et al. 1994, 70).

Humiliation was also a purpose for its own sake. The particular forms of sexual violence in many cases seem to be especially focused on humiliation. These include rape in public spaces, gang rape, rapes over a protracted period of time, forced fellatio, and forcing detainees including family members to perform sexual acts with one another. The effects on victims of these forms of sexual violence include, as intended, humiliation and degradation (Askin 1999, 114–19).

Humiliation could go hand in hand with ethnic-based hatred and the desire to impregnate women to ethnically cleanse the Bosnian population. Part of the Slobodan Milošević regime's ideology revolved around the so-called "white death," a phenomenon caused by low birthrate and high emigration rate in a Serbian area located next to Muslim areas with high birthrates. Propaganda images depicted "good" Serbian boys unable to find wives due to female emigration, which translated into violence when Serbian soldiers raped Bosnian Muslim women while using ethnic slurs and speaking of the Serbian babies that would result (Schwartz et al. 1994, 73).

Čelebići and Furundžija

These two cases, involving Serbian victims, demonstrated that rape would be treated as a violation of international law regardless of the identity of the perpetrators (Engle 2005, 798). In the *Čelebići* case, four Bosnian and Croatian men in positions of authority at the Čelebići prison camp were found guilty on multiple counts including torture and rape (Askin 1999, 114). The case was important in that it developed command responsibility for crimes of sexual violence, recognized rape of women as torture and as sex discrimination under the CAT framework, and recognized the effect of public ostracism in considering the torture charge (Askin 1999, 114; Engle 2005, 789–802; Wagner 2005, 236). The tribunal found that nonphysical suffering could include fear of public ostracism, humiliation, fear of a husband's reaction, or fear for family reputation (Engle 2005, 802). These findings are important because for rape to constitute torture, it must first meet the "severe pain or suffering" element in the CAT's definition (Art. 1, §1). However, the sentences for all the charges ran concurrently, so that one man's rape sentence, for example, was subsumed within a longer sentence for murder (Askin 1999, 114–15). This is a particular issue with rape because the sentence tends to be shorter than for other crimes, meaning that, for example, one can rape women in addition to mass murders constituting genocide and not suffer any increased penalty.

The *Furundžija* case involved charges for rape under the Geneva conventions, and thus is outside the scope of this chapter. However, it is important because the ICTY established a definition of rape in the case. In doing so, it used much narrower terms than the ICTR and came closer to a definition typical of US or European domestic law (Askin 1999, 113).[1] It limited rape to either (a) penetration of the vagina or anus by the penis or an object or (b) penetration of the mouth by the penis. In addition, it required coercion, force, or threat of force (Wood 2004, 296). However, this definition still sweeps more broadly than that of some US and European jurisdictions in that it is not gender specific.

Kunarac

The *Kunarac* case charged three Serbian military officers with crimes arising from a particularly horrific set of incidents that took place in the town of Foča. Conduct included repeated rape, forced fellatio, public rape, "exceedingly painful and reproductively destructive rapes," sexual violence as punishment for women who complained of their conditions, and the use of ethnic slurs connected with the desire to impregnate women. Individual soldiers or groups of soldiers also held women in houses and raped them repeatedly, in at least one case with the aim of punishing women for reporting the conditions in Foča (Askin 1999, 119–20).

The indictment for this case was notable in that it focused exclusively on sexual crimes, but it has also been criticized for not including genocide charges. Despite the severe effects on the victims and comments about pregnancy and ethnicity that might indicate a genocidal intent, the perpetrators were charged not with genocide but with lesser crimes, including crimes against humanity for torture and rape (Askin 1999, 118–19).

The superior officer, Kunarac, was charged individually and under command responsibility for a number of crimes, including crimes against humanity for torture and rape. The court took note of the torturous nature of rape, the pattern of sexual assault, permanent gynecological harm, and the psychological and emotional harm for all victims. However, despite evidence that Kunarac told a woman he raped that she would have Serbian babies and humiliated another woman with comments about her baby's ethnicity while three soldiers were raping her, and despite the fact that Kunarac was in a position of control over the other perpetrators, he was not charged with genocide (Askin 1999, 120–21).

At the time of the *Kunarac* case the ICTR had found that rape could constitute genocide, but the ICTY had not. The ICTY did recognize that systematic mass rape such as at Foča was legally distinguishable from "ordinary" rape, as this was the first case before the ICTY to convict defendants for rape as a crime against humanity. There were also references to ethnic cleansing, and it would be a plausible interpretation to find that the decision links rape with ethnic cleansing, though not with genocide (Engle 2005, 798–99).

The treatment of rape as a gender-based crime is uncertain in this case. On the one hand, this case gave the tribunal a chance to focus exclusively on crimes against women and specifically on the detention and rape of Bosnian women. On the other hand, the tribunal found that the sole basis for victimizing Bosnian women was their ethnicity, as opposed to their gender. Even so, it may be significant that the tribunal noted women and girls were "systematically taken" to the camp, which could be read to say that the motivation was gender-based (Engle 2005, 799–800). In other words, the focus on females was not simply incidental—the defendants purposefully focused on women in detaining and raping only female Bosnians. Aside from being important for the "widespread and systematic" language under the crimes against humanity rubric, this also is a baby step in the direction of admitting that rape might be genocidal. Perhaps under the same fact pattern, with more evidence to show intent to destroy a group of women, genocide might be found.

Other Proceedings Before the ICTY

Along with trials, the ICTY also heard Rule 61 proceedings, which were hearings that took place before a judge but were not full trials on the merits. In one proceeding focused on camps that were exclusively devoted to rape with an aim of producing Serbian babies, there was a finding that forced impregnation can be evidence of genocidal intent. The features of the sexual assaults involved, including their systematic nature and the victims' ethnicity, were used to infer their place in a "widespread policy of 'ethnic cleansing.'" Another noteworthy proceeding is the Miljkovic (and Others) indictment. Part of this indictment involved charges of rape as a crime against humanity for forcing detainees to have sex with one another, rather than a soldier raping a victim. Unlike an indictment in an earlier case where rape charges were not brought because the soldier was not the rapist, in this indictment the same charges were brought for the soldier who ordered these acts and another soldier who failed to stop him (Askin 1999, 115–18).

Analysis of the Law on Paper and Its Application

Based on the evidence of these two conflicts, there appear to be a number of reasons for the use of systematic mass rape in wartime. These include humiliation or harm to dignity, mental or physical harm, ethnic cleansing through terrorizing a population or through forced impregnation, and simple convenience where perpetrators did not have the military resources to physically conquer territory without resort to illegal means.

The effects of rape vary, but the documented harm is extreme. Emotional and psychological harm are common, including risk of suicide. Rape has been called a "crime worse than death." Brutality in some cases resulted in death or permanent physical harm including sterility. Children resulting from rape were stigmatized and mothers are ostracized from family and community. In Rwanda, HIV infection was one serious consequence of rape. The question that this section tries to answer is whether the legal framework described in the previous section sufficiently addresses these purposes and effects.

For the most part, the law sufficiently addresses the purposes and effects of systematic mass rape of women in wartime. The biggest problem is that tribunal statutes are vague on rape and the case law is not entirely consistent. The tribunal statutes do not define rape, and rape is not explicitly put into the framework of torture or genocide. On the latter points, the case law makes up for this problem by stating that rape can constitute torture or genocide, but the differing definitions of rape used by the ICTY and ICTR are troubling. The ICTR's language of physical invasion sweeps most broadly, encompassing various methods that might meet the same purposes and cause the same effects as a narrower definition like the ICTY's. The ICTY definition could conceivably allow perpetrators to "get around" the prohibition on mass rape by orchestrating a campaign of sexual violence that used nonpenetrative means. However, the Rome Statute of the ICC shows clear progress by focusing on rape and including a definition. The definition is a compromise, not quite as broad as that used by the ICTR, but it is still progressive in comparison to domestic definitions of rape.

The ICTY's and ICTR's recognition that rape can in some cases constitute torture or genocide is particularly important to meeting the purposes and effects of systematic mass rape in wartime, in addition to the recognition by the tribunal statutes that rape can be a crime against humanity. This interpretation of the conventions and customary law recognizes the severity of the crime and the possibility of a genocidal purpose to eliminate a particular group or a purpose to intimidate particular women for discriminatory reasons. Though the ICC statute does not mention rape in the context of torture or genocide, the ICC "Elements of Crimes" do enumerate rape as falling under "serious bodily or mental harm" when determining whether genocide was committed (2000).

How Does Enforcement of the Law Match the Purposes and Effects of Systematic Mass Rape in Wartime?

Indictments and Convictions

Though recognition of rape as a war crime and a crime against humanity is an important first step in deterring the use of mass rape in future conflicts, recognition will not be an effective deterrent if prosecution is ineffective (Wood 2004, 277). As of October 1998 the ICTY had 19 public indictments of 56 suspects in addition to sealed indictments, with at least half of the indictments charging gender-based violence (Askin 1999, 99). The ICTR had 22 indictments of 35 officials with two gender-based charges at that time (Askin 1999, 100). By 2002 the ICTR had indicted 17 men and 1 woman for gender-based crimes, and the ICTY had handed down 8 rape convictions (Goldstone 2002, 278).

Feminist scholars especially criticize the tribunals for an inadequate number of sexual violence charges and convictions and unduly short sentences. Kunarac, for example, was sentenced to only 28 years in prison, despite guilty findings on 11 counts, including rape, other crimes against humanity, and war crimes (*Prosecutor v. Kunarac,* ¶ 883–85). Another defendant in the same case was sentenced to only 12 years in prison for rape and torture as crimes against humanity and war crimes (*Prosecutor v. Kunarac,* ¶ 888–90). These sentences, involving a fact pattern that revolved entirely around sexual violence against women, can be contrasted with the life sentence for Akayesu, who was charged under command responsibility for torture, crimes against humanity, and genocide for events that included sexual violence against men and murder (*Prosecutor v. Akayesu,* Sentencing Decision, ¶ 3). Though it is difficult to make a simple comparison and it would be easier to draw a conclusion about inadequate sentencing if there were more cases to compare, it is noteworthy that the sentence for multiple crimes against humanity could be only 12 years in prison. When the sentence for rape runs concurrent to another crime, the deterrent effect is further limited because there is no additional penalty for rape if one is already committing serious crimes in a war. It is hard to imagine that such limited penalties serve as a sufficient warning for those who might commit systematic mass rape in future wars.

Other criticisms of the tribunals in dealing with systematic mass rape revolve around delays in arrests and prosecutions, especially at the ICTR. This is not surprising due to limited resources, but it is difficult for a tribunal to be effective in punishing violators and deterring future violations if the process takes many years and many violators are never brought to justice. The ICTY, on the other hand, is recognized as a leader in enforcing prohibitions on gender-based violence. Hopefully the ICC will follow its lead.

Working With Witnesses

When the only witnesses are rape survivors, there can be tension between the needs of justice and the needs of the survivors. Prosecutors may ignore the stigmatization women can experience if they report sexual violence, so policies are needed to ensure fair treatment of witnesses that balance the need for justice and the survivor's needs, including safety and empowerment (Wood 2004, 283, 299–300). One example of these tensions occurred in the *Furundžija* case mentioned previously.

In this case, the only available witness was the rape victim. Her credibility was attacked and the case was reopened to determine whether her testimony was still credible after the prosecutor revealed evidence of psychological treatment to the defense. In fact, it was common knowledge that rape victims received counseling, and the defense could have accessed that information through discovery requests. Though the defendant was convicted and the chamber did note that someone with posttraumatic stress disorder (PTSD) can be a reliable witness, it is troubling that the court allowed broad access to medical records and did not conduct an in camera review of the records to determine what would be relevant for the trial (Askin 1999, 111–13).

There are, however, some ICTY rules designed to protect witnesses. There is no corroboration requirement for testimony of sexual violence and other gender-based crimes, unlike in many domestic legal systems where women's testimony of sexual violence is treated as less reliable (Askin 1999, 104–5). Evidence of prior sexual conduct is prohibited, and use of consent as a defense to crimes of sexual violence is limited (Goldstone 2002, 284). The ICC also has procedural protections, including in camera review, but again this is at the discretion of the judge. Judges need to be properly trained in the special issues that might come up around rape victims as witnesses to be prepared to use these procedural devices (Rome Statute, Art. 68, 1998).

It is important to note that not all feminists agree on these protections, particularly the limiting of consent as a defense. Feminist scholar Karen Engle objects to the ICTY's treatment of consent insofar as it presumes female victimhood, refuses to acknowledge women's involvement in wartime, and treats women as passive by taking away the option to consent to sexual relations. She challenges the presumption that, based on non-Serbian ethnicity and the circumstances of the case, none of the women at Foča could consent (2005, 804). She believes that affirmative proof of coercion, force, or threat of force should have been required, rather than presuming this element to be met based on circumstances. She further argues that allowing circumstances to negate a consent defense could be broadened to apply to all sex in wartime, which would be unfair to women who choose to have sexual relations with a soldier on the opposing side (2005, 805).

This objection does have some weight—clearly there are circumstances in which a woman could have consensual sexual relations with a soldier. On the other hand, the agency problem does not compromise the entire legal framework. This problem could be solved in future cases by allowing the "victim" to testify in defense of the accused. The presumption made in coercive circumstances still seems appropriate, however, especially when limited to circumstances where the need for a presumption of nonconsent can be factually proven. It may be difficult to prove nonconsent, and when the facts show a policy of using rape as a weapon of war, combined with facts that suggest mass rapes being carried out in a certain place and time, it would be unnecessarily burdensome to require proof of nonconsent in every case.

Investigation

Similar concerns come up in the context of investigating crimes of sexual violence in wartime. Tribunals have been criticized for failing to adequately investigate crimes, which is crucial not only for criminal justice but also to create an accurate historical record (Wood 2004, 277, 300). Sexual crimes can be especially difficult to document because women tend to conceal their injuries to avoid retribution, ostracism, expulsion from refugee camps, and further emotional harm (Schwartz et al. 1994, 77; Wood 2004, 285). A conspiracy of silence makes it difficult to find survivors (Schwartz et al. 1994, 78).

Richard Goldstone, former chief prosecutor for the ICTY and ICTR, notes that the investigators in Rwanda were mostly male army and police officers who had cultural reasons not to consider gender-based crimes (2002,

280). Even when independent groups track down rape survivors, victims can find constant storytelling with no results and the commodification of their experience frustrating. Immediate survival needs are most important to a rape survivor, and talking about the experience may be traumatic rather than therapeutic. Even doctors have broken their patients' trust by sharing stories with fact-finders, such as in the case of Serbian doctors highlighting cases involving Serbian victims for propaganda reasons. Local groups need training in how to properly document survivors' experiences so that the perpetrators can be identified and held legally accountable in the international tribunals. Investigators also need to be made aware of the importance of documenting PTSD for credibility reasons in the event of a trial (Schwartz et al. 1994, 76–79).

Prosecutorial Initiative

One problematic element in the treatment of sexual violence before international tribunals is that prosecutors initially took limited initiative in this area. Human rights organizations were first to alert the international legal community of the importance of pursuing gender-based crimes. Judges also became unusually active in suggesting that prosecutors amend indictments, such as in the *Akayesu* case or when an ICTY judge suggested that the prosecutor pursue crimes not specifically listed in the ICTY statute, such as rape as a grave breach or a war crime.

Of course some may object that judicial activism is an improper and even partial role for a judge. Though this may be a concern, the fact that rape was *not* included in the charges of the original *Akayesu* indictment, for example, is sufficiently troubling to suggest that the judge was making the suggestion in the spirit of fairness rather than desire for a particular outcome. If the law ignores "female concerns" or does not concern itself with rape, as was the case historically, armies can easily use rape as a tactic without reprisal. Considering the severe harms of systematic mass rape and the purposes for using this tactic, it is important that rape be brought before international tribunals. The involvement of international groups and individuals lobbying for inclusion of rape charges also suggests that this was not simply a case of judicial activism run amok.

Procedural Protections

There are some special protections that have been used in this context, such as counseling and support for victims in Yugoslavia or the appointment of a special legal advisor for gender-based crimes at the ICTY. Article 68 of the Rome Statute also provides special protections for victims of sexual violence and allows consideration of gender in determining what protections to use, including in camera proceedings (§1). The in camera provision specifically references the victim's or witness's own views (§2), which is particularly promising for the agency of women in such a trial. Another improvement with the ICC is the number of females involved in the court. For example, only one female permanent judge serves on the ICTY (ICTY 2011). At the ICC, 11 of the 19 judges, including the first vice president, are female (ICC 2011).

Domestic Law Involvement

Finally, some may object to the involvement of international law at all in this area, if domestic law also criminalizes rape. This, of course, is part of a broader question of whether international tribunals should try severe crimes carried out in war in the first place. In the area of rape, it is important to note that the cultural problems addressed previously are likely to color domestic processes, and that in very severe cases such as systematic mass rape, international law involvement may be necessary to protect universal human rights.

Rwanda is one example of a case where international involvement provided an impetus for domestic law improvements. Rwandan domestic law criminalizes rape; and in the years following the ICTR's rape-related rulings, the government has introduced improvements to the law and its enforcement, including prioritization of rape cases, 20- to 30-year prison sentences for rape, and classification of rape committed during the genocide as a category I genocide crime (U.S. Department of State 2007). Police investigated 2,476 rape cases in 2005 alone, and the government also improved victim protection for victims testifying in local Gacaca courts (U.S. Department of State 2007). When such domestic legal changes occur, international actors may be able to ease off and allow the domestic process to do its work, stepping into a role of resource provision—training police and other investigators, providing shelters for rape victims, or training medical and legal professionals to protect women's privacy. The needs of the local population, especially the victims, should always be at the forefront. International actors that can provide resources must collaborate with domestic actors that understand cultural norms and victims' needs. This collaboration can help minimize the intrusion of the international legal process in the aftermath of a conflict.

Analysis of Enforcement

Though the law itself meets the purposes and effects of systematic mass rape in wartime, there are practical problems that must be addressed if it is to effectively deter future crimes and account for the harm already caused to victims. First, international courts and tribunals need to prosecute crimes when they occur and issue sentences that match the seriousness of systematic mass rape. Concurrent sentencing, especially when the sentence for rape is subsumed within another sentence, is a particular problem because it sends the message that rape is more acceptable than other crimes and does not constitute a separate violation. Even in a case where a victim is raped and then killed, the harm is greater than death alone. The tribunals have acknowledged the harm to the community, as well as to the individual, but this needs to be effectively addressed through prosecution and sentencing of the perpetrators. Similarly, charges such as genocide should be used where they are appropriate. The Foča case is one example in which the charges sought were perhaps less serious than the crimes committed.

Second, those who investigate rape in wartime and work with witnesses need to be effectively trained and consider issues such as the possibility of reprisals and ostracism by the community. It would be particularly effective to train female investigators from the culture concerned, so that investigators are sensitive to particular needs of the victims. Investigators and prosecutors must balance the need for justice with the needs of the victims. Even if a less sensitive process can address the perpetrators' purposes, it does not address the effects.

Third, law cannot address everything. Purposes such as humiliation, ostracism, and the reputation-based harm can only effectively be eradicated through cultural change and education. If men in a culture believe that rape is acceptable, this immediate social understanding will contribute more to their actions than some vague understanding of international law. For example, one recent study by the Republic of Rwanda Ministry of Gender and Family Promotion (2004) found that 53.8 percent of women surveyed had experienced some form of domestic violence, with psychological violence particularly prevalent, even in peacetime. Though the number of women reporting sexual violence was only around 8 percent, it is possible that taboos on reporting rape contributed to underreporting.

Focus groups also revealed that Rwandans believe wives can avoid domestic violence by being a "good wife," and that Rwandan men believe that violence is justified by women's behavior. Adolescent boys were insistent that a wife's disobedience was an acceptable justification for violence, and adolescents of both genders believe that local authorities are responsible for solving the problem of what they perceive as frequent rape in the country, as opposed to ordinary individuals (Republic of Rwanda Ministry of Gender and Family Promotion 2004, 52–74). This example seems to clearly show that Rwandan society, at least, might have benefited from education, especially for boys, about rape and gender relations in general, and that perhaps rape during the conflict would not have been so prevalent or easily accepted by those ordered to use it as a tactic had this education been the norm.

Even commanders who understand international law and consciously break it might be less likely to use rape as a tactic if they were not educated into a patriarchal value system. Similarly, communities might evolve over time not to stigmatize rape victims, eradicating some of the harm to victims and nullifying some of the purposes. Any educational changes, however, should be carried out by local actors and informed by local cultural understandings. The frustrations of women's groups in Rwanda with ineffective fact-finding missions that commodify rape show that an entirely Western-driven response is inappropriate, and that international actors may be able to assist more effectively by providing resources and training that local actors can adapt. Western activists also should consider working toward education efforts in their own countries, as patriarchy and rape culture are far from a "developing world problem."

Conclusion

Above all, it is important for law to respond effectively to the purposes and effects of systematic mass rape of women in wartime. It is possible that these may change over time, especially as the legal response to current methods becomes more effective, and so the law must adapt to changing circumstances. As the ICTY and ICTR have done in some cases, the ICC will need to use its interpretive powers to keep perpetrators from escaping this crime with impunity. Communities will also need to address the social ills that allow perpetrators to accept the use of this weapon in wartime.

Note

1. Many US jurisdictions, for example, require "sexual intercourse," and some jurisdictions even define rape with reference to gender so that a man cannot rape another man and a woman cannot rape anyone. The UK definition, contained in the Sexual Offences Act 2003, refers specifically to penetration with a penis.

5

International Criminal Justice: Advancing the Cause of Women's Rights?

The Example of the Special Court for Sierra Leone

Kiran Grewal

TRANSITIONAL JUSTICE HAS BECOME AN INCREASINGLY IMPORTANT FEATURE OF INTER-national community discourse in the post–Cold War period (Teitel 2000; UN Secretary-General 2004). Moreover, while the concept of transitional justice potentially incorporates a range of institutions, courts are frequently identified as playing an important role. Whether through the International Criminal Tribunals for Rwanda (ICTR) or the former Yugoslavia (ICTY), the establishment of various internationalized or hybrid tribunals and courts in the late 1990s and early 2000s, or the establishment of the first perma-nent International Criminal Court (ICC) in 2002, the paradigm of inter-national criminal justice has emerged as central to discussions about how to address the legacies of conflict and build postconflict peace. Many human rights and feminist scholars and activists have embraced this development. In particular, they have argued that international criminal justice provides the potential for developing recognition and protection of women's rights in conflict and postconflict situations as well as in "peacetime" (Amnesty International 2005; Askin 2003, 288; Goldstone 2002).

However, while many normative claims are made regarding the utility of legal interventions to postconflict human rights projects, there remains a dearth of empirical evidence. This chapter addresses this gap by consider-ing the work of the Special Court for Sierra Leone (SCSL), a hybrid court established in 2002 to prosecute those deemed most responsible for inter-national crimes committed during the 10-year civil war in the small West African republic. By looking at two specific aspects of the SCSL prosecutions for gender crimes, this chapter explores both the asserted promise of the SCSL in terms of promoting women's rights in Sierra Leone and what it has delivered. In doing this I highlight what I consider to be a number of problematic features of international criminal justice, features that must be recognized and challenged for international criminal justice to contribute to genuinely improving the lives of women.

The SCSL: Advancing Women's Rights?

The SCSL was established in August 2000 as a joint initiative of the United Nations and the Sierra Leonean government. Aside from being charged with prosecuting high-ranking representatives of the various fighting factions, the hybrid nature of the SCSL was identified as providing other advantages. With local institutions in ruins and plagued by corruption and inefficiency, the SCSL was argued to be not only a necessary measure to address past crimes but also to be a useful model for future justice sector development. Moreover, its location in the country and the heavy emphasis placed in the early days on outreach were identified as key to enhancing the peace process (UN Secretary-General 2000, para. 7; see also Sriram 2006).

At the same time, the decision by the chief prosecutor to include charges of rape and sexual slavery in four of the five indictments as well as to include the new and previously untried charge of forced marriage was met with great enthusiasm. Not only was this move identified as reflecting a real commitment to condemn violence committed specifically against women, it was also argued to reflect a desire to incorporate victims' experiences of the violations they suffer into international criminal trials (Muddell 2007, 95–96). As a result there has been real enthusiasm for the SCSL in terms of its potential contribution to develop a more gender-sensitive body of international law (Damgaard 2004; Frulli 2008; Muddell 2007; Nowrojee 2005; Park 2006) as well as its capacity to "mark a turning point for the women of Sierra Leone, who are gaining both a measure of control over their bodies and a chance to assert control over their own lives through prosecution of such crimes" (Eaton 2004, 908). The rationale provided was as follows:

> The overall effect of including violations against women in the international human rights rubric is that women gain power. With this power and newfound voice, women may expand their role outside of the Tribunals, expose issues that have traditionally been subjugated by male power structures, and begin to address the root causes of such violations against

them. Providing women with this voice and power is where the Tribunals will truly have the greatest deterrent effect. (Eaton 2004, 906)

Equally ambitious, Karine Bélair, in writing about customary law and forced marriage, concluded that in the SCSL's naming of crimes committed against women "it is not only the visibility of the crimes in conflict that will be increased; it is also the visibility of the same crimes in times of peace" (2006, 605–6).

So what did the SCSL prosecutions achieve? The next section of this chapter explores two aspects of the gender crimes prosecutions, which sadly did not live up to the expectations of the cited advocates of the SCSL. In fact, ironically, it was actually through a perversion of the very feminist efforts at including women that women's experiences ended up marginalized within the trial process.

Sexual Violence in the Civil Defence Forces Case

It is interesting that many commentators note with approval the inclusion of gender crimes in all the indictments except those of the three Civil Defence Force (CDF) defendants. In their special report on the issue, the independent trial monitors at the SCSL reported that it was widely known that the CDF troops and at least one of the accused had been personally responsible for rape and forced marriage (Kendall and Staggs 2005, 2–3). However, due to the failure on the part of the prosecutor to include specific counts of sexual and gender-based violence in the original indictment, this evidence was completely excluded. Although there was an attempt by the prosecutor to later amend the indictment to include these charges, this application was rejected by the majority of the judges. Added to this, the Trial Chamber went on to rule that any evidence related to sexual violence was inadmissible as it had to be specifically pleaded and could not fall within the general category of "inhumane acts."[1] This decision was heavily criticized by the trial monitors who noted: "In a disturbing outcome of the Chamber's majority rulings, the beatings, amputations and imprisonments that the witnesses described could qualify as physical violence and mental suffering, whereas rape and sexual violence could not" (Kendall and Staggs 2005, 4–5).

The CDF case in fact highlights two problematic features of the rape prosecutions conducted by the SCSL. The first is that the Trial Chamber's treatment of sexual violence as a distinct and completely separate experience from physical violence ultimately ignored the experiences of the very people it was supposed to be assisting: the victims. Female witnesses were allowed to give evidence of harm that they had witnessed toward others, damage to property, and physical assaults but were expressly forbidden from talking about the harm that for many was their principal reason for coming to the court. As one woman told interviewers:

> I feel so bad, because they raped me very brutally, and that was the main reason for going to court to testify. As soon as I got there, my lawyer told me that I should not talk about that anymore. And up until now, that still causes me pain. It makes me feel bad. (Staggs Kelsall and Stepakoff 2007, 357)

The separation of "sexual harm" from "physical harm," a move advocated by feminists in an attempt to redress the general inertia toward confronting the former as well as its frequent added dimension of stigma, in this case actually allowed for sexual violence to once again be marginalized. By the Trial Chamber finding that sexual violence could only be dealt with under the specific heading of "gender crimes," sexual harm was rendered unrecognizable as violence. Added to this, at the same time as sexual violence was treated as discrete from other forms of violence, it was also specifically gendered.

In reporting their trial observations, the Berkeley monitors noted that one of the judges insisted on referring to the evidence relating to sexual violence as "gender evidence" and "gender testimony." They also reported:

> Judge Itoe stated that if the women were captured and retained "on the other side" against their consent, this was enough to suggest that the women were either raped or retained as wives. Judge Itoe appeared to suggest that not only evidence relating to sexual violence, but also evidence about *women* that *may lead to evidence* of sexual violence, should be considered inadmissible. In refusing to hear testimony relating to the treatment of women at Base Zero, he effectively silenced testimony based on the gender to which it related: the story of how women were treated was being omitted on the grounds that it was somehow "tainted" with sexual violence even before those acts had been alleged. (Kendall and Staggs 2005, 16, original emphasis)

In this way the feminist efforts at engaging international criminal justice to achieve recognition for the specific and underappreciated harm of sexual violence as well as the greater proportion of female than male victims produced a highly ironic outcome. Rather than *enhancing* the inclusion of women, the judge's approach paradoxically excluded women on the basis that they were automatically assumed to be rape victims. This seems an extreme example of what Sharon Marcus (1992) identifies as the tendency to construct women as "automatically" rape victims (actual or potential): a situation she also partly attributes to feminist responses to rape.

At the same time, the judges were largely unsympathetic to both the submissions of the prosecutor and the ICTR jurisprudence that suggested some flexibility was required to recognize the differences between investigating other crimes and those involving sexual violence. Instead they noted, "if any gender offence or offences existed at all against those accused persons who are the subject matter of this motion, this should have been uncovered through the exercise of the ordinary and normally expected professional diligence on the part of the prosecution and the investigators."[2] Once again the exclusion of women's experience from criminal processes was reinforced. Although it was acceptable to recognize difference when it meant the automatic exclusion of women's testimony on the basis it would necessarily lead to evidence of sexual violence, it was contradictorily ruled *in*appropriate to recognize difference when it required greater sensitivity and consideration for women's experiences as different from men's.

The other outcome of the CDF case that excluded sexual violence is that it has resulted in jurisprudence that maintains "rape as a weapon of war" as completely separate and unrelated to other forms of rape. In the CDF case, aside from the stigma that prevented many women from identifying themselves as rape victims, there was an added obstacle to them coming forward. The CDF was in fact a group established to protect civilians during the war. As a result the CDF members were viewed as heroes by many and had been welcomed back into communities. The hero status of the CDF had made many women reluctant to speak out about the sexual violence they had experienced because, unlike those women who had been raped by rebels, this involved accusing men in their own communities. The SCSL's decision to exclude sexual violence from the CDF case resulted in only rape perpetrated by opposing factions being recognized and punished by the CDF. Rape committed by men in the victim's own community, indeed the men supposedly protecting them, was rendered invisible.

Aside from the problematic assumptions this perpetuates (a point discussed further in the following section), this occlusion of certain rapes within the SCSL's jurisprudence has very direct implications for the lives of Sierra Leonean women. The local Sierra Leonean human rights organization, the Campaign for Good Governance (CGG), noted in its 2004 report that it was *only* in the context of the war that women were able to openly speak about sexual violence (Peace Women 2004, 10). Moreover, the report refers to an interview with the director of a provincial rape crisis center suggesting that, "[a]lthough women during the war experienced support when they were raped because of the widespread nature of rape and human rights violations, this trend rapidly reversed after the war and women are once again blamed as their sexuality is seen as invitation to force" (CGG 2004, 26). Thus, by excluding all references to the sexual violence committed by the CDF against the civilians it was allegedly protecting, not only were those specific victims denied recognition but a poor example was set in terms of addressing the broader issue of impunity for sexual violence. Staggs Kelsall and Stepakoff reach a similar conclusion: "[t]he silence surrounding the prosecution of wartime rape in the CDF case may only reinforce the stigma associated with prosecuting crimes of sexual violence that exists at the local level in Sierra Leone, where rape—other than rape of a virgin—is still largely not considered a crime" (2007, 362).

Forced Marriage

The problematic ways in which the SCSL's work interacted with feminist demands emerges perhaps even more clearly in the context of the forced marriage prosecutions. As discussed previously, many scholars and activists have noted with approval the prosecutions and the subsequent convictions of the crime of forced marriage in the Revolutionary United Fund (RUF) and the Armed Forces Revolutionary Council (AFRC) trials. However, I would argue this support has all too often paid little attention to the actual nature of the violation as defined by the prosecution and the judges.

In praising the SCSL prosecutor's decision to specifically and separately prosecute forced marriage, various feminist legal scholars have asserted the positive function such a charge could play in recognizing a particular form of gender-based violence (Frulli 2008; Jain 2008; Oosterveld 2009). Yet in asserting this as an important means of recognizing harm that is specifically suffered by women but not necessarily sexual (Oosterveld 2009, 86), they do not seem to address why the specific situation of bush wives should be considered separate and worse than those women and girls who were abducted and *not* kept as wives. Furthermore, why were the crimes of enslavement, deportation, abduction, and forced pregnancy—all contained explicitly within the SCSL Statute and capable of being charged cumulatively—not sufficient to capture the nature of the violations suffered by these women? The failure of feminists to sufficiently address these questions themselves before supporting and advocating for the separate charge of forced marriage has had important implications, as a consideration of the prosecutorial and judicial reasoning will demonstrate.

Particularly influential in the development of the definition of forced marriage as an international crime, Justice Theresa Doherty drew the following distinction between those kept as wives and other victims of sexual and gender-based violence: "The evidence of witnesses shows victims had no protection from rape and were available to any rebel but were not stigmatized as 'rebel wives' or 'bush wives.'" Doherty added: "I am satisfied that the use of the term 'wife' is indicative of forced marital status which had lasting and serious impacts on the victims. I find the label of 'wife' to a rebel caused mental trauma, stigmatized the victims and negatively impacted their ability to reintegrate into their communities."[3]

As with the cited feminist legal scholars, Doherty, in making this finding, did not address the fact that both the prosecution's expert witness and some of the victims themselves noted that their experience was preferable to those who did not have the "protection" of a "husband." Various researchers have noted that bush wives in many circumstances fared much better than women who were not associated with a particular rebel husband (Coulter 2005; MacDonald 2008; Mazurana and McKay 2003; McKay 2004, 22). Indeed some gained status and rose to command positions. Nor did Doherty explain how the stigmatization or difficulties of reintegration experienced by those who had been bush wives was substantially worse than those who had been abducted, forced to fight, kept as sex slaves or forced labor, or raped. Even the prosecution's expert witness noted that many of the girls or women after they were abducted chose to remain with their husbands in preference to the worse fate of *not* being attached to a particular rebel.[4] This is not to suggest that those forced into marriages were not victims, but the emphasis is placed on their trauma and stigmatization risks, masking the very similar experiences of trauma, violence, and an inability to return to traditional communities that other women experienced in the war. It also raises the question of what message is being conveyed by such a prosecution, a question that requires greater consideration of how the nature of the violation was understood.

Despite her optimistic comments on the SCSL prosecutor's decision to include charges of forced marriage, Binaifer Nowrojee added a note of caution: "The Prosecutor and the Court should take care that patriarchal gender stereotypes of a wife's role, such as household cooking and cleaning, are not inadvertently incorporated into jurisprudence that nominally seeks to make gains for women" (2005, 102). Such cautionary advice proved to be both prophetic and sadly unheeded. Returning to Doherty's rationale for recognizing "forced marriage" as a crime, she focused on what she understood to be the creation of a "forced conjugal association."[5] This approach was subsequently endorsed by the Appeals Chamber, which provided the following definition of forced marriage:

> [T]he Appeals Chamber finds that in the context of the Sierra Leone conflict, forced marriage describes a situation in which the perpetrator through his words or conduct, or those of someone for whose actions he is responsible, compels a person by force, threat of force, or coercion to serve as a conjugal partner resulting in severe suffering, or physical, mental or psychological injury to the victim.[6]

As Valerie Oosterveld observes, "The Appeals Chamber's reliance on the term 'forced' added to 'conjugal association' implies that the 'conjugal association' aspect naturally consists of sex, cooking, cleaning, pregnancy, childbearing, and child-rearing" (2009, 87). However, what Oosterveld does not explain is why she is surprised by this. Indeed, the prosecution's very use of the term *marriage* was always a reflection of a patriarchal conception.

Michael Scharf and Suzanne Mattler were responsible for providing advice to the SCSL prosecutor on the viability of prosecuting the practice of forced marriage as a new crime against humanity. Their explanation for what is the core of the offence is informative: "forced marriages demean and distort the institution of marriage itself" (2005, 77). For Scharf and Mattler, what emerged as a central policy reason for prosecuting forced marriage had less to do with what the women endured as a result of this practice and more about protecting the sanctity of the institution of marriage itself. In an illuminating section of their analysis, they noted what they considered to be the detrimental change in status experienced by women in forced marriages:

> By virtue of attaching the rights of a spouse to [the victim of forced marriage], her "husband" traps her within the forced marriage through cultural and social mores in place to protect valid marriages. For example, in Sierra Leone, strong taboos exist regarding victims of rape. A woman who has been raped may be seen as unfit for marriage but if she is "married" to her rapist, then the sexual violence is deemed a part of the marital relationship and the woman is spared censure. (2005, 86)

Scharf and Mattler appeared unconcerned by this rather problematic situation for both married and unmarried women who suffer sexual violence, and they went on to conclude:

> The institution of marriage enjoys protected status because it facilitates the betterment of the individual and of society, objectives that cannot be

met in a forced marriage. The international community, therefore, has a clear interest in sending a strong message that forced marriage is an unacceptable perversion of a protected and valued institution, and it, and the threat it poses to the family, will not be tolerated. (2005, 86)

Following directly from their observation that sexual violence within marriage is not only tolerated but normalized in Sierra Leone (and as many feminists have pointed out), Scharf and Mattler's conclusion is deeply troubling. Certainly they seem oblivious to the argument many feminists have made that in fact marriage and the family have *not* always been sources of betterment in the lives of women (Coomaraswamy 1994, 117). Their own observation that women can be raped with impunity within legitimate, state-sanctioned marriages seems to provide a bizarre justification for why the institution of marriage should be protected! What becomes clear is that the interests being protected in the decision to prosecute forced marriage are not that of gender equality.

This impression is reinforced by the evidence ultimately presented to the SCSL by the prosecution via local civil society representative Zainab Bangura. Bangura's evidence provides a fascinating insight into the tensions and contradictions associated with the forced marriage prosecution. It also addresses a central issue that emerged in the trial regarding whether and how the practice of forced marriage during the conflict could be distinguished from the more general practice of early or arranged marriage common in rural Sierra Leone. Although this distinction was *legally* necessary, as Justice Julia Sebutinde pointed out to justify criminal prosecution,[7] it led to a highly unhelpful outcome for women's rights and human rights activists in Sierra Leone.

On the one hand, Bangura's description of her early life—facing marriage against her wishes at the age of 12, being thrown out of her father's home, and then denied the right to attend her mother's funeral—presented a powerful picture of the wide-reaching implications of patriarchy and its violence in the lives of young Sierra Leonean women. On the other hand, her later evidence asserted a fundamental distinction between forced marriage and arranged or early marriages conducted under customary law on the basis that the young woman or girl in the former had none of the protections of her family or community accorded in customary marriages. Given her own life experience, this seems a bizarre and contradictory position.

Based on my own conversations with human rights and women's rights activists in both 2006 (when I was working at the SCSL for three months) and in 2011 (during a follow-up trip exploring the legacy of the SCSL in relation to women's rights), this position was also at odds with that taken by many within the local human rights community. For example, Brima

Sheriff, the local director of Amnesty International Sierra Leone, stated that initially he and various other human rights activists had been eager to work with the SCSL for the very reason that they hoped its decision to prosecute forced marriage would lead to local law reform to abolish the practice of early or coerced arranged marriage (personal communication, May 21, 2006). They were therefore extremely disillusioned when they discovered the narrow scope of the SCSL's definition. By drawing an express distinction between those forced marriages within the conflict and the everyday practice of early or arranged marriage, not only did the SCSL not assist the human rights activists' work, it in fact made it harder. Added to this, the specific ways in which forced marriage was characterized as a crime highlights further troubling tendencies.

In the AFRC case Doherty made the following startling observation:

> On the evidence I find that the intention of the "husband" was to oblige the victim to work and care for him and his property, to fulfill his sexual needs, remain faithful and loyal to him and to bear children if the "wife" became pregnant. In return, he would protect the "wife" from rape by other men, give her food when food was available and, depending on his status, confer a corresponding status upon the wife. In effect, these are rights and obligations of the type referred to by the Defense expert as being involved in traditional marriages but in there is no agreement of the family or kin of the "wife" and the status is forced by violence or coercion upon the female partner.[8]

What is striking in this paragraph is the way in which Doherty does not seek to problematize the assumed role of the wife in a traditional Sierra Leonean marriage but simply qualifies the acceptability of this state of affairs as dependent on whether the wife's family or kin have agreed to this arrangement. Similarly, Scharf and Mattler, while noting the potential for overlap between those practices identified as "arranged marriages" in peacetime and those identified as "forced marriages" in times of war, identified what they considered to be the distinguishing features of the latter. The former was a lack of consent: a requirement they considered if not from the prospective spouse at least from her family, accompanied by the payment of bride wealth (2005, 81). The latter was the intention of the practice:

> The practice of arranged marriage is not injurious to the groups that practice it in intent or result. Forced marriage, in contrast, has no basis in the benevolent parental objectives to assist children or to perpetuate important values, and it is highly injurious to its victims. (Scharf and Mattler 2005, 89)

Certainly it would be wrong to assert that all forms of arranged marriage are deeply injurious or ill-intentioned. However, so too is Scharf and Mattler's assumption that arranged marriage in Sierra Leone is automatically seen as a "benevolent" and legitimate practice. As noted previously, this was certainly not the view of many within the Sierra Leonean human rights community who had been actively seeking reform of customary law and practice to better protect the rights of women and girls.

Furthermore, the extended definition of consent—which allowed for this to be given not by a woman or girl alone but also potentially by her family—specifically deviated from the international human rights standard. In this way, not only did the emphasis on the distinction between international criminal law and international human rights law do little to enhance the latter's authority, it actually undermined it. Added to this, the reference to the failure on the part of the perpetrator to follow custom and in particular pay the bride wealth left the impression that this was essentially a violation of the property rights of the victim's family. In light of this definition of forced marriage, it becomes debatable whether international criminal justice has really come that far from the traditional characterization of women's rights violations as "a crime against the family honor or family property" (Doherty 2009, 2).

As occurred in the CDF case, feminist demands on international criminal justice to specifically respond to crimes committed against women paradoxically resulted in a marginalization of women's experiences from the central accounts of the conflict. Rather than inflecting understanding of enslavement or forced labor with a gender perspective (i.e., recognizing the gendered ways in which this violation may occur), crimes committed against women were set up as separate based on a patriarchal conception of the harm. Not only did this preclude recognition of the harm suffered by some women and girls (those abducted, raped, and enslaved but *not* identified as wives) during the war, it also placed another obstacle in the way of those seeking greater gender equality in times of peace. Moreover, I argue that while the factual scenarios may be unique to the SCSL, they are illustrative of a number of problematic features underlying the international criminal justice project more broadly.

The Symbolic Significance of "Woman"

As various feminist scholars on nationalism have identified, men and women have been incorporated into communal identities in different ways. In particular, women have frequently performed a symbolic function—

operating as the embodiment of the national or ethnic community—rather than occupying the role of active citizen subjects (Eisenstein 2000; Yuval-Davis 1997). Although this role has been increasingly recognized by those concerned with sexual violence committed in conflict, I argue that insufficient steps have been taken within the international criminal justice project and many feminist engagements with it to actually problematize and deconstruct this role. Rather, as I have discussed elsewhere (Grewal 2010), the prosecution of rape as a "weapon of war" (and thus distinct from rape in times of "peace") has frequently reinforced the status quo. As the CDF case demonstrates, the symbolic role ascribed to women has worked to the detriment of rape victims whose experience cannot be generalized to hold greater communal significance. Moreover, the symbolic rather than the actual significance of the women identified as victims emerged as even more clearly problematic in the conceptualization and prosecution of forced marriage.

Although the initial inclusion of the charge of forced marriage was alleged to be responding to women's experiences, the particular definition adopted by the prosecutor and the judges in fact rendered invisible many women's experience of harm both during and beyond the conflict. Not only did it exclude those women and girls who were abducted, raped, and forced to work but were *not* kept as wives, it legitimated a perverse situation where women and girls forced to marry in times of "peace" were left without legal recourse. In the end the nature of the violation identified by the SCSL relied not so much on the subjective experience of the individual woman or girl, but on the violation of family rights to decide to whom a woman or girl should be married. This was a point also made by the defense counsel for the accused Brima in the AFRC trial.[9]

The Problem With Cultural Sensitivity

At the same time, one of the justifications given for the narrow and extremely conservative approach to prosecuting forced marriage was a regard for the cultural relativity of such intimate practices as marriage, reproduction, and family life. However, as Lori Handrahan points out: "The international community engaged in post-conflict needs to recognize that 'cultural sensitivity' does not mean supporting systems of violence, oppression and gender inequality even if these are 'couched' as a prevailing ethnic identity" (2004, 440–41). The unquestioned acceptance of the benevolence inherent within customary marriage practices, despite the assertions by local women's rights and human rights activists to the contrary (and indeed evidenced by the prosecution's own expert witness's life experience), reflects a selective and superficial approach to cultural sensitivity. It also reinforces Handrahan's view that:

> It is rarely considered that encouraging a return to what is considered "normal" after a conflict may reflect the patriarchal order before the conflict, where women's rights might have been routinely violated. Or that the international community's definition of "normal" tolerates high levels of violence against women in their own societies. (2004, 440)

The failure on the part of both the prosecutor and the judges to reflect more critically on the institution of marriage before accepting the importance of its protection seems to exemplify Handrahan's point as well as demonstrate the patriarchal foundation of international criminal justice.

The recruitment of a local expert to give evidence in the trial process may seem to add legitimacy to the approach taken. However, this in itself raises two issues. First, as noted previously, given Bangura's life experience, it seems highly unusual that she would conclude that customary marriage could be distinguished from forced marriage due to the better protections offered in the former to women and girls. Second, it also seems to run contrary to much of the women's rights campaigning in Sierra Leone, exemplified in the campaign that led to the passing of three gender acts[10] in 2007.

One possible explanation for the inconsistency is the contradictory pressures faced by many feminist activists located in the global south to address the culturally specific nature of oppression, the demands of a universalizing discourse of suffering required by the international human rights movement, and the need to resist colonial discourses of the backwardness of certain cultures and traditions (Mohanty 2003; Narayan 1997). Unfortunately, what these pressures frequently produce is a discourse in which the "culturally specific" and the "universal" remain uncontestedly defined by the status quo. The contradictory understandings of forced marriage as either or both a result of backward traditional practices or a perversion of the natural institutions of marriage and the family ultimately serve to mask the contested nature of both these assertions. Indeed Bangura's evidence makes little reference to the ongoing resistance by local women to the acceptability of customary marriage practices in the name of tradition (resistance that some saw as undermined by the SCSL's characterization of the violation of forced marriage). At the same time, her definition of what constituted the harm in forced marriages during the conflict seemed to suggest women otherwise experienced being married as an undisputedly positive status. Not only does this not seem to have been the case in her own life, it runs contrary to what women's rights actors in both the Sierra Leonean and many other contexts have asserted.

International Experts and Authentic Locals

This brings me to my final observation. I consider it noteworthy that Bangura's report ultimately mirrors the views set out in the brief provided to the prosecutor's office by a male US law professor and his student who have no particular familiarity with the Sierra Leonean context nor with women's rights in that region. Furthermore, although Scharf and Mattler provided their advice to the SCSL prosecutor in 2004, the prosecution itself told the Trial Chamber that Bangura was not selected to act as an expert witness and compile a report on the issue until February 2005.[11] Added to this, as a member of the AFRC defense counsel pointed out, Bangura's prior experience was as an insurance broker and advocate in the area of governance and democratization rather than with survivors of sexual or gender-based violence.

Acknowledging her own limited experience working with bush wives, Bangura in her own testimony stated,[12] as have others (McKay 2004, 27), that it was the nongovernmental organization (NGO), Forum for African Women Educationalists (FAWE), that had worked with bush wives, female combatants, and rape victims throughout and after the conflict. This is noteworthy as when a colleague and I were invited in July 2006 by the SCSL defense office to conduct a gender competency training workshop, we approached FAWE. In agreeing to help us, the two representatives remarked that this was the first time their experience and expertise had been recognized or called upon by anyone at the SCSL. On the one hand, this anecdote highlights the farcical circumstances of our invitation, two young women from the global north who had been in Sierra Leone no more than two months and both with limited gender training experience being allowed to run a training that long-term local practitioners had been unable to organize. On the other hand, it seems to beg the question: How and why was Bangura selected as the forced marriage expert?

In commenting on the current status of the human rights discourse, Gayatri Spivak (2004) urges a complication of the straightforward binary frequently drawn between international and local perspectives. This is important given the increased lip service paid to local consultation within international community discourse. Apart from identifying the potential limitations of metropolitan human rights' construction of "the colonial subject transformed into the new domestic middle-class urban radical," as representing the "below," Spivak notes: "To be able to present a problem intelligibly and persuasively for the taste of the North, is itself proof of a sort of epistemic discontinuity with the ill-educated rural poor" (2004, 527), the very people the human rights industry claims to be concerned with helping.

My aim here is neither to criticize Bangura's engagement with the international community nor to suggest that this automatically disqualifies her from speaking on the situation of women in her home context. This would indeed be a perverse refashioning of the traditional disregard for global south perspectives and voices. Rather, by understanding the processes through which Bangura is constructed as an authentic local voice situated as speaking authoritatively and, therefore, incontestably, a more complex picture of the international community and its engagement in postconflict societies emerges.

In the context of international involvement in postconflict societies, all too often only select local voices have been endorsed or engaged with. Although this is often argued to be the only feasible approach—clearly engaging with everyone is not possible—I do not believe this to be simply innocent pragmatism. Rather, all too often the only local voices heard are those that reflect what the international community expects (wants) to hear. Making a similar argument, Julie Mertus notes that following the war in Kosovo, many international donors that focused on issues related to women preferred to work with newly created local NGOs and women's sections of political parties rather the local women's projects that had existed throughout the 1990s. A particular source of tension was the identification of expertise: "'They find us difficult to deal with,' one longtime Kosovar women's rights activist explains, 'because they want to *train us* and we don't want their training'" (quoted in Mertus 2003, 165). My own observations and conversations with many prominent Sierra Leonean women's rights and human rights figures, while anecdotal, seem to mirror this finding.

For this reason I see Bangura's expert testimony as effectively allowing international criminal justice to kill two birds with one stone. On the one hand, the fact that she was hired some time after the initial expert advice was obtained and her report differed little from this advice allowed the prosecution to maintain their view on the issue unhindered by the contestation of local women's rights activists. On the other hand, it offered the badge of legitimacy by virtue of being delivered by an authentic local, thus avoiding the potential charge of cultural imperialism.

Not only does this do little to produce *genuine* local engagement, it also potentially limits our understanding of the various complex—and locally contested—factors at play within both conflict and postconflict contexts. Instead, international criminal justice institutions like the SCSL push toward the adoption of a simplified and decontextualized understanding of what has happened during the conflict and how it relates to peacetime. Not only does this achieve little in terms of women's rights development within the particular postconflict society, it also does little to destabilize the patriarchal foundation of international legal institutions. Indeed as Charlesworth reminds us:

> The lives of women are considered part of a crisis only when they are harmed in a way that is seen to demean the whole of their social group. For example, international law regards massive and organized rapes of women in times of armed conflict as illegal because they affect the honor of a community. Other forms of systemic violence, or structural discrimination against women, do not constitute a crisis for international lawyers. This is rather seen as part of the status quo and not truly the business of international law. (2002, 389)

The example of the SCSL would seem to suggest that not only is the positive potential of international criminal justice for improving the lives of women not often lived up to, but potentially detrimental consequences can come out of this selective approach to understanding and punishing crimes against women.

Conclusion

Although many feminist scholars have sought to engage positively with international criminal justice on the basis that it may hold potential for providing the redress long denied women, the example of the SCSL unfortunately does not inspire optimism. If it started out as a potentially positive step toward enhancing women's rights in Sierra Leone and beyond, it fell victim to a number of deep-rooted problems within the international framework. In particular, the need for crimes committed against women to be characterizable as about something *other* than *just gender* in order to be punished means that not only do some women's experiences never receive recognition, but the implicit construction of women as symbols rather than rights-bearing individuals remains unchallenged. Added to this, the gender and cultural assumptions imported by many of the internationals working within the system ultimately raises the question: Do more gender crimes prosecutions necessarily mean positive change? Having sought to demonstrate the ways in which the SCSL's incorporation of feminist agendas has led to counterproductive and sometimes perverse outcomes, my answer to this would be not without much greater critical reflection.

Notes

1. *Prosecutor v. Sam Hinga Norman, Moinina Fofana and Allieu Kondewa,* SCSL-04-14-T-434 (CDF Trial Chamber), Reasoned Majority Decision on Prosecution Motion for a Ruling on the Admissibility of Evidence, May 24, 2004.

2. CDF Trial Chamber, Decision on Prosecution Request for Leave to Amend the Indictment, May 20, 2004, para. 58.

3. *The Prosecutor of the Special Court v. Brima et al.,* SCSL-2004-16-T (AFRC Trial Chamber), Trial Chamber Judgment, *Partly Dissenting Opinion of Justice Doherty on Count 7 (Sexual Slavery) and Count 8 (Forced Marriage),* June 20, 2007, para. 50 and 51.

4. AFRC Trial Chamber transcript, October 3, 2005, 54; 56-57. www.sc-sl.org/CASES/ProsecutorvsBrimaKamaraandKanuAFRCCase/Transcripts/tabid/158/Default.aspx, accessed August 30, 2011.

5. Above note 3, para. 53.

6. *The Prosecutor of the Special Court v. Brima et al.,* SCSL-2004-16-A, Appeals Chamber Judgment, February 22, 2008, para. 196.

7. AFRC Trial Chamber, *Separate Concurring Opinion of the Honorable Justice Julia Sebutinde Appended to Judgement Pursuant to Rule 88(C),* June 21, 2007, para. 12.

8. Above note 3, para. 49.

9. Above note 6, 118.

10. These acts cover domestic violence, the registration of customary marriage and divorce, and inheritance: www.socialedge.org/blogs/alyson-in-africa/archive/2008/01/29/implementing-the-gender-acts-in-sierra-leone, accessed August 30, 2011.

11. AFRC Pre-Trial Chamber, *Separate and Concurring Opinion of Justice Doherty on Prosecution Request for Leave to Call an Additional Witness Pursuant to Rule 73bis (E) and Joint Defense Application to Exclude this Expert Evidence of Zainab Hawa Bangura or Alternatively to Cross-Examine Her Pursuant to Rule 94bis,* October 21, 2005, at para. 5.

12. Above note 4, 97.

6

Combating Postconflict Violence Against Women

An Analysis of the Liberian and Sierra Leonean Governments' Efforts to Address the Problem

Peace A. Medie

ALTHOUGH THE AFTERMATH OF WAR IS EXPERIENCED DIFFERENTLY IN EACH STATE, HIGH LEVELS of human insecurity is a common thread that runs through postwar societies. Violence against women is one such type of human insecurity that is present preconflict, becomes widespread during war, and persists in its aftermath (Meintjes, Turshen, and Pillay 2001; Sweetman 2005).[1] The end of conflict ushers in a transitional period in which the ultimate goal is to prevent a relapse into conflict, engender human security, and promote development. Nongovernmental organizations (NGOs), governments, and the international community work independently and collaboratively to accomplish these goals (Dobbins et al. 2007; Ndulo 2007).

The reduction in levels of violence against women is heavily dependent on the decisions that are made by the state and the steps taken to implement them. Postconflict governments, however, are considerably constrained in their attempts to implement policies that benefit their citizens. This is partly because the majority of these governments have weak institutions (Bolongaita 2005; Gantz 2007; Rotberg 2004). Consequently, many of their efforts do not have the intended effects. This challenge is compounded in the area of women's rights policy implementation because of patriarchal norms that engender violence against women (Dobash and Dobash 1972; Petersen 1992). These norms pervade institutions and hinder effective policy implementation.

This chapter examines the behaviors and conditions that impede the implementation of anti–violence against women policies and contribute to ineffective policy outcomes in Liberia and Sierra Leone. Violence against women continues to be a major problem in both states several years after the conflicts officially ended, in spite of a variety of policies and programs that aim to ameliorate the problem. Although the case of Sierra Leone highlights the difficulties of responding to violence against women in the absence of a strong female presence within the government, the situation in Liberia reveals that this presence alone is insufficient to protect women from violence. Both cases presented in this chapter demonstrate that reducing levels of violence against women depends heavily on the erosion of deeply engrained patriarchal norms and the reformation of weak state institutions.

Postconflict Violence Against Women

Many violent conflicts in the past two decades have been characterized by the targeting of civilians by all warring factions (Kaldor 2007), and research indicates that violence against women occurs at elevated levels during such wars (Rehn and Johnson Sirleaf 2002). The costs of conflict, however, extend beyond physical harm and include economic, social, and environmental devastation. The end of conflict does not automatically result in significantly increased levels of human security, as high levels of human insecurity usually persist in the initial postconflict phase (Coulter, Persson, and Utas 2008; Kumar 2001).

Violence against women is one form of insecurity that is prevalent during this period. It sometimes occurs as domestic violence, which ranges in form from verbal attacks to physical assaults that maim and kill victims. Sexual violence, which can also occur in tandem with domestic violence, is also a major problem in most postconflict states (Ertürk 2008). Trafficking in women and girls for sexual slavery and physical labor is also an area of concern during this period (Bastick, Grimm, and Kunz 2007; Ward and Marsh 2006). Other forms of violence against women, including forced and early marriage, dowry killings, infanticide, and female genital cutting, also occur and may be largely unchecked within postconflict societies.

Working both independently and in collaboration with government agencies, international organizations and NGOs implement a range of programs with the aim of engendering human security for both women and men. These organizations also serve as women's rights advocates by pressuring governments to introduce and enforce existing legislation related to violence against women. Yet governments vary in their responses to violence against women, and while some states have introduced policies to address the problems, others have been considerably slower and sometimes even reluctant to implement measures to tackle violence against women (Tripp et al. 2009).

Postconflict Governments' Responses to Violence Against Women

Grassroots women's organizations, NGOs, international organizations, bilateral agencies, and postconflict governments are the major actors that work to reduce incidents of violence against women. The United Nations is one of the most visible bodies that promotes initiatives to reduce the problem. Working through the UN Development Fund for Women, the UN Development Program, the United Nations Population Fund, and the Security Council, the United Nations has lobbied governments to adopt measures that have the potential to reduce various forms of violence against women. It has also introduced resolutions that recognize the extents and effects of violence against women in conflict and postconflict societies. UN Security Council Resolutions 1325, 1820, and 1888 have raised awareness of sexual violence during and after conflict. Regional bodies such as the African Union have also developed women's rights agendas. The African Union's Protocol to the African Charter on Human and People's Rights on the Rights of Women in Africa (Maputo Protocol), which entered into force in 2005, addresses issues of women's security and protection from all forms of violence.

Bilateral agencies and international organizations also partner with local organizations and governments or work independently to raise awareness of women's rights and to provide health, education, and other services for women. Some of these organizations also directly lobby governments to take actions to protect women's rights. They sometimes serve as nodes for local and international women's rights networks. Local women's groups have also created a variety of programs to assist survivors of violence against women. In many areas, grassroots groups and women's NGOs fill the programmatic gaps that result from the governments' inability to function effectively. These groups provide a range of services, which includes shelters for battered women and free legal advice to rape survivors. Advocacy by women's groups has been central to placing women's rights on the agenda and has also positively influenced the formulation and implementation of policies to enhance these rights in many postconflict states. Postconflict governments, however, vary in their responses to this call for action, and in many cases where governments pass and implement policies, evidence indicates that violence against women (VAW) remains a major problem.[2] This is the case in Liberia and Sierra Leone.

Violence Against Women in Liberia: Laws, Policies, and Programs

Women's experiences of violence have varied across ages, geographic locations, identity groups, and socioeconomic classes in pre- and postconflict Liberia (Bledsoe 1980; Liberia Ministry of Gender and Development 2009). The atrocities that the warring factions committed against women during the country's conflicts led to the introduction of new policies and programs to protect women from some forms of violence. There were multiple warring factions in both of Liberia's wars, the first of which began when Charles Taylor's National Patriotic Front of Liberia launched an attack against the government of Samuel Doe in 1989 (Kieh 2008). Taylor won national elections in 1997, but by April 1999, his government was under attack from a group called Liberians United for Reconciliation and Democracy. These attacks launched the second civil war, which contributed to Taylor's eventual resignation in August 2003 and culminated in the signing of the Comprehensive Peace Agreement, which officially brought the conflict to an end.

All factions considered civilians to be legitimate targets and participated in their kidnapping, rape, torture, and murder. An estimated 200,000 people were murdered during the wars and close to half of the country's population of 2.5 million was displaced. Studies reveal that physical and sexual violence against women was rampant during both civil wars and was particularly brutal. A health needs assessment revealed that 81.6 percent of women experienced some form of violence during the wars, of which 72.1 percent were raped (Omanyondo 2005).[3] Women were also captured to serve as porters, cooks, and sexual partners for combatants (Swiss et al. 2008).

Sexual and physical violence have continued in the aftermath of the conflicts, and an estimated 22 percent of women experienced violence in 2008.[4] In 2007, rape was the most reported crime in the country, and 46 percent of the cases involved children.[5] Many more incidents have gone unreported because women lack faith in the judicial system and often cannot afford the socioeconomic costs that come with seeking justice under statutory and customary laws. Despite the high report of rapes, research demonstrates that it is not the most prevalent form of violence against women (Tomzyck et al. 2007), as women and girls continue to experience domestic violence and have also been trafficked for prostitution, sexual exploitation, and forced physical labor (U.S. Department of State, 2010a). Forced and early marriage and female genital cutting are harmful practices that women and girls have had to undergo in Liberia. The UN's *World Marriage Data* (United Nations Population Division 2008) reveals that in 2008, just over 7 percent of girls between the ages of 15 and 19 were married. According to the United Nations Children's Fund (2009), 53.8 percent of women between the ages of 15 and 49 had been subjected to the practice of female genital cutting.

Women's vulnerability is structural as well as physical; according to Liberia's 2007 Demographic and Health Survey, 17.6 percent of men between the ages of 15 and 49 have no education, while the percentage for women within that same age group is 42.4 (Liberia Institute of Statistics and Geo-Information Services, Ministry of Health and Social Welfare 2007). Liberian women are also exposed to high levels of economic insecurity due to high national unemployment levels and the overrepresentation of women in the low paying informal sector (Liberia Institute of Statistics and Geo-Information Services 2007). Liberia also has very high maternal and infant mortality rates (Liberia Institute of Statistics and Geo-Information Services 2007), and HIV/AIDS is more prevalent among women than among men (WHO, UNAIDS, and UNICEF 2008).

Liberia's postconflict governments, due to pressure from local women's groups, NGOs, and international organizations, have amended existing legislation to address violence against women and introduced new laws to provide women with more rights and opportunities in all spheres. Both postconflict governments have also developed multiple women's rights policy documents and programs, largely in collaboration with NGOs and the international community.

Since the election of President Ellen Johnson Sirleaf in 2006, Liberia has created three national gender action plans, one of which is the Liberian National Plan for the Implementation of UN Security Council Resolution (UNSCR) 1325, which proposes practical steps to implement the recommendations made in UNSCR 1325. These new laws and policies have led to a range of initiatives to protect women from violence as well as to empower them. They include the 2007 Anti-Rape Campaign to highlight the problem of rape in Liberia. In February 2009, the government created Criminal Court E exclusively to try rape cases and established the Women and Child Protection Section of the police force.

Local women's organizations and the international community have applauded these steps on the part of both postconflict governments, and yet simultaneously acknowledge that the government needs to do more to combat the problem of violence against women (IRIN 2009a). Although comprehensive periodic surveys to measure changes in the levels of physical and sexual violence and to evaluate existing initiatives are lacking, reports demonstrate that sexual and physical violence continue to be major problems in the country (CEDAW 2008; UN-INSTRAW 2009; U.S. Department of State 2010a). The question remains as to why violence against women remains pervasive in Liberia in spite of the government's initiatives to resolve the problems, and, as the following section will illustrate, the case of Sierra Leone raises the same question.

Gender-Based Violence in
Sierra Leone: Laws, Policies, and Programs

Throughout Sierra Leone's history, women's positions and roles in society have varied based on the ethnic, religious, and socioeconomic groups to which they belong. Similarly, women's experiences of violence and society's responses have also varied across these groups. The Sierra Leonean civil war was notorious for the egregious acts of violence perpetrated against noncombatants by warring factions. The war officially began when the Revolutionary United Fund (RUF), a rebel group led by Foday Sankoh, launched an attack against the government of Major Joseph Momoh in 1991. Rebel and government factions murdered more than 50,000. The RUF was particularly brutal and made the mutilation of the Sierra Leonean population one of the principal tenets of its warfare strategy. Both progovernment militia and rebel forces, which were composed of both women and men, forcefully conscripted, impregnated, displaced, raped, trafficked, tortured, enslaved, and murdered women (Mazurana, Carlson, and Anderlini 2004; UN Economic and Social Council 2001). An estimated 250,000 women experienced some form of sexual violence during the civil war (Physicians for Human Rights 2002). These human rights abuses have resulted in grave physical, psychological, and social consequences for women.

The postconflict governments of presidents Ahmed Kabbah and Ernest Bai Koroma have introduced new laws with the aim of reducing some forms of violence against women. In 2005, the Sierra Leonean government passed the Anti-Human Trafficking Act, which criminalized all forms of human trafficking; in 2007, it passed the Domestic Violence Act as well as the Child's Rights Act, which outlawed early and forced marriages. The Kabbah government established the Family Support Unit (FSU) in 2001 within the police force to deal with domestic violence; as of March 2010, there were 40 FSU stations across the country. There has also been an increase in women's participation in the political sphere and in the security sector. Female participation in the police force increased from 5 percent preconflict to 20 percent postconflict (Kabia 2010).

In spite of these measures, women continue to be highly vulnerable to all forms of violence, with an estimated 67 percent of urban women subjected to domestic violence in 2008 (Integrated Regional Information Network 2009b). In 2007, the FSU reported that the rape of girls was becoming increasingly common, as 65 percent of cases reported to the police in 2006 involved females who were under 18 years old (IRIN 2007). Civil society organizations described an "alarming spate" of rapes between January and March 2010 (UNDP 2010a), and yet none of the 927 cases of sexual abuse in the country reported to the FSU in 2009 resulted in a conviction

(IRIN 2010). This occurs in a particular context in which early marriages and female genital cutting are common practices (Statistics Sierra Leone and ICF Macro 2009), poverty is endemic, and Sierra Leone ranks 180 of 182 on the Human Development Index. Health care remains inaccessible to many, and HIV/AIDS prevalence is disproportionately higher among women (WHO, UNAIDS, and UNICEF 2008).Women also lag behind in education and are underrepresented in the formal sector (Statistics Sierra Leone and ICF Macro 2009).

Similar to the situation in Liberia, these figures reveal that existing policies and laws have not adequately protected women from physical and sexual violence. They seem to have failed to sufficiently deter the violent acts and harmful practices they were created to address. Furthermore, survivors are frequently denied justice. I argue that these trends can be attributed to two sets of factors. The first set is internal to the state bureaucracy and includes the deeply engrained patriarchal norms that are held by many in the public sector, weak institutions, the lack of accountability, a shortage of skilled personnel, and governments that face severe fiscal constraints. These factors create an implementation deficit by hindering the successful enforcement of laws and implementation of policies.

The second set of factors consists of socioeconomic conditions within both countries that affect the lives of the citizenry and engender and facilitate violence against women. These conditions also hinder measures that are introduced by the state to address the problem. These categories are not mutually exclusive because government agencies and the people who work within them influence the social and economic conditions within the state and vice versa. This chapter employs these categories mainly to structure the discussion.

Explaining Policy Outcomes

Weak States, Weak Institutions, and Violence Against Women

One factor that significantly hinders the effective enforcement of laws and implementation of policies is the weak institutions that characterize postconflict states. States that are recovering from extended periods of conflict, including Liberia and Sierra Leone, tend to have institutions that lack the mechanisms needed to engender efficiency, transparency, and accountability (Bolongaita 2005; Rotberg 2004). This adversely affects how these institutions function and the quality of public goods and services they are tasked with providing.

Both Liberia and Sierra Leone have institutions that were compromised before the civil wars and that continue to face considerable organizational challenges. Each country's national government has taken steps, in conjunction with the international community, to reform these institutions, especially those in the security sector. Nevertheless, reports argue that significant sections of the police force and judiciary in both states are corrupt and lack professionalism. Low pay among officials within the public sector and delays in payment of salaries have contributed to these problems (Amnesty International 2009; Malan 2008). The Liberia National Police is also plagued by a general lack of infrastructure and is largely ineffective due to the scarcity of vehicles, radios, handcuffs, and other necessary equipment (Malan 2008). The scarcity of resources also directly affects the prosecution of cases, partly because of a low forensic capacity that precludes the use of DNA evidence in cases of sexual violence.

These problems are mirrored in Sierra Leone, where police officers frequently demand bribes to perform their duties and to pervert the course of justice (Chikwanha 2008). The FSUs have a shortage of trained staff and lack necessities such as vehicles or forensic equipment (Barnes, Albrecht, and Olson 2007). The challenges extend to the judicial sector as well; in Sierra Leone, the limited number of lawyers has resulted in police officers serving as prosecutors in the national courts. Chikwanha (2008) explains that these officers often come to court unprepared, causing the victims to lose their cases. The prison sector also suffers from a lack of equipment and infrastructure. There have been several prison breaks in Liberia due to security lapses and weak prison infrastructure. The health sector is also affected by the lack of infrastructure. In Liberia, many survivors of violence against women, particularly rural women, are unable to access health care or must walk long distances to see a medical professional (Greenberg 2009).

The effects of weak and underfunded institutions are compounded by norms that condone, engender, and trivialize the problem of violence against women. Police officers in Sierra Leone are reluctant to intervene in domestic abuse cases unless they result in grave physical injuries or death (UN Population Fund 2005). This is mostly because some officers and a considerable proportion of the population—including women—still think that it is acceptable for men to physically punish their wives. These norms also sanction harmful practices. Similarly, politicians have openly supported the practice of female genital cutting in order to curry favor with powerful traditional leaders during elections (German Technical Cooperation 2007).These patriarchal norms are also present in Liberia (Liberia Ministry of Gender and Development 2009) and similarly negatively impact the formulation and implementation of legislation on violence against women.

The limitations of state institutions have created the space for traditional leaders to employ informal rulings to adjudicate cases. Studies reveal that chiefs illegally preside over cases and make rulings that often abuse women's rights; for instance, some chiefs in the Kenema District of Sierra Leone have responded to domestic disputes by locking up the survivors (UNFPA 2005). In Sierra Leone and Liberia, evidence reveals that traditional rulers often force rape survivors to marry their rapists (UN General Assembly 2007). Many women therefore find themselves in a situation where they cannot get justice under statutory law and are subject to abuse in the customary legal systems.

The governments' efforts to address VAW are also affected by the lack of data on the subject, a problem both Liberia and Sierra Leone have begun to address. Liberia's 2007 and Sierra Leone's 2008 Demographic and Health Surveys were important steps in ameliorating this problem. In 2008, both states launched a National Strategy for the Development of Statistics. The Liberian government has made data collection an essential part of its plan to implement Resolution 1325. Despite these efforts, there is still a need for current, comprehensive, and sex-segregated data in both states. The inadequacy of data has hindered the governments' efforts to evaluate the scope of problems and to respond accordingly, and it also makes it difficult for both governments to evaluate existing programs and to determine changes that need to be made (Piah 2009).

Such conditions negatively affect the governments' ability to combat violence against women and result in policy implementation deficits whereby government agencies are unable or unwilling to implement policies as outlined in legal and policy documents. This leads to policy outcomes that do not adequately tackle violence against women and are largely ineffective. This ineffectiveness contributes to the state of insecurity that puts women at risk of violence and engenders impunity. Weak state institutions also cause survivors to lose faith in the criminal justice system and compel them to turn to customary laws and, in extreme cases, to mob justice.

Socioeconomic Conditions and Violence Against Women

The patriarchal norms that pervade state institutions are also present across Sierra Leonean and Liberian society. These norms promote and facilitate the occurrence of VAW within homes and communities. They also provide protection for perpetrators of VAW and hinder survivors' attempts to get justice (Barnes, Albrecht, and Olson 2007; Liberia Ministry of Gender and Development 2009; Park 2006). The effects of these norms are compounded by the economic and social conditions within both states.

The majority of Liberians live in abject poverty, and Sierra Leone is one of the poorest countries in the world. In Sierra Leone, poverty has forced many girls and women into prostitution, putting them at risk of all forms of violence (John-Langba 2008). The social dislocation caused by the conflict has resulted in a breakdown in the family structure, and there are many households where a sole parent—usually the mother—is responsible for supporting extended family members. This requires some mothers to be away from home for long hours, leaving many children unsupervised and unprotected for long periods of time and exposing them to all forms of violence (Barnes, Albrecht, and Olson 2007). Children also sell on the streets to support their families.

Young girls are especially vulnerable in such situations because they are often lured into homes and other secluded areas by people who pretend to be interested in their wares but then proceed to sexually assault them. The poverty that pervades these societies also creates fertile conditions for international peacekeepers and humanitarian workers to sexually exploit girls and women (Nordic Africa Institute 2009). Furthermore, poverty in both states and the weaknesses in the security sector have led survivors of violence and their families to accept financial compensation from rapists in exchange for not reporting rapes to the police. It has also made it difficult for many women to access health care in the aftermath of attacks.

The years of conflict have normalized violence in some areas of both societies (Barnes, Albrecht, and Olson 2007; UN-INSTRAW 2009). Furthermore, many young people are unemployed and idle in both states. This, combined with the experiences of conflict and the high levels of poverty, has created conditions that breed violence. In Liberia, armed robbery is on the increase, and rape during robberies has become a common phenomenon (Malan 2008). Although prevailing poverty and social dislocation do not cause violence against women, they create conditions in which the problem thrives due to the socioeconomic vulnerability of women and girls. These conditions contribute to the high incidence of violence against women, which overburdens the already weak state institutions and limits program effectiveness (Zuckerman and Greenberg 2004).

Lessons Learned

Although the state is only one of several actors playing a role in addressing violence against women, its actions are determinative to a reduction of the problem. The cases of Liberia and Sierra Leone provide valuable insight into the challenges that confront governments as they implement policies. Both cases reveal that there is a major implementation deficit in the protection of women's rights. Weak institutions constitute a key impediment to effectively implementing policies. It is therefore imperative that the international community continue to provide support for institutional reform in all sectors of government. Security sector reform programs in both Liberia and Sierra Leone have improved the performance of the police forces and judiciaries, but weak accountability, corruption, and lack of professionalism and equipment are problems that persist. There needs to be a sustained effort by all stakeholders to reduce the levels of these problems and to improve the performance of all state agencies.

Patriarchal norms and customs that engender and condone violence against women are prevalent in state institutions in both Sierra Leone and Liberia. Their existence underscores the inadequacy of legislative and policy reforms for provoking behavior change. There is, therefore, a need for the continual education of public servants. Governments have to make gender-sensitivity training an ongoing aspect of professional development for all public servants. This is necessary because the social norms that promote violence against women have emerged over centuries and cannot be removed with brief training sessions that target specific state agencies but neglect others.

Related to this is the need for a transformation in societal norms and attitudes toward women. Although this is a monumental task, it can be accomplished to a degree if it is prioritized by policymakers. In both Liberia and Sierra Leone, women's rights groups and international organizations have taken the lead in this area, implementing a range of awareness-raising programs. For their part, the governments have to make women's rights a constant and integral part of their message to the public and to emphasize their nontolerance of violence through rhetoric and action. The governments also need to make trauma and counseling services more available to the population. These services are necessary to provide rehabilitation for ex-combatants and other members of society who have become used to a violent culture and to help heal those who were victimized during and after the conflicts.[6]

The challenges that confront both governments also illustrate the need for a women's rights approach that transcends all spheres. The Liberian government has taken a positive step in this direction; in its 2009 national action plan to implement UNSC 1325, it outlined a comprehensive approach that recognized that substantial progress in the area of women's rights cannot occur in a society that is crippled by illiteracy, unemployment, and poverty. A reduction in the levels of violence against women requires actions in all sectors of the state. Women must be represented in all sectors of government and must have a voice in the decision-making process at all levels. This is not only important to empower individual women, but also to open the door for the creation and implementation of more gender-sensitive policies. Both Liberia and Sierra Leone have made significant strides in this area, but women are still underrepresented in all governmental sectors.

This comprehensive approach also has to recognize, and address, the problems that confront men. The governments and the international community have to create programs that provide education and employment for the thousands of barely literate and unemployed young men in both states. The welfare of men plays a central role in women's experiences of violence. The implementation of anti-VAW policies in the face of high levels of poverty makes it more difficult to produce favorable outcomes. Efforts to end violence against women, therefore, have to occur concurrently with those that aim to reduce poverty among all groups and to socially empower women.

Governments also need to educate and, where possible, work with religious and traditional leaders to prevent and respond to violence against women. This engagement with traditional leaders has to be combined with the strict enforcement of the law to deter illegal adjudications on the part of these community heads. Both states have only superficially overridden traditional authority with statutory law, and there is the need to strengthen these efforts by bringing to justice traditional leaders who illegally interfere in cases of violence against women. When possible, the governments and women's rights advocates should strive to coopt these leaders into promoting women's rights. Since this is not likely to succeed in every community, both governments have to invest in making the formal justice system accessible to all, so that women are not compelled to turn to traditional leaders to adjudicate cases.

The Liberian and Sierra Leonean governments must also harmonize existing gender laws and policies to prevent confusion on the part of those who are responsible for enforcing them. It is also imperative that both governments and NGOs take measures to fill the gaps in existing legislation. Furthermore, policy documents should clearly outline the steps that need to be taken, the agencies that are responsible for implementing them, and frameworks for evaluation. Related to this is the need for further education on the gender laws for members of the security sector.

The cases also highlight the very important role that exists for local and transnational women's rights advocates. Women's organizations in both Liberia and Sierra Leone have played pivotal roles in getting women's rights onto the national agenda. These organizations need to sustain their advocacy efforts beyond the introduction of laws and policies. The implementation stage is equally important, and women's rights advocates should increase their demands for a voice in how programs are structured and implemented. This sustained advocacy is necessary to hold governments accountable and to increase the effectiveness of policy outcomes. The international community should support the efforts of these local organizations and provide them with the technical expertise to achieve their goals.

There is also the need for a higher level of coordination across NGOs and government agencies. As much as the autonomy of civil society is important, these organizations have to work with the government wherever possible to enable it to more efficiently implement policies and to fill implementation gaps that result from weaknesses in state agencies. In Liberia, the Ministry of Gender and Development regularly meets with civil society organizations to share vital information on violence against women and to discuss ways to address these problems. This is a step in the right direction. It is also important for civil society organizations to collaborate in order to strengthen and avoid duplication of their programs.

Women's rights advocates also have to lobby for policy action on forms of violence against women that are often below the radar in postconflict states. They often focus their attention on rape, but it would be useful to shine the spotlight on other less discussed problems such as forced prostitution and human trafficking. There are multiple forms of violence against women, and stakeholders should not limit the conversation to rape.

Conclusion

This chapter discussed the major factors that have constrained the efforts of the postconflict governments of Liberia and Sierra Leone to reduce the level of violence against women. It demonstrated that myriad factors negatively influence policy outcomes and showed that the measures to clear these hurdles call for significant resources and often require extended periods of time to produce favorable results. These requirements do not mean that it is impossible to reduce levels of violence against women, but rather that these governments, local women's organizations, and the international community have to invest more resources to address the problem. Reducing violence against women is a collaborative effort between both state and nonstate actors, each of which has a distinct role to play, as well as unique constraints, in addressing violence against women.

Notes

1. The experience of the postconflict phase also differs for individuals within the state according to social position, religion, ethnic group, geographic location, and so forth. There is no common countrywide postconflict experience.

2. For details on postconflict VAW see CEDAW Country Reports www.un.org/womenwatch/daw/cedaw/reports.htm.

3. According to Swiss et al. (1998), the levels of rape varied based on where women were located during the conflicts.

4. See Committee on Elimination of Discrimination Against Women, "Liberia Is Writing New History for Its Women and Girls, Delegation Tells Women's Anti-Discrimination Committee, Admitting Great Challenges in That Endeavour." www.un.org/News/Press/docs/2009/wom1748.doc.htm.

5. For more data on sexual violence see A Joint Program of the Government of Liberia and the United Nations. 2008. "Combating Sexual and Gender Based Violence in Liberia." http://stoprapenow.org/uploads/features/SGBVemail.pdf.

6. See Zuckerman and Greenberg (2004) for a discussion of how to break the cycle of violence.

7

Gender-Based Violence, Help-Seeking, and Criminal Justice Recourse in Haiti

Benedetta Faedi Duramy

PLAGUED BY DESTITUTION, POLITICAL INSTABILITY, AND BLOODY CONFRONTATIONS AMONG rival armed groups, Haiti suffers widespread sexual violence as a consequence of civil and political conflict affecting 50 percent of women and girls living in and around Port-au-Prince (Geneva Centre for the Democratic Control of Armed Forces, International Sector Advisory Team 2009, 7). Poor social conditions, domestic unrest, and rampant poverty afflict the majority of the Haitian population, and women and girls are most often the most vulnerable to the violence that grows out of such crises. Sexual assault and child sexual abuse are so pervasive in Haiti that women and girls describe being victimized by relatives, gangs, militiamen, law enforcement officers, peacekeepers, and strangers—they are at risk in every area of social life. However, in Haiti, as in developing and developed countries around the world, sexual violence against women and girls is widely undercounted, and a complex and interrelated set of circumstances lead to underreporting.

This chapter presents findings from a study conducted in the Haitian capital of Port-au-Prince between 2006 and 2008 (Faedi Duramy 2008). Thus, it does not include data from events occurring after January 12, 2010, when a 7.0-magnitude earthquake devastated Port-au-Prince and much of the surrounding countryside. However, insights, analyses, and recommendations drawn from the study have become increasingly relevant given the increase in sexual violence perpetrated against women and girls in the aftermath of the earthquake.

In particular, the study presented in this chapter focused on female survivors' decision-making process relative to help-seeking and resistance; because

103

sexual violence primarily affects women and girls in Haiti, the research project excluded male victims. The fieldwork employed individual interviews and small group discussions involving 100 participants, which included 85 survivors, and 15 professionals providing medical assistance and psychological support to rape victims. Local health and international aid workers confirmed high incidence of patients' reluctance to report sexual violence to the authorities, even after victim services staff had encouraged and supported them in this effort. Of the 85 survivors interviewed, only one had reported the assault. Tragically, she revealed having been raped twice but reported only the first assault to authorities. As a result, the victim services staff was exploring programs to include client assistance within the criminal justice system. They needed answers as to why victims of sexual violence so seldom seek state recourse and why the criminal justice system so miserably fails the few who do.

As a result, these findings emphasize both the cultural and institutional barriers Haitian women face in attempting to report sexual assault. This chapter groups the social contexts in which women make these decisions into the following sections: political conflict and instability; sexual violence and social uncertainty; criminal justice, dysfunction, and insecurity; underreporting rape as survival strategy; and gender stereotypes—the cornerstones of discrimination. Analyses explore three cases that won convictions and include examination of law enforcement, prosecutorial, and judicial performance during the proceedings. The conclusion identifies key incentives for the victims to report and participate in the criminal proceedings and encourages a response to violence against women in Haiti that directly includes survivors' experiences and needs.

Conflict Against Women: Haitian Contexts

Political Conflict and Instability

The ouster of Jean-Bertrand Aristide's government in late February 2004 resulted in the massive breakdown of the shantytown communities in the capital city of Port-au-Prince, the north region, and Artibonite, which supported the exiled president. After the overthrow of Aristide, violence in Haiti gradually turned into an urban guerrilla war among the former president's militias—Chimeries—and other armed groups, including former members of the disbanded military forces, officers of the Haitian National Police dismissed for criminal activities, members of organized criminal gangs, as well as zonal vigilante groups (Faedi Duramy 2008). The Chimeries were aggressively soliciting the return of Aristide, while other politically and criminally motivated armed groups, financed by Aristide's opponents, favored the new transitional government. By April 2004, determining that the critical situation of Haiti endangered the international peace and security of the entire Caribbean region, the UN Security Council adopted Resolution 1542 and established the UN Stabilization Mission in Haiti (MINUSTAH). Since Haiti was not torn by civil strife, but it was experiencing a situation of political violence, the mandate of MINUSTAH did not include the achievement of a peace accord or the promotion of a peace process. Rather the mission was tasked with assisting the transitional government in restoring the rule of law and public order so that constitutional and democratic process in Haiti could take root. Despite internal tensions and several confrontations among rival armed groups, an interim government, supported by the peacekeeping mission, ruled the country until February 2006, when René Préval was democratically elected the new president of Haiti.

In the following two years, the UN peacekeeping mission primarily focused on providing stabilization and security to the Haitian government as well as supporting the longer process of reforming its key institutions. Indeed, following the successful and peaceful political transition to an elected government, the United Nations continued its strong commitment to the sovereignty, independence, territorial integrity, and unity of Haiti. Security, rule of law, institutional reforms, national reconciliation, and sustainable economic and social development remained fundamental to the UN mission.

In particular, the UN mission, in cooperation with the international community, urged the new Haitian government to complete a comprehensive reform of the police, judiciary, and correctional systems. This objective was ultimately aimed at protecting human rights and fundamental freedoms as well as promoting a fair judicial system and fighting impunity. However, the United Nations calculated that a firm response to the escalating gang violence, widespread insecurity, and human rights violations, especially violence against women and children, was the key to successfully implementing such institutional reforms.

Therefore, on July 6, 2005, MINUSTAH forces led a full-fledged military attack on Cité Soleil, the *favela* (shantytown) of Port-au-Prince most affected by armed violence. The target of the military action was an alleged gang leader, Dread Wilme, who was killed during the operation along with an unspecified number of his associates, but civilian casualties were high, with the death toll estimated at 30 people. Doctors Without Borders, operating at a nearby hospital, reported treating 26 gunshot victims, 20 women, and at least 1 child. Civilian causalities resulted in powerful criticism from nongovernmental organizations (NGOs) operating in Haiti. However, MINUSTAH argued that it had warned the Haitian government and NGOs of predictable damage and death, due to the flimsy construction of shantytown structures in Cité Soleil, and the nature of such missions conducted in densely populated urban areas.

Again, on December 22, 2006, MINUSTAH launched another large-scale attack on the residents of Cité Soleil. Hundreds of peacekeeping troops with aerial support confronted armed groups with the goal to apprehend gang members. According to MINUSTAH 9 civilians were killed; independent sources reported over 20 dead and more than 40 injured, and other estimates counted up to 70 victims. The International Red Cross recounted that the UN soldiers prevented its vehicles from entering the zone to assist wounded women and children.

A recent report by the Security Council's mission to Haiti stated that, in the past few years, positive progress had been made on the overall security situation due to strategic military actions conducted by MINUSTAH with the cooperation of the Haitian National Police (UN Security Council 2009). In spite of such interventions aimed at dismantling some of the armed gangs responsible for much of the violence in the capital, criminal activities, particularly gender-based violence, remained rampant. Instances of civil unrest involving violence largely affected the entire country, undermining public confidence.

The establishment of René Préval's elected government in 2006 represented an unprecedented democratic development in the political history of Haiti. For the first time, political opposition and journalists had the freedom to express their positions without fear of retaliation and prosecution. However, profound divisions within Haitian society and stagnant political tensions among diverse contending groups still undermined the stability of Haiti's democratic institutions (Faedi Duramy 2008). Indeed, relations between parliament and the executive branch remained fragmented, as did their intent to cooperate and reach agreement on joint legislative and reform agendas.

During 2008, further political uncertainty arose when the president announced that eight elections would take place over the subsequent 36 months. On the occasion of the first round of elections for the renewal of one-third of the Senate, the Provisional Electoral Council rejected the Fanmi Lavalas candidates who had supported former president Jean-Bertrand Aristide. Representatives of political and civil society organizations emphasized the potential for renewed social unrest and confrontations. In response, the Provisional Electoral Council and the United Nations promised free, fair, and inclusive elections. However, several political parties decided to withdraw their participation in the elections due, at least in part, to financial constraints.

On a positive note, during Préval's presidency, specific commissions on education, competitiveness, information technology, security forces, and constitutional reform were established. Political parties, the private sector, and civil society organizations engaged in dialogue to restore public confidence in the political process and to ensure the future of the country. In particular, Haitian political leaders and representatives of MINUSTAH indicated that reforming the Constitution was essential to improve the functioning of Haiti's democratic institutions, and, thus, to effect better governance in the country. Despite such intentions, internal divisions, burdensome administrative structures, lack of coordination, and imbalance of powers between the executive and legislative branches of the government have hampered the commissions in delivering concrete results and implementing the reform process in the country.

Haiti's history of political instability and violence, its poor governance, and the persistent deterioration of security severely hamper the country's economic growth and development. The detrimental impact of political conflicts, the intermittent cycles of foreign assistance followed by the withdrawal of international aid, and the high degree of inequitable and inadequate access to productive assets and public services make the country the poorest in the Latin American and Caribbean region and the most disadvantaged of the Western Hemisphere. Haiti's population is approximately 8 million, and 54 percent of its citizens live on US$1 or less a day and 78 percent on US$2 or less a day (World Bank 2006). Large pockets of urban indigents in slum areas in Port-au-Prince, including Martissant, Gran Ravine, Carrefour, Cité Soleil, and Bel Air, register even higher poverty rates.

During 2008, the combined effects of the food crisis, the global financial and economic collapse, and the hurricane season had a devastating effect on the socioeconomic situation in Haiti. According to the postdisaster needs assessment conducted with the assistance of the World Bank, the European Union, and the United Nations, the 2008 storms and hurricanes resulted in some US$900 million worth of damage, the equivalent of 14.6 percent of Haiti's GDP (UN Security Council 2009). Degradation and the lack of infrastructure, including basic services such as potable water, electricity, and sanitation, characterize the wretched living conditions of the slums' inhabitants and exacerbate their anger and malcontent.

Persistent poverty and youth unemployment in urban communities created an environment susceptible to civil unrest and gang activity. Among the active armed groups, the distinction between political motivation and organized crime is often indistinct. Drug trafficking is the dominant illegal enterprise of Haitian gangs, and according to the UN mission this is one of the most destabilizing factors facing the country. Political groups use criminal violence to advance a legitimate political platform or social agendas, further undermining the sustainability of Haiti's security. As control by rival armed groups splintered between the pro-Aristide Lavalasian organizations and their opponents, the Haitian purlieus around the capital became breeding grounds for sexual and gender-based violence. To be sure, the earthquake of January 12, 2010, further exacerbated tensions and disparities in the Haitian community and severely impaired the already dire conditions of women and girls.

Sexual Violence and Social Uncertainty

In the shantytowns of Port-au-Prince, armed gang violence is commonplace and sexual violence is epidemic. It is estimated that 50 percent of girls have been victims of rape, often by more than one perpetrator (Geneva Centre for the Democratic Control of Armed Forces 2009). A study on factors impacting youth development in Haiti revealed that violence is part of everyday life and that sexual violence is rampant: 46 percent of Haitian girls have been sexually abused, among whom 33 percent were between 5 and 9 years of age and 43 percent between 10 and 14 (Justesen and Verner 2007). Findings from a random survey of households in Port-au-Prince suggested that, between 2004 and 2006, 35,000 women were sexually assaulted, half of whom were under the age of 18 (Kolbe and Hutson 2006). Aggregated figures showed that sexual violence against women is the most prevalent form of violence in Haiti, affecting 35 percent of women over 15 years of age, with a higher incidence in provincial areas (41 percent) than in the urban settings (34 percent). Disaggregated data collected from medical and psychological assistance organizations that provide aid to victims of sexual violence in Haiti reported that the number of rape cases per annum increased between threefold and 12-fold from 2002 to 2005 (Table de Concertation Nationale 2005). Among the victims, 96.1 percent were single women, and between 34 percent and 76.1 percent were girls under 18 years of age (Table de Concertation Nationale 2005). One organization operating in Port-au-Prince showed the prevalence of sexual violence in the conflict areas of the capital: 63 percent of rape cases occurred after intimidation with a firearm, 71 percent were committed by strangers, and between 41 percent and 62 percent by more than one perpetrator. Estimates of the prevalence of sexual violence in 2006 ranged from 64 percent in Port-au-Prince to 69 percent throughout the entire country (Kay Fanm 2006). Among the victims, 65 percent were girls between the ages of 3 and 18, 17 percent were between 19 and 25 years of age, and 16 percent were over 26. Among the rape cases documented, 53 percent were committed by armed groups and 29 percent by more than one of their members (Kay Fanm 2006). More recently, a survey of households in Port-au-Prince estimated that 3 percent of women and girls had been victims of sexual violence between January and March 2010 (Haiti, Republic of 2011).

Examining patterns of risk factors for sexual violence in Haiti shows the interplay between political violence and forced sex since the Haitian military coup in 1991–1994 (Magloire 2002). Since then rape has been employed as a weapon of political oppression and remains deeply entrenched in Haitian society, shaping gender relationships in both private and public spheres. Correlations between practices of gender discrimination and sexual abuse in the private realm and gender-based violence in the public domain have also been suggested (Faedi Duramy 2008). Other studies acknowledged the challenges of Haitian women in both rural and impoverished urban settings, forced by extreme poverty and gender inequality to become entangled in survival strategies, including continuing in abusive relationships and trading sex for food, money, and protection (Maternowska 2006).

Recent studies acknowledged the normalization of violence in Haitian society, reporting that over 58 percent of residents in the metropolitan areas feel unsafe in their own homes and that particularly women are the primary targets of the assaults. Gender disparities clearly emerged from women's accounts collected for the purpose of this study. Most of them seemed to passively accept their condition, confiding hopelessly that "women can only be victims, victims of everything." Others became very quiet when the discussion moved from violence committed by armed gangs to the general understanding of women's role in society, and, particularly, in the household. However, the most loquacious women frankly claimed that their status as victims had very little to do with being raped by gangs, but rather it commenced in their childhood when inequality and sexual abuse became their very first memories.

Victim service professionals interviewed for this study confirmed that Haitian girls experience sexual initiation at the age of five or six, primarily with relatives or neighbors. In particular, one psychologist revealed the lack of boundaries among family members and the prevalence of discrimination, neglect, and incest against girls behind closed doors. Another staffer providing psychological support to rape victims explained that women are so accustomed to sexual abuse that by now they have accepted violence as part of their daily lives, simply resigning themselves to their unfortunate condition. Nonetheless, failure to report sexual and gender-based violence skews the data in even more painful ways. According to a UN Special Rapporteur report in 2000, an estimated 66 percent of rape victims never reported the sexual violence to authorities for fear of reprisal and social stigmatization (UN Economic and Social Council 2000).

Criminal Justice, Dysfunction, and Insecurity

The classification of sexual assaults and rape under the Haitian criminal justice system evolved over time. Originally based on the French Penal Code of 1810, it stated that anyone who committed a crime of rape or was responsible for any other assault on morals, executed or attempted, with violence against individuals of one gender or the other, should have been punished with detention (Haiti Penal Code of 1835, Art. 278). In the event that the crime was committed against a child under the age of 15, the perpetrator should have been punished with imprisonment (Haitian Penal Code of 1835, Art. 280). This initial taxonomy of rape among the "*atteintes aux bonnes moeurs*"—assaults on morals—reflected the common understanding that the harm inflicted by sexual violence caused damage to the victim's honor and dignity rather than being a crime against her physical integrity and well-being. The language and wording adopted in the Haitian criminal provisions revealed the patriarchal perception of girls' and women's social role as keepers of the family honor, responsible for the community's moral system, as well as the customary misconception of women's bodies as men's property.

More recently, the Decret Modifiant le Régime des Agressions Sexuelles et Éliminant en la Matière les Discriminations Contre la Femme (Decree Changing the Regulation of Sexual Aggressions and Eliminating Forms of Discrimination Against Woman), adopted in July 2005, acknowledged that the provisions under the Haitian Penal Code established practices of discrimination against women, which contravened the precepts of the Constitution and the international commitments undertaken by the Republic of Haiti. Further, it redefined rape as a criminal offense and as sexual aggression against the victim rather than a moral assault.

Included under a new section of the Haitian Penal Code titled "Sexual Aggressions," the amended Article 278 provides that anyone who commits a crime of rape or is responsible for any other type of sexual aggression,

executed or attempted with violence, threats, surprise, or psychological intimidation against an individual of one gender or the other, shall be punished with 10 years of forced labor. Similarly, the amended version of Article
280 states that in the event that the crime is committed against a child under
the age of 15, the perpetrator shall be punished with 15 years of forced labor.

Ministry of Justice staff revealed that although significant amendments
have been made to the Haitian Penal Code and important enactments have
been adopted, in practice, little substantive change has occurred, and the Haitian legal culture still remains deeply saturated with discriminatory and macho
attitudes and beliefs. The legacy of social hierarchies and patriarchal values as
well as the lack of capacity and resources in security and justice services impede the pace and undermine effective application of the revised penal code
and its promise of justice for survivors of sexual and gender-based violence.

Underreporting Rape as Survival Strategy

Representatives of the Ministry for the Status of Women who were interviewed asserted that the lack of official national statistics on violence against
girls and women significantly limits any accurate evaluation of the situation
in the country and, ultimately, compromises any attempt from women's associations and civil society institutions to raise awareness and promote the
political legitimacy of the issue. According to a study of 1,705 women undertaken by the Centre Haïtien de Recherches et d'Actions pour la Promotion Féminine (CHREPROF) in November 1996 and as reported by the
Special Rapporteur on violence against women on the mission to Haiti in
2000, an estimated 66 percent of girls and women victims never reported
the aggressions for fear of reprisals and social prejudice, as well as due to the
lack of adequate legal mechanisms and support structures (UN Economic
and Social Council 2000).

More recently, respondents from MINUSTAH and national civil society organizations confirmed that the majority of sexual abuses and rapes
against girls and women are never reported to the police or other competent
organizations. Staff from Kay Fanm (a creole expression that means "wom-
en's house") in Port-au-Prince reported that in 2006, 224 cases of violence
against women were taken to the judicial system. Among those, 120 cases
were dismissed before the judgment and, of the remaining 104 cases, only
one rape case ended in a conviction. In 2007, Kay Fanm reported that at
least 155 cases of violence against women were taken to court. Of the 41
rape cases, 13 were perpetrated against young girls, 21 against teenagers,
and 7 against women—only one ended in a conviction.

The lack of reporting and the extent of rape case attrition in the Haitian criminal justice system result from the combination of several factors, including the victims' internalization of gender inequalities and stereotypes, fear of social stigmatization and reprisal, the corruption and dysfunction of the security and formal legal systems, as well the exercise of discretionary power by criminal justice personnel at various stages of the process. Whether discretionary decisions are motivated by reluctance or complicity, the significant loss of rape cases from the criminal justice system reveals a troubled pattern of incentives aimed at the recurrent denial of justice for victims of sexual violence and abuse.

Gender Stereotypes: The Cornerstones of Discrimination

The internalization process of customary norms that place men at the top of the gender hierarchy and women at the subordinate levels of family and community structures was corroborated in all the victims' narratives. The common pattern of male dominance and female subservience experienced in Haitian households was rooted in the social role of men as the providers and property owners and women's role to serve spouses and comply with their commands. The interviews revealed unanimously the perception of the household as inclusive of an extended family and the pervasive attitude of maintaining secrecy about child sexual abuse, incest, and sexual assaults.

Participants from MINUSTAH as well as representatives of the Ministry of Justice that contributed to this research contend that in Haiti, as in other countries affected by postconflict or sociopolitical crises, violence often arises from a shift of the gender system under heavy economic, social, and political pressures. By undermining men's ability to find paid work in legitimate income-generating activities, the economic decline of the Haitian society results in undermining men's role and identity. In these shifts of gender roles, power is expressed in multiple ways: through machismo and aspirational male sublimation as well as, in its most extreme form, through structural violence in the household and community (Maternowska 2006). Although indigence and unemployment significantly diminish male sources of self-esteem, sexual violence becomes a tool for reclaiming men's identity and overcoming their plight of emasculation.

Victims' accounts revealed that the impact of gender roles on their decision making was threefold. First, the internalization of gender stereotypes determined a victim's attitude to accept sexual aggression as an inevitable by-product of the socioeconomic collapse in the Haitian communities and the resultant troubled state of masculinity. Second, survivors of sexual violence failed to take any action because they were aware that holding relatives, intimates, or even gang members accountable would be socially unacceptable.

Third, the fear of being stigmatized and abandoned by husbands or partners as well as of being subject to reprisals either against their families or themselves paralyzed any genuine attempt to ask for help and justice.

The following synopses of the experiences of two rape victim exemplify rational fear of social stigmatization and rejection by their own families and community:

> Tamara is a 27-year-old merchant. She also manages to look after her husband and their two children of six and eight years of age. Every day she goes to the poor area of Martissent to sell her merchandise at the local market. One day, she went to the market and earned 125 *gourdes* from a client. On her way back home, two young men around 20 years old approached her, dragging her into a car parked at the corner of the street where two other men were waiting. The four men were members of one of the armed groups of the area responsible for many kidnappings. Tamara was kidnapped by the group for 22 days, beaten, and gang raped multiple times per day. Upon the payment of 150 *gourdes,* she was finally released and abandoned at the edge of the street. Initially, she was so weak that she could not even walk and, thus, remained there for a while listening to cruel comments made about her by the passers-by. Fearing abandonment by her husband and rejection by her community, Tamara decided to keep quiet about the aggression. She refused to go to the hospital or to consult a doctor. Her injuries still hurt.
>
> Mary decided to ask for medical assistance at the Haitian Group for the Study of Kaposi's Sarcoma and Opportunistic Infections (GHESKIO) medical center in Port-au-Prince after she was sexually assaulted and discovered that she had contracted HIV. She reported that she had been rejected by her family. Her father held her responsible for the rape and her aunt threw her out of the home. Tragically, she attempted to kill herself several times until she was finally committed to a psychiatric institution.

These accounts strengthen social understanding that sexual violence is a normal everyday fact in the lives of women and girls. Little tolerance for resistance is demonstrated by family and community groups, and tolerance for violence against women is conceived of as a natural expression of the Haitian culture.

Analysis, Criminal Cases, and Proceedings

Law Enforcement Operations

Survivors' accounts of their engagement with police forces revealed a common pattern of further victimization against girls and women who report sexual assaults. Ridiculed and blamed by the officers receiving them at the police station immediately after the assault, they are often discouraged from filing complaints. Some are dismissed because rape is perceived as a non-serious crime. In other situations, where the sexual violence occurred within the family or was committed by acquaintances of the victim, the assault is regarded as an unfortunate event that needs to be settled among the parties involved as a strictly private matter. Survivors' interactions with law enforcement substantiate the harm this pattern of discriminatory norms and gendered stereotypes plaguing Haitian law enforcement is doing to reporting rates for sexual violence and prevention efforts to slow the ever-increasing number of victims.

On the other hand, rape victims who did not report the aggression to the police displayed an overwhelming distrust in the system. They felt that law enforcement personnel would not believe them and would fail to protect them from retaliation. Further, they perceived that they would be blamed for the attack and were apprehensive of the challenges presented by a criminal court process. One victim described reporting to police and pressing charges with a prosecutor would be the equivalent of a "death wish."

Informants from MINUSTAH Child Protection Unit and the International Committee of the Red Cross (ICRC) contended that victims not only fear being humiliated and derided by police officers, but possibly being subject to further acts of violence from law enforcement officers themselves. Haitian police stations have earned a reputation for depravation and brutality, with tales of 15-year-old girls entering jail as virgins and becoming pregnant by police officers while in custody. Some victims describe being safer "in the middle of the street" than in a police station.

Victim service staff who work within Port-au-Prince recount stories of rape survivors who identified police officers using their weapons to intimidate and threaten them before perpetrating the sexual assault. Haitian Women's Solidarity (SOFA) staff detailed this tragic experience of one of their patients:

> The woman was sexually assaulted in 2006 in the area of Carrefour, in the southern part of the capital. That night the victim was at a friend's party. When she left, a policeman and his accomplices followed her down the street and attacked her smashing her against the wall and beating her with a firearm. . . . The aggressors raped and sodomized the woman for several hours. In the end, although she tried to wriggle herself out of their control, the men lifted up her legs and lacerated her flesh from the vagina to the anus with a razor.

A professor of sociology at the University of Port-au-Prince explained that women living in the shantytowns profoundly distrust the security forces. In fact, they believe that police officers either are not willing to enter the conflict zones to eradicate armed violence or, if they actually access the areas, they become perpetrators of sexual assault against women and girls. A representative of MINUSTAH Police Department reported that a specific project has been designed but not yet funded to train female police officers of the Haitian National Police on gender issues and to make them responsible for receiving rape victims' complaints as well as dealing with women associated with armed groups in detention. Indeed, very few female police officers have been hired. Moreover, very few police stations have provided their female officers with training courses on gender issues, most of which have been discontinued due to financial shortages.

Criminal Prosecutions

The Haitian judicial system has been widely credited for corruption, dysfunction, and military interference throughout the history of the republic. Currently, due process and judicial redress in criminal proceedings are extremely difficult to obtain. Very few cases are adjudicated each year, and prisoners are commonly held for lengthy periods without trial or sentence. The resolution of these cases often depends more on money and power than on justice. Corruption and abuse of discretionary power interfere with judicial process from case investigation to decision, compromising the independence, transparency, and performance of judges, prosecutors, and attorneys at every level.

Rape, incest, and child sexual abuse more than other crimes fall prey to the culture of impunity for sexual and gender-based violence in Haiti. Judges and prosecutors claimed that the unresponsiveness of the system to sexual assault originates from the lack of capacity and resources. Low salaries compel them to engage in second jobs, and intimidation by violent criminals puts their own lives at stake. Police officers from the Haitian National Police confirmed that the lack of basic resources and services, including cars, computers, telephones, and electricity, severely impedes the pursuit of investigations and arrests in general and in sexual assault cases even more since they are not taken seriously as crimes from the start.

Ombudsman Haiti, a neutral and confidential moderator that serves as a dispute resolution advocate and peacekeeper diplomat, contends that rape is seen as a crime to be settled man to man outside the courtroom. They report that the parents of a rape victim are often willing to dismiss the case out of financial desperation for small compensation from the perpetrator. Rape victims lament that "money often pays other hands to shuck off the case." One survivor described having been raped twice by members of different armed groups. The first time, she decided to report the assault and seek legal assistance through Kay Fanm. The case was taken before the tribunal of Port-au-Prince, but it was soon dismissed. The defendant was released upon the payment of a bribe to the judge. The second time she was raped, the victim understandably decided there was no point in reporting the assault.

When seeking justice for the aggressions committed against them, girls and women in Haiti confront not only the obstacle of a corrupt and inefficient judicial system, but also procedural hurdles to gathering the evidence necessary to support a rape allegation. Being required to provide a medical certificate verifying that forcible sexual intercourse has occurred, the majority of victims struggle to reach medical institutions that can perform the examinations and issue the certificate because they are located a distance from the shantytowns where they live.

Ministry for the Status of Women staff emphasized that girls from rural areas or urban *favelas* of the capital often arrive at the hospital too late to demonstrate the fact that forcible sexual intercourse has occurred, or, even worse, they are provided with medical certificates, which eventually prove to be incomplete or illegible. Despite the fact that a protocol of the agreement stated that a free medical certificate is to be provided to rape victims (signed by the Ministry for the Status of Women, the Ministry of Justice, and the Ministry of Public Health on November 17, 2006), the practical obstacles and perils women face in trying to reach hospitals or private doctors are still far from being overcome.

Aggregate data from Unité de Recherche et d'Action Médico-légale and Médecins du Monde reported that between 2002 and 2005, of the 372 victims of sexual violence, 76.1 percent were minors and only 23.9 percent were adult women (Table de Concertation Nationale 2005). Yet, data from SOFA collected between 2003 and 2005 revealed that all the victims who visited the police and pressed charge after the aggression were minors (Table de Concertation Nationale 2005). Participants in this study from MINUSTAH Gender Unit explained that in Haiti it is easier to report a case of sexual violence against a girl than against a woman, since the latter is more exposed to shame and social reprobation. While young girls are perceived to be, after all, innocent victims of an unfortunate damage, adult women are often blamed or held accountable for the aggression itself.

Another Haitian myth surrounding rape is the belief that rape is a crime *only* when it is committed against a virgin. Patriarchal misconceptions and gender bias classifying the girl's body as the property of a family and commodity to be transferred from man to man still deeply pervade the Haitian culture and society. While judges interviewed for the purpose of this study declared that no distinction is made before the law, victims revealed that in practice anyone who alleges rape must endure public scrutiny of her own virtue. NGOs and national rape prevention and victim service organizations denounce the fact that raping a nonvirgin, whose honor has been already compromised, is commonly considered a less serious offense. Based on this assumption, rape charges by nonvirgin victims are often dismissed, as if, because of their previous sexual experiences, they could no longer be raped but rather they would just consent to any further sexual contacts.

Judicial Outcomes and Sentencing

Kay Fanm testified that there are two principal motivations that encouraged victims to report and resulted in criminal prosecutions: first, victims were supported by their own families in embarking on such a painful process; and second, victims could benefit from legal aid provided by the organization and funded through international programs. The first case involved an assault committed by the police officer James Montas against a 20-year-old woman, Carline Séide, as she was entering her house in Delmas 19, Port-au-Prince, on November 2, 2003. The man threatened and beat the victim with his weapon, dragged her to the bedroom, and, after having handcuffed her to the bed, raped her. Subsequently, Montas called his six accomplices, who also raped the woman one after the other. Following the multiple aggressions, the policeman threatened the victim with death in the event that she decided to report the attack.

In spite of several acts of intimidation, Séide resolved to report the aggression to competent authorities and pursue legal action with the assistance of Kay Fanm. On August 3, 2006, the case was adjudicated by the Criminal Court of Port-au-Prince. The public prosecutor requested the penalty of unlimited detention for the police officer in compliance with Articles 279 and 281 of the Haitian Penal Code. In fact, according to Article 281, if the rape is committed by an individual who has abused his authority, the maximal penalty should be applied. On the other hand, the defense requested the immediate and unconditional release of Montas, arguing that he was a victim of conspiracy.

The final verdict, released by Judge Jean Carvez on August 8, 2006, condemned the accused to six years' detention. The sentence acknowledged that the weapon and handcuffs used by the police officer during the aggression were found in his residence; the crime was perpetrated with free deliberation, violence, and lack of the victim's consent. Montas was a police officer on duty at the time of the assault, who abused his authority, weapon, and handcuffs to rape the victim. The medical certification, issued by the Hospital of the State University of Haiti, confirmed the injuries and the penetration of the victim; and finally, although the public prosecutor requested the maximum penalty for the accused in compliance with the

Haitian Penal Code, the judge decided to condemn him to six years' imprisonment. Kay Fanm reported that despite the reduction of penalty, the condemnation of Montas was the only rape case successfully prosecuted in 2006 and, thus, held symbolic importance for the struggle to eradicate violence against women in Haiti.

They also reported that, similarly in 2007, another rape case was successfully prosecuted with a substantive reduction of penalty. The case regarded a 12-year-old girl who was brutally raped by a neighbor. The man, who was an electrician and knew the girl and her mother very well, entered the victim's home while she was taking a shower. He drugged her and brutally raped her until she fainted. When the girl regained consciousness she found blood between her legs. Even in this case, the public prosecutor requested the permanent detention of the aggressor considering the fact that the victim was a minor. However, the judge sentenced the man to 15 years of prison. In 2008, two more rape cases were adjudicated in Port-au-Prince with the legal assistance of Kay Fanm. The first one involved a 27-year-old woman attacked by an armed group as she was exiting church in 2005. The group dragged the victim to a nearby cemetery, forced her to walk naked around the graves, and then viciously raped her. Only one of the aggressors was successfully prosecuted and sentenced to 9 years' detention.

The other case regarded a 15-year-old girl who was attacked by a 51-year-old man in the city of Leogane. The victim was going to visit her father when she was kidnapped by her aggressor in the middle of the street. The man abducted the girl for an entire week, raping her multiple times per day. The judge asserted that since the victim did not scream at the moment of the aggression, she had consented to the sexual relationship. Therefore, the man was not held accountable for either the kidnapping or the rape, but only of having engaged in a consensual sex relationship with a minor, thus punishable by two years of imprisonment. The director of Kay Fanm grieved over the gender bias that pervaded this case, but acknowledged that any condemnation of rape, even with the lowest penalty, represents an important achievement in the struggle of Haitian activists to eradicate gender-based violence.

Conclusion

Key Incentives to Report and Participate

The previous analysis investigated rape victims' decision-making process in seeking help to report sexual violence and participate in the criminal prosecution. Several factors were identified as creating barriers for rape victim participation in the criminal justice process: internalization of gendered stereotypes, widespread lack of law enforcement for sexual assault, judicial corruption, and lack of resources, which contribute to reluctance to report the sexual assault. The conclusions drawn are twofold: weak or corrupt security and judicial systems have an enormous impact on women's decision to report sexual violence and an equally negative effect on deterrence since fewer than three cases per year see a conviction.

Indeed, despite the international commitments undertaken by the Haitian government and the recent efforts made by the national legislature to comply with the international human rights standards as applied to women and girls and sexual violence, criminal justice responses to gender-based violence still remain largely inadequate. However, analysis has revealed that two principal motivations encouraged women to report the aggression: first, victims were supported by their own families in embarking on such a painful process; and second, victims could benefit from legal aid. The results of this study seek to stimulate an innovative and sensitive debate about gender-based violence in Haiti and adequate responses to guarantee women's protection.

Part Three

Conflict-Related Sexual Violence
and Its Aftermath

8

The Afghan State and the Issue of Sexual Violence Against Women

Carol Mann

MY RESEARCH INTO THE IMPACT OF WAR-RELATED GENDER VIOLENCE ON AFGHAN WOMEN began in 2001 with interviews in Afghan refugee camps in Pakistan. This work continues today, focusing on educational and health issues for rural women survivors of war-related violence in the Farah province of rural Afghanistan, near the Iranian border. In addition, the research from the start included work being done via my own humanitarian organization, Femaid, based in Paris. The analysis in this chapter was developed to introduce researchers and aid workers to the history and legal frameworks at play in Afghanistan that impact violence against women in war zones. The data presented are a result of field research, practical experience, and literature review.

If sexual violence is generally described as an overarching term used to describe "[a]ny violence, physical or psychological, carried out through sexual means or by targeting sexuality" (UN Economic and Social Council 1998, 7–8), its legitimacy or illegitimacy is variously recognized from nation-state to nation-state and in times of peace and times of war. The case of present-day Afghanistan is a poignant example of some of the worst gendered and sexual violence that women and children face on a daily basis as a consequence of over 30 years of warfare (Soviet intervention 1979–1985 and US invasion in 2001 to the present). This chapter presents how the Afghan government's efforts to reform the legal system since 2002 have incorporated contradictory aspects of constitutional, Islamic religious, and customary law, which has resulted in women being deprived of their most basic rights, including the right to live free from violence. This chapter examines (a) the political and military contexts for women; (b) women of pre- and post-Taliban rule; (c) the customary law and violence against women; and (d) the progress that could be made for women's safety and rights. The chapter will present a new direction for Western feminists' thought and action in terms of creating changes in Afghanistan.

Political and Military Contexts for Women

Since the early twentieth century, progressive Afghan monarchs have been trying to reform the country according to Western criteria. The initial influence was the nearby British empire, which itself caused considerable adverse reactions, as they were targeting women and children especially in typical imperial social policies, which Leila Ahmed has aptly named "Colonial Feminism" (Ahmed 1992). In the 1920s, the most progressive of all Afghan rulers, Amanullah (1892–1960), took up the lead from Mustafa Kemal, known as Ataturk, the Turkish reformer of the newly founded republic, himself much inspired by Lenin (Dupree 1973). Heralding the communist government later, he simultaneously attempted reforms concerned with land tenure and marriage customs, all of which remain at the heart of Pashtun identity and self-definition. When he ordered the population of Kabul to wear Western clothes (something the British never dared attempt in India), the enforced unveiling of women (1929) was designed to turn them into equal partners of their freely chosen husbands (1924) in the national quest of modernity, reinforced by coeducation. As a result, he brought the country to near revolution, coming from the staunchly conservative southern part of the country, and had to flee into exile.

This reconfiguration of Afghan identity with Western-style aspirations to bring together British, Turkish, and Soviet influences did not help unite the Afghan population and indeed achieved the opposite. The absence of communication and mutual incomprehension between the ruling class and the vast rural majority was largely caused by the foreign and secular criteria for modernization. They meant cultural alienation for those who felt threatened by these new norms, a situation that became acute when the Marxist modernizing elite began to exert its influence within the government from the mid-1960s onward. This feeling of alienation is being experienced once again today, even though popular reaction is far less violent than what it had been in the past.

At present, Afghan women theoretically enjoy constitutional rights that ensure equality and freedom, but at the same time, they are subjected to Sunni Islamic law and customary practice, which undercut these liberties. In addition, policymakers in the United States or at the United Nations and nongovernmental organization (NGO) aid agencies have not made the religious and customary applications regarding sexual violence central to crime prevention and services for sexual violence in Afghanistan. For example, a 2009 report issued jointly by the UN High Commissioner for Human Rights (OHCHR) and the UN Assistance Mission in Afghanistan (UNAMA) stated:

> The limited space that opened up for Afghan women following the demise of the Taliban regime in 2001 is under sustained attack, not just by the Taliban themselves, but by deeply engrained cultural practices and customs, and—despite a number of significant advances in terms of the creation of new legislation and institutions—by a chronic failure at all levels of government to advance the protection of women's rights in Afghanistan. (UNAMA 2009a)

Customary practices that intersect with political Islam (or Islamism) are particularly to blame for gender-related humanitarian tragedies such as conflict-related sexual violence; so-called "honor killings"; the exchange of women and girls as a form of dispute resolution; trafficking and abduction; early and forced marriages, and attacks on girls' schools and on girl students," including gas and acid attacks, domestic violence, and threats against women in public life. *Political Islam* as a term includes adherents who believe that "Islam as a body of faith has something important to say about how politics and society should be ordered in the contemporary Muslim world and implemented in some fashion" (Fuller 2003, xi). Political scientist Guilian Denoeux defines *Islamism* as "a form of instrumentalization of Islam by individuals, groups and organizations that pursue political objectives. It provides political responses to today's societal challenges by imagining a future, the foundations for which rest on reappropriated, reinvented concepts borrowed from the Islamic tradition" (2002, 61). The terms *political Islam* and *Islamism* are used interchangeably throughout this chapter.

It is a contradiction to see grave gendered human rights violations so widespread in contemporary Afghanistan, where the constitution includes a 25 percent quota for female members of parliament, one of the highest such quotas in the world. It is best explained by exploring how generations raised in war (the Taliban) have responded to imposed democracy underwritten by the West (Mann 2005). The Taliban are fundamentalist Sunni

Muslims, mostly from Afghanistan's Pashtun tribes, arising in the wake of Soviet withdrawal in 1989. During the decade-long occupation, thousands of Afghan orphan refugees grew up in Pakistan. They were schooled in Pakistan's *madrassas,* religious schools that develop militantly inclined Islamists. "Hundreds of thousands of youths, who knew nothing of life but the bombings that destroyed their homes and drove them to seek refuge over the border, were being raised to hate and to fight, in the spirit of Jihad, a holy war that would restore Afghanistan to its people" (Laber 1986). As students at *madrassas,* the name they chose for themselves was *talib,* an Islamic student who seeks knowledge, as opposed to *mullah,* one who gives knowledge. The Taliban neither recognize nor tolerate forms of Islam divergent from its own. It rejects democracy or any secular or pluralistic political process as an offense against Islam.

Initially, the war against the Soviet intervention provided a focus for all opposition and helped unite people who had very little in common, such as Kabuli intellectuals, peasants, *mullahs,* and Islamists (Roy 1985). The latter evolved from being mujahideen guerrillas to becoming military commanders and eradicated opponents who could have constituted a secular political alternative in Afghanistan after the demise of the communist government. Posing as the legitimate representatives of the Afghan people, they benefited from major US military help and directed humanitarian aid into the narcotics trade (Cooley 1999). The warlords were ideologically endorsed by the local extremist Wahabbi Mullahs. With the further support of Pakistani dictator General Zia-Ul-Haq, thousands of *madrassas* were built in the region with additional Saudi Arabian funds.

Beginning in 1994, the Taliban rose to power and established totalitarian rule, in direct ideological continuity of the warlords' creed developed in the refugee camps. Until July 2011, the Taliban's long lists of edicts and decrees took an especially misogynistic view of women. Schools for girls were closed. Women were forbidden to work or leave their homes without verifiable permission. Wearing non-Islamic dress was forbidden. Wearing makeup or sporting Western products such as purses or shoes was forbidden. Music, dancing, cinemas, any form of nonreligious broadcasting, and entertainment were banned. Lawbreakers were beaten, flogged, shot, or beheaded (Womenaid International and Institute for Afghan Studies 2000).

The Bill Clinton administration initially supported the Taliban's rise, but by 2001 the Taliban were overthrown by the George W. Bush US-backed invasion of Afghanistan. The Taliban were never defeated; they retreated, regrouped, especially in Pakistan, and by 2006 were again controlling vast swaths of southern and western Afghanistan where the war wages on today. Further, new generation Taliban are far from the "primitive" warriors Orientalist journalists would have us believe (Porter 2009). Today's Taliban are sophisticated experts in communication, technology, and business. Its knowledge of the workings of global capitalism is best demonstrated by its command of the shadow economy in narcotics and smuggling.

The violent consequences of the past 30 years of war and the upsurge of the Taliban have been incalculable for Afghan women. Despite attempts made by the US-backed Hamid Karzai government to put women's and human rights at the center of the political agenda, conditions have worsened for most women, including the political elite. Afghan women participate in almost all sectors of public life, including as parliamentarians, civil servants, and journalists, and they "have been targeted by anti-government elements, by local traditional and religious power-holders, by their own families and communities, and in some instances by government authorities" (UNAMA 2009b). Karzai's political rhetoric is not closely aligned with his government's political action. In terms of financial expenditures, much money has been wasted and in fact far more has been spent on war than on development (Rashid 2008). Furthermore, General Stanley McChrystal, former commander of the North Atlantic Treaty Organization (NATO) and US Afghanistan forces, had been pushing compromises with Taliban leaders prior to his forced resignation in June 2010, demonstrating a lack of respect for women's and human rights by Western leadership in the region.

He was replaced by General David Petraeus (until July 2011, when General John Allen took over), who theoretically did not accept the notion of talks with Taliban leaders, embracing a policy of "reintegration," which aims at splitting and weakening the Taliban, and not "reconciliation," which meant negotiating with them. Nevertheless, those the US military are negotiating with today are all united behind a misogynist banner where human rights do not have a place. The Taliban has become very much an umbrella term that no longer means much outside armed opposition to foreign intervention. Ironically, Secretary of State Hillary Rodham Clinton, the woman who coined the phrase "women's rights are human rights" in her now famous speech in Beijing, China (September 1995), has embraced a "three red lines" policy for reconciliation with the Taliban: "They must renounce violence . . . abandon their alliance with Al Qaeda, and abide by the Constitution" (quoted in Lieven and Lodhi 2011). Such contradiction at the highest level of leadership confirms that Afghan women's lived experiences are not central to policy development or implementation in terms of ending wartime violence against women.

Afghan Women Pre- and Post-Taliban Rule

The particular brand of Afghan Islam, a product of the war, is very different from earlier, gentler versions of Afghan Islam, which were suffused with mysticism (Barry 1984). In rural pre-Taliban Afghanistan, women informally negotiated their place, older women were respected, and the eldest daughter was often the father's favorite. In farms and rural enterprises in Afghanistan, men and women always worked hard together in complementary ways, even if the woman's contribution was never recognized at its full worth. This way of life was largely destroyed during the Soviet intervention when over three million Afghans fled to neighboring Pakistan, dwelling in refugee camps in the North-West Frontier Province (NWFP). These refugees from villages and the camps reflected the social demographics of the country, which remains 72 percent rural and illiterate, ranking it 202 of 204 countries, despite 10 years of Western intervention and funding (CIA World Factbook, Afghanistan, confirmed July 2011).

The basis of the misogynistic gender laws the Taliban used to rule Afghanistan were laid out in exile, in Pakistan, and in the refugee camps and the *madrassas*. The impoverished refugee population was drawn to the camps with reassurances of regular meals and provision of a minimum education. The reality of these *madrassas* reveals frequently appalling conditions and mistreatment for children (Amnesty International 1998). Many of the refugees were widows who eagerly sent their sons to the *madrassas'* schools, the training grounds for the Taliban. Herded in decrepit boarding houses, cut off from contact with mothers and sisters, the boys and young men were taught political Islam, which became the Taliban creed.

In 1990, 80 Afghan *mullahs* exiled in Peshawar, representing all conservative Islamic fundamentalist factions, decreed an official *fatwa* forbidding women to wear perfume, anything that was deemed jewelry, or Western clothes (Moghadam 1994). A full veil covering the entire body became mandatory, and it was henceforth forbidden for women to talk, laugh, or joke with unknown persons, such as unrelated males, as decreed by Koranic law. This came as a shock to women who had been brought up in the communist regime and who saw life in exile as a form of intolerable repression. Yet these *mullahs* and warlords provided the guidelines to postwar life in Afghanistan.

When they came to power in Kabul in 1992, the Islamist warlords brought with them this ideological mix from exile, a basis on which the Taliban could build. The fall of the last pro-communist premier Mohammed Najibullah (1947–1996) heralded the beginning of an extraordinarily bloody civil war (1992–1996) between former "freedom" fighters allied to two major political formations, the Jamiat-e-Islami (Society of Islam) led by

Barhanuddin Rabbani (b. 1940) and the Hezb-e-Islami (Party of Islam) run by ultrabrutal Gulbeddin Hekmatyar (b. 1947). In Kabul, the deaths were numbered in the thousands, food convoys were blocked by daily battles, and an unarmed civilian population was taken hostage by battling factions. A pogrom against the Shi'ite Hazara people living in the Afshar district in western Kabul in 1993 was masterminded by the fabled Ahmad Massoud (1953–2001), allied to Barhanuddin Rabbani (Rashid 2008). The same year, French intellectuals put forward Massoud as a candidate for the Nobel Prize for Peace.

The West's support for these warlords had tragic consequences (Mann 2005). In Kabul, during the civil war, rape was used as a weapon of ethnic cleansing. The loss of virginity and therefore private and family honor is the most potent threat for girls and has led to suicide in some instances. The story of Nahid fleeing potential rapists during the civil war by throwing herself out of the window is part of Kabul folklore. Even the *burqa* became a way of hiding. According to a woman who was interviewed, "in those days, I was glad to be able to conceal myself from these brutes who preyed on young girls in the streets." In talking with women in Kabul after 2002, life was worse under the reign of the warlords than in Taliban times. "We lived in fear, day and night, no place was sacred to them." I was told by Shafiqa, a physiotherapist, "I slept in the hospital, I was afraid to go home after work. Under the Taliban, at least I could treat my patients and go home at night."

The Taliban arrived with an idiosyncratic set of rigid rules and regulations based on their own sectarian interpretations of Islam, resulting in true gender apartheid (Rashid 2000). The violence toward women was simultaneously enacted publicly as well as within the private domain. A ministry, copied from the Iranian model, was set up "for the promotion of Virtue and the repression of Vice" (Amr Bil Maruf awa Nahi Al Munkar), employing a special police force whose duty was to bring the human body in the public sphere to conformity with Taliban edicts. Men were forced to wear turbans and big beards, and every inch of female flesh, hair, and clothing needed to be hidden from view. This fixation on the sexual potential of women meant that whips and sticks came down on visible ankles, feet, and fingers. The female body became *haram,* that is to say impure, forbidden, and the status of women plummeted accordingly.

Afghan traditions were chiseled away by what Oliver Roy (2002) has termed *neo-fundamentalism,* that is to say an extreme form of modern political Islam that is at once religiously ultraconservative and politically radical. It aims at a globalized, totalitarian application of religion with no regional or cultural differences, in which women are confined to domesticity and passive subservience. The Taliban banished women from the public sphere in every possible way and at the same time attempted to destroy any form of solidarity within the home, which led to a quasi-totalitarian domination of one gender over the other.

Under the Taliban women lost their time-honored status as transmitters of culture and tradition. This became particularly acute in refugee camps, where the only link with the home country was the one fostered by the older female generation's memories. Yet the Taliban never offered any form of symbolic compensation to women, something that today Islamic feminist movements have been attempting to negotiate. Henceforth, women were forbidden in workplaces, hospitals, schools, and universities, those that were left after the massive destruction of the civil war (Dupree 1996). Widows were reduced to begging for a living and sometimes prostitution. According to one informer, these women painted the nails of just one hand: when begging they would hold out the grubby hand; while selling their bodies, they would display the manicured version.

Most restrictions only affected the urban minority and therefore did not concern the vast majority of the population living in rural areas. Women's health and education suffered severely, but also those of boys as many of the civil servants and hospital and teaching staff were female in communist times. Only religious education in *madrassas* was open to boys along with the learning of Arabic. Mullah Omar's minister of education proudly declared that the only training a future doctor might need was an internship at a butcher's shop, which aptly summarizes the Taliban view on education.

Apart from a few mosques and gas stations, the Taliban did not build anything, nor did they create jobs. Furthermore, they maximized the obstructions for the few NGOs, such as the Red Cross, that were attempting to help the population through a famine brought on by a five-year drought. The Taliban wanted UN agencies to impose gender discrimination, which led to a call for unilateral withdrawal from all forms of assistance for Afghanistan. However, in remote villages of the country, nothing had really changed with Taliban rule because the government does not reach that far. As explained to me by an aged grandmother, "Frankly, we did not feel any difference. Life was hard before they came along and after they left; nothing ever changes women's lives here."

Customary Law and Violence Against Women

Despite the Taliban's official fall from power, the fate of women in Afghanistan remains one of the most brutal on earth. The kind of Islam that is officially meant to be the basis of its administration remains close to its Wahhabi model into which customary practice has been woven, producing one of the world's harshest regimes ever inflicted on women. Most people in Kabul are apt to say, "The Taliban have merely shaved their beards off, they're still here." It comes as no surprise that President Karzai's first minister of justice, the much-feared Mollah Shinwari, solely versed in Koranic law, in power from 2001 to 2006, decorated his office with a copy of the Koran and a hefty whip. Taking his cue from George W. Bush, he ensured his continuing domination well beyond his reign by nominating supreme judges all over the country. The public promotion of women's rights is a disguise affected to curry favor from Western nations and potential aid donors while application has no legal state backing in terms of advancing women's safety and security from violence. Religious and customary law dominates the lives of Afghani women.

In Afghan society the notion of a communal national good is weak, and ethnic, tribal affiliation, and solidarity groups (known as *qawm*) form the basis for identity and association. Customary law (of which the strictest is the *Pashtun* kind, known as *Pashtunwali*) is a pre-Islamic code that provides at once identity and guidelines, as described by Fredrik Barth in his numerous works from the 1960s onward. It is based on the tenets of "*melmastia,* hospitality and the honorable uses of material goods; *jirga,* councils and the honorable pursuit of public affairs; *purdah,* seclusion and the honourable organization of domestic life" (Barth 1981, 106). The principles are validated through territorial connection to inherited land through the male lines only, which is difficult for returnees who have lost their land and who nevertheless continue to refer to their patrimony as a framework for the visible practice of their *Pashtun* identity.

Collective decisions about such issues as building roads or schools are taken by dominating elder males in councils called *jirgas,* where all have to be in agreement (Akbar 1980). Everything else is left to the head of the family's discretion, no one will intervene unless it is to reinforce the application of his rights—in the case of stoning a wayward young girl, for instance, or turning a blind eye to so-called honor killings.

An Afghan woman's rights from sexual agency to claims to any inheritance are additionally curtailed by customary law, which denies this right altogether and is reinforced by Article 3 of the Afghan Constitution: "no law can be contrary to the beliefs and provisions of the sacred religion of Islam." Child marriage is not a crime according to Afghan law but is forbidden under the Civil Code, yet no punishment is prescribed for offenders, which is why at least 60 percent of brides are under the age of 15, a year younger than the official minimum age as recommended by Article 70 of the Code of Civil Law: "Marriage shall not be considered adequate until the male (reaches) the age of 18 and the female the age of 16" (Human Rights Watch 2009).

Article 71 provides a loophole in two cases: (1) when the girl does not complete the age provided under Article 70 of this law, the marriage may be concluded only through her father or the competent court, and (2) the marriage of a minor girl whose age is under 15 shall never be permissible. Forced marriage is theoretically considered a crime under Afghan law, but once again, punishments are rarely enforced (Human Rights Watch 2009). Another example is that of "adultery," which requires four eyewitnesses. In tribal law, mere suspicion of some potentially sexual conduct (even the vaguest flirting) warrants stoning.

According to the Koran, men and women do not enjoy identical rights; for example, in the Koran a woman inherits admittedly half of what her brother receives, but according to tribal custom she gets nothing, which explains why so many people resort to tribal councils to solve inheritance problems and cheat women out of property.

The word *honor,* for which there are several synonyms in Pashto, conveys different interconnected aspects (Barth 1981) and is key to understanding women's lack of rights in Afghanistan. Afghan attitudes regarding gender exemplify a classic patriarchal society with built-in hierarchies and oppositions between male and female values.

Male honor is proactive and expressed through exacerbated virility, which includes physical strength, military prowess, and a continuous display of authority. For females it is necessarily passivity, submissiveness, and centered around avoidance of shame. Its members are organized according to a tight patriarchal hierarchy with one dominating male at the top of the pyramid, followed by his married sons; single sons and grandsons; then his wife; and, at the bottom, the youngest as yet childless (or, more precisely sonless) daughters-in-law, just above the daughters of the family.

Male domination is never questioned; indeed it is seen as God given even by women themselves who perceive the frequent marital brutality as a normal part of marriage. Girls join the household of their husbands upon marriage, which is one of the reasons they are often poorly treated at home. "Why feed someone else's property?" is the recurring explanation. Of course there are exceptions and there is room for leverage, at least there used to be, and families managed to work out some kind of compromise until political Islam radicalized male authority and turned misogyny into a God-given mission.

Exchange is at the heart of social life: no action, positive or negative, is undertaken without the expectation of some kind of counteraction. Murder, for instance, invites revenge (known as *badal*), and cycles of transgenerational vendettas go on forever, until some other form of compensation can be found, often by giving one or two very young girls from the murderer's kinship to the victim's family (a system known as *baad*). This officially stops the hostilities between the two families, but of course the girls are dealt the worst possible treatment, being close relatives of the assassin. Yet women have their own value even in this case, and the girls are sacrificed to their clan's respectability, which they carry about their persons (Grima 1998).

The honor of the family is indeed its principal "cultural capital," as pioneering French sociologist Pierre Bourdieu showed throughout his work, especially in *La Distinction* (1979). Following Max Weber, he demonstrated that beyond financial capital, families and social groups transmitted specific values, behaviors, and codes of honor that would entail recognition and respectability for all those who function with the same criteria. Women in Afghanistan, even at the cost of their own lives, traditionally avoid any display of independence and agency, which could betray failings (or criminal doings) of male kin and therefore tarnish the group's reputation.

In the most traditional settings, this is the justification for the strict seclusion as women are personally responsible for the desire they may ignite among the men they could meet in public spaces, such as at schools, hospitals, parks, or markets. This is the meaning of the all-covering *burqa*, already traditional in the area and legally imposed by the Taliban, which indeed acts as a means of portable seclusion (Papanek 1982). This is an example of how religious politics and tradition conspire coherently to further restrict women's autonomy. As every female simultaneously carries her father's and her husband's honor, she is expected to passively submit to all forms of violence committed in their names. In the most rural areas, going to the law courts is practically unheard of as it would mean denouncing unacceptable family practices.

Women are not just the victims of men. The *khushu* (mother-in-law) is a feared figure in a young Afghan woman's life and justifiably so. She is the guardian of patriarchal tradition within the family: adding sons to the clan has conferred her respectability and power; she is willing to defend these hard-earned privileges that, more often than not, entail active subservience to the whole system of domination. The mother-in-law may indeed be the one to stop her daughter-in-law from giving birth in a hospital, which is considered a public place, and therefore dishonorable, especially in front of strangers (Mann 2008). For the same reason, a woman may not receive any vaccinations or other medical treatments.

International aid organizations and political powers have failed to take customary law into consideration when creating programs or policy often because the power of unwritten law seems misunderstood in the West. Furthermore, the Afghans themselves are unwilling to discuss these customs with *farangi* (foreigners). It is up to the government in Kabul to take a real stand in order to enforce a notion of state, which necessitates a powerful legislative system and a sense of the common good and shared goals, thereby criminalizing the privatized violence of antiquated customary codes (Mann 2009).

The practices of customary law have been made more rigid since the rise of militant political Islam, which seeks to legitimize the ascending violence, especially against women, through religious texts. However, customary law and privatized violence are precisely what founding prophet Muhammad sought to ban through Koranic law by introducing spiritual references that went beyond the private domain and instituting a real code of law that gave some rights to women. But these do not apply to Afghan women's everyday reality.

Violence Against Women: Failed Promises

According to a survey conducted in 2008, some 87.2 percent of women of all ages have suffered at least one act of brutality: physical, sexual, or psychological (Global Rights 2008). Less than 15 percent of the victims dare complain. Although quantitative research is very difficult to establish in a country where the year of birth is mostly unknown, it is probable that half of Afghan girls are married off before the age of 16, according to Medica Mondiale, in most cases without their consent (Bahgam and Mukhatari 2004). The youngest brides are given up generally in *baad* marriages or for debt by opium farmers.

The increase of such marriages has less to do with ancient tradition than modern catastrophes that cannot be resolved by Karzai's state. The young brides are usually immediately removed from school. Early pregnancy follows, in a context of chronic malnutrition and frequent abuse, that results in the rate of maternal mortality in Afghanistan being the highest on earth (Hogan et al. 2010), the world record having been achieved in the region of Badakhshan. As most girls cannot read, no public health campaign, let alone efforts to promote any awareness of human rights, is likely to be effective.

Furthermore, the female literacy rate is one of the lowest, with a national average for women of 12.8 and a rate of almost zero in Kandahar, despite massive literacy campaigns organized by UNESCO (UNDP 2010b).

It comes as no surprise then that infant mortality in Afghanistan is also ranked the highest, with some 850 children dying per day for entirely avoidable causes, according to Save the Children (Save the Children 2011a). Even so, the statistics for maternal mortality only account for mothers aged 15 and upward, excluding the vast number of children who become mothers before reaching that age. Despite the lack of official statistics, if we presume that at least 50 percent of girls are married off before the age of 16, we may presume that half of them will give birth before the age of 15, meaning that up to 25 percent of infant deaths in Afghanistan may be unaccounted for.

A UN International Children's Emergency Fund official described this anomaly in quantitative terms, explaining that there is no specific category for such deaths and the problem remained under the radar. Afghanistan has been named the worst place in the world to give birth (Save the Children 2011), despite the colossal aid the country has received. There is no single answer to explain these gendered statistics and the humanitarian catastrophe they represent. Some combination of factors, such as a lack of government organization and coordinated aid distribution, is to blame. Corruption is another, described in terms of aid money not filtering to those in need and being confiscated at the upper echelons of government for high salaries and expensive executive lifestyles. Military budgets continue to be a priority over aid in general but especially aid to women.

However, problems within the administration of aid itself have also been identified. Female empowerment projects popular with donors today are developed with little or no sensitivity to the realities of Afghan women's daily lives. The notion of the individual, so typically Western, disastrously collides with the centrality of the family, the institution of marriage, and importance of religion. In the West, Afghanistan is inevitably reduced to being a primitive Muslim country thirsting for Western salvation, a theme that runs throughout other aspects of discourse on Afghanistan (Abu-Lughod 2002). Empowerment programs that comply with the conventional secular feminist views held by Western aid agencies are developed thousands of miles away from Afghanistan and are incongruent with the lived experience of Afghan women. In addition, projects that promote women's empowerment in terms of sexual agency and bodily autonomy would likely be rejected by the local *jirgas,* and enforcement of laws criminalizing violence against women would be unlikely by the state judiciary.

In Afghanistan, female sexuality is criminalized when it involves a sexual act without the consent of the dominant males of the concerned woman's immediate kinship (father, brother, husband). This includes disparate incidences like stranger rape or a partner chosen by the woman herself, known as *zina,* unregulated sexual activity, or extramarital sex criminalized as adultery. The situation is indeed a paradoxical one as the injured party is seen to be the male of the family whose honor has been tainted. The woman is not perceived to be the victim of a crime: she is considered "damaged goods" and may be killed or socially excluded by her own kin, even in the case of rape, child sexual abuse, or incest.

The perpetrator is considered to be the woman or child who is deemed to have provoked such sinful activity, even in the case of rape. Corruption is rampant and female victims often find themselves convicted of *zina* because the perpetrators bribe judges. A study by the United Nations on unjustified imprisonment revealed that in 30 of 34 provinces, rape victims of all ages were systematically sentenced and jailed as guilty of *zina,* sometimes for years (UNAMA 2009a). Running away from marital brutality is also a crime, which also carries a prison sentence. A survey showed that some 54 percent of "crimes" for which women were jailed in Afghanistan consisted solely of *zina* and escaping domestic brutality (Women and Children Legal Research Foundation 2008).

Afghan construction of masculinity is dependent on preserving personal male honor, and judicial bribery is seen as an extension of this power. A measure of honor can be redeemed by personally tackling the legal system through subornation and failure to convict sex offenders and in some cases murderers. Purchasing a favorable judgment becomes a symbolic way of simultaneously vanquishing an enemy (the state) and paying one's dues (directly to the judge). The offended party, in the case of rape, is seen to be the victim's family whose honor has been besmirched.

This customary code also occurs in other countries like Kurdish Turkey and the Democratic Republic of the Congo. Section 398 of the Afghan Penal Code sentences any murderer who claims to defend his honor (that is to say, by killing his wife, daughter, or sister) to two years' jail maximum, far less than for killing a male. This is why fathers and brothers often take the law into their own hands and execute the hapless victim themselves, before even considering vengeance against the rapist. In addition, customary law of the local *jirgas* at the village level may advise a rapist to marry his victim, which is considered the best option. The woman victim's opinion is routinely discounted.

The Ministry of Women's Affairs has made the fight against these customary and statutory legal practices a priority, but it lacks the means to put pressure on the courts. This ministry receives the least financing of all the ministries. Arguably its resource-starved work can be seen as camouflage intended to attract potential aid donors. It is therefore almost impossible for women to lodge a legal complaint for gender-based violence.

Few women in Afghanistan can stand up to such a monolithic rejection of women's and human rights. Maria Bashir is an exception; she is the leading attorney in the country and works at the court of Herat. She specializes in defending the women who are confident enough to lodge a complaint against an abusing husband and their often equally brutal mother-in-law. Yet Bashir's recommendations are often rejected by the judges. "It's very difficult here to achieve any form of justice," Bashir told me in Herat. She also engages in health-related disputes involving the Herat hospital, where many young women are treated for injuries related to suicide attempts or attempted murder by fire committed by a mother-in-law or spouse. "As there are no proper police records every murder is labeled suicide," Bashir explained. In addition, her attempts to prove the collusion between hospital administration and perpetrators have put her own life and that of her children in danger: she has removed them from regular school and now carries a gun in her handbag. Her experience goes far to explain the dearth of lawyers willing to advise and counsel women in Afghanistan.

NATO-sponsored projects have attempted to train the police academy in Kabul to view domestic violence as a crime under constitutional law and not protected by concepts of privacy to which males are entitled. It is particularly hard to reinforce this message to police trainees because their rate of literacy is 29 percent (Human Rights Watch 2009). The Afghan and foreign NGOs are trying to motivate more women to join the forces to help mitigate violence against women and police it fairly, while at the same time the Taliban are targeting these female law enforcement professionals with intimidation. One of the best-known high-ranking officials, Malalai Kakar, in charge of the department of crimes against women, was murdered in Kandahar. Her crime was threefold: this mother of six children worked for the government, intruded on private space, and confronted patriarchal domination head on (BBC 2008).

In February 2009, Karzai attempted to further entrench violence against women by proposing the Shi'a Personal Status Law, restricting the rights of Hazara women, of a level of severity that had not been seen since the Taliban (Human Rights Watch 2009). It legalized domestic rape by authorizing men to withhold financial and other support from wives who did not comply with their sexual or other wishes. Furthermore, the law forbade women to leave the house without permission from their husbands. Despite the international outcry that followed, a watered-down version of the selfsame act was passed the following April. Karzai's motive was political; he wanted to make sure he got the Hazara vote for the impending elections. To remain in power, Karzai has continued to compromise women's rights to achieve his ends.

Commitment to women's rights in Afghanistan is publically demonstrated in terms of signing onto international charters and conventions against gender-based violence. For example, in July 2009, President Karzai signed the UN Convention on the Elimination of All Forms of Discrimination Against Women (CEDAW). However, ratification has proved daunting. The head of international relations, the warlord Abdul Rasul Sayyaf, obstructed ratification on the grounds that (a) rape is not a crime, (b) for orphan girls, marriage of minors and forced marriages are acceptable, and (c) violence (the term used is *qahr,* anger) against a girl or woman by an angered husband or a father is not a crime. CEDAW was blocked by Islamist members of parliament who sought to deny women human rights. The preservation of patriarchal privilege and the nonintervention of the state in private life means violence against women in Afghanistan remains strictly a private matter. From the male's point of view, resorting to outside police or judicial intervention would signify being unable to fight one's own battles, in brief admitting defeat and (symbolic) castration.

Women's rights signify the most extreme invasion of the state into the sacred areas of personal administration and male honor. The latter, as we have seen, depends on the male right to administer private justice, namely a death sentence on whomever threatens these values. And women personify such an unacceptable threat when claiming a right to bodily autonomy and sexual agency. The very notion of state intervention is incompatible with these customary, religious, and tribal norms and with the preservation of such a system.

Conclusion

Times are changing. From 2002 to 2005, there seemed to be a real improvement in women's lives and expectations: enrollment in girls' schools was high and new avenues to employment were opening, especially for girls who had learned English in Pakistan and other skills in Iran. Through humanitarian aid, the vast majority of the younger generation of rural refugees had been exposed to schooling abroad they never would have had access to had they remained in Afghanistan. Women's associations were established, recommencing structures that existed in the far more progressive 1960s and

1970s. Aid agencies have sponsored programs that foster educated young women in cities to find paid employment and make financial contribution to their families. This in turn has had a beneficial influence on the status of women, generally simultaneously improving the chances of autonomy for the new female workforce itself.

Families who traditionally arranged marriages are now increasingly reluctant to let this new source of revenue go to a potential husband's family. Naturally such examples of success—unfortunately limited to cities—bring out the value of schooling for families otherwise reluctant to send their daughters to school. An awareness of alternatives is seeping through the media, however limited. There are now three television channels in the provinces, one local, two national (compared to at least 20 in Kabul), and rural women's expectations are changing along with those of their urban sisters.

The news and the much-loved Indian television serials, however limited, reinforce efforts to empower women and are changing their worldview and self-assessment of gender. Add to that the direct experience of having lived abroad as refugees and for the more fortunate urban inhabitants, the benefits of schooling and access to paid employment. Girls are beginning to realize that there are other options to being sacrificed without their consent to an increasingly unacceptable customary code. This is especially the case for those who have been to Iran, after living in a Muslim theocracy that allows women the freedom to study and work.

A quarter of parliamentarians in Afghanistan today are women, which constitutes indisputable progress. But this does not mean that human rights are a priority for these female members of parliament. Their solidarity goes first to their political family and the clan to which they belong. One of the problems is that they have little to no leadership training and are powerless in conceptualizing problems and promoting possible solutions. Left to follow the male model of governance, parliamentary assemblies take place in an atmosphere of recriminations and insults hurled across the hall by men and women alike.

In May 2007, a woman member of parliament from Farah, Malalai Joya, was excluded from Parliament following the remarks she had made on television, comparing the National Assembly to both a zoo and a badly kept stable. Talking in such blunt terms, she was in fact voicing a steadily discontented public opinion. However, members of parliament, lawyers, and activists who voice opposition are constantly threatened. Murders are frequent, perpetrated by Taliban and their allies, and are intended to inhibit any female ambition through intimidation and terror. As a result, the number of women in the civil service is steadily declining. Because of the impunity for these crimes, the government is in fact amplifying the deterrent effect of this campaign of persistent intimidation.

Perhaps it is time to look elsewhere and away from the Western paradigm. Perhaps imposing secular democracy according to Western standards is simply not possible in Afghanistan. After all, the United States and NATO, by backing conservative Islamist warlords first in the 1980s and today, have all but sabotaged their own aid agencies. And ultimately these cannot be allowed to be the sole representatives of women's rights in this country (Khattak 2004). Nearby Iran, while being far from ideal for its sophisticated urban populations, has achieved a considerable measure of progress for its rural citizens, in terms of public health and education, including access to university in accordance with locally acceptable standards.

From one side of the frontier to the other, women in Iran live 20 to 30 years longer than their counterparts in nearby Afghanistan. On average they have two children rather than eight and are nearly totally literate, while Afghan women, as we have seen, are among the most illiterate in the world. Furthermore, a powerful state has been able to supersede the customary practice. The Iranian example has had a particularly potent influence in the western part of Afghanistan. Young rural female refugees who spent years there in exile, despite continuous hardship, experienced a truly acceptable form of empowerment within Islamic norms.

The young Afghan women born in the 1980s and 1990s in Pakistan, and especially Iran, nearly all of rural origin, are poised to create and lead an Afghan movement for women's rights. With intelligent and culturally sensitive support, a transformation could take place, led this time by women who have benefited from post-Taliban aid and who will stake their claim in the public sphere. This naturally depends on the degree of enlightenment of the government, which will follow after total US forces withdrawal. Although the prospects are grim and include the possibility of civil war, it is hoped that the younger generation of women, born in the 1980s, will demand their rights, even within an ultraconservative regime. Western feminism could learn from and contribute to these exciting potentialities for change.

9

The Experiences of Male Intimate
Partners of Female Rape Victims From
Cape Town, South Africa

Their Journeys From Secondary Victims
to Secondary Survivors of Rape

Evalina van Wijk

THIS CHAPTER PRESENTS A PHENOMENOLOGICAL EXPLICATION OF THE EXPERIENCES OF NINE
male intimate partners of female rape survivors from Cape Town, South
Africa, who shared their stories of how the rape of their partners affected
them and described their journeys along the path of healing. Following introductory comments about the magnitude of rape in South Africa and a
summary of the literature pertaining to the impact of rape on the intimate
partners of female rape survivors, I introduce a model for understanding
intimate partners' journeys from being secondary victims to secondary survivors of rape. This chapter concludes with the implications for practice and
recommendations for implementation.

Magnitude of Rape in South Africa

South Africans recognize sexual violence as a scourge and legitimate public health problem (Meel 2005). The country has the reputation of having one of the highest incidences of rape in the world (Itano 2003), which
has reached "epidemic proportions" (Vogelman 1990, 1). South Africa has
been referred to as the "rape capital" of the world (Artz and Smythe 2007,
13). Although no accurate rape statistics are available because of gross underreporting, approximately 55,000 cases are reported annually within a
population of around 48 million. Most rapes occur at the victims' homes,
and while the offenders are known to the victims in 90 percent of cases,

conviction rates remain disappointingly low (Meel 2005, 2). Many South Africans blame the rape statistics on the "violence, repression, poverty and psychological degradations of the white supremacist, apartheid regime that ended 15 years ago" (Jacobson 2009, 1–2).

A previous South African study by Van den Berg and Pretorius (1999) emphasized that cultural background, ethnicity, community, and personal values may all have an impact on intimate partners' experiences and the manner in which the experiences and losses are interpreted, expressed, or experienced. Although South Africa is not recognized as one of the countries where rape has been used as a weapon of war (Clifford 2008), the country is host to a substantial number of foreign nationals from other African countries. Although most foreign nationals are economic refugees, others have fled conflict in their own countries. Violence, including rape, has been perpetrated against foreign nationals as part of growing xenophobic intolerance. Isolated violent incidents against foreigners have occurred since democracy came to South Africa in 1994, though large-scale outbursts occurred in 2008 (Kapp 2008). Although rape is a traumatic event for anyone, the situation and impact of sexual violence is even more complicated for refugees (Naparstek 2006).

Three of the nine intimate partners involved in the research were foreign refugees who voiced their frustration and anger toward the local Xhosas, as the perceived perpetrators of xenophobic violence, and the South African government for not protecting them and their partners. Fuller has asserted, "being both foreign and female increases the vulnerability of women during the xenophobic violence in South Africa" (2008, 1). Foreign women in the townships have been disproportionately affected by the attacks brought on by xenophobia, and "the violence has played out on their bodies through beatings and rape" (Fuller 2008, 1). Fuller further states that criminals targeted foreign women as scapegoats for the domestic problems facing South Africa, such as unemployment, crime, and limited access to services.

Literature Review

Rape has both primary and secondary victims, as it has a substantial impact on the intimate partners, such as boyfriends or husbands, of women who are the primary victims of rape (Clifford 2008). Of the available literature concerning sexual assault–related issues, most literature demonstrates the perspective of the rape victims, with less information available about intimate partners' experiences and the manner in which they cope over time after the rape of their partners (Remer 2001). Holmstrom and Burgess (1979) and Remer (2001) have described that intimate partners go through similar phases as their partners after rape, such as trauma awareness, crisis and disorientation, outward adjustment, and finally, reintegration. Morrison, Quadara, and Boyd (2007) have found that for the intimate partner of a rape victim, the emotional and psychological impact of rape will be multifaceted.

A lack of understanding of and support for an intimate partner contributes to his or her inability to deal with and overcome problems. Hence, as secondary victims, partners of rape survivors have to cope not only with their own reactions and emotions but also with their partners' responses to the rape. The deleterious effects on the relationship can escalate into severe social, mental health, and physical problems for the intimate partners (Emm and McKenry 1988; Figley and Kleber 1995; Orzek 1983; Smith 2005). Previous South African research into intimate partners' experiences is remarkably sparse. This dearth in information draws attention to the need for a scientific basis for intervention strategies for the intimate partners of rape victims (Van den Berg and Pretorius 1999).

From a Concern to a Research Study

As a practicing mental health nurse, I became aware that the partners of rape victims in South Africa remain unrecognized as a vulnerable population worthy of support or therapeutic intervention. Nothing is known about how the rape of Cape Town women affects their intimate partners, how the partners cope over time, and to what extent a healing process occurs. The postulated need for improved services for sexual assault victims requires sound academic information generation, based on local circumstances. With these unanswered questions in mind, a qualitative, interpretative, longitudinal study was designed and implemented between 2007 and 2010. The main research question was: "What constitutes intimate partners' experiences of living with a rape victim, and how do they cope within the first six months following the rape?"

The Study Findings:
Development of an Integrated Conceptual Model

The nine study participants were recruited from a rape treatment center in Cape Town, South Africa. Three of the nine intimate partners were foreign nationals who had left their home countries with their families for economic reasons. Four semistructured interviews were conducted with each of the men two weeks after the rape and then one, three, and six months later. The recorded interviews of their lived experiences were transcribed, read, reread, and interpreted, then coded to categorize the participants' statements within each case and across cases into four categories of developmental stages, two core themes, and various subthemes and patterns (Speziale and Carpenter 2003). The findings of the thematic analysis are discussed in the context of a conceptual model of the lived experiences of the intimate partners of female rape survivors within the first six months after the event (see Figure 9.1).

All of the study participants experienced a psychological crisis after the rape of their partners; however, not all of them attached the same meaning to their experiences. Orzek (1983) found the manner in which intimate partners react to the trauma depends on the situation, the person, and the amount of support they receive following the rape. Although some intimate partners felt the study period was too short (in that they were not completely "healed" after six months), it was an enlightening experience to observe most of them evolve from initially traumatized secondary victims to secondary survivors of the rape of their partners. All participants, in a unique way, attempted to give meaning to their experiences while grappling to make sense of their partners' rape. During the final interview six months after the traumatic incident, most were able to reflect on their experiences, and, as one said, "I'm back on my feet again, thank you!"

The four main categories follow the well-described phases of psychological adaption after a traumatic experience: (1) trauma awareness, (2) crisis and disorientation, (3) outward adjustment on the personal and the relationship level, and (4) reorganization on the personal and the relationship level. In most cases, healing will occur, and a return to the pretrauma level of functioning is evident (Janoff-Bulman and Frieze 1983). Two themes reflecting the broad life-worlds of intimate partners were identified: (1) being-in-the-world as a secondary victim of rape and (2) living in multiple worlds, or the worlds of their female partners, family, friends, society, employers or colleagues, health professionals, and the justice system, respectively. The categories and themes, as well as the various subthemes and patterns, are all based on the thematic analysis of participants' narratives. A few selected excerpts from the narratives gathered of the nine male intimate partners are included.

Discussing the Framework:
The Pretrauma Level of Functioning

An awareness of the prerape functioning of intimate partners, pertaining to their relationship with their partners, their coping styles, and their

Figure 9.1 An Integrated Conceptual Framework to Understand and Conceptualize Male Intimate Partners' Lived Experiences

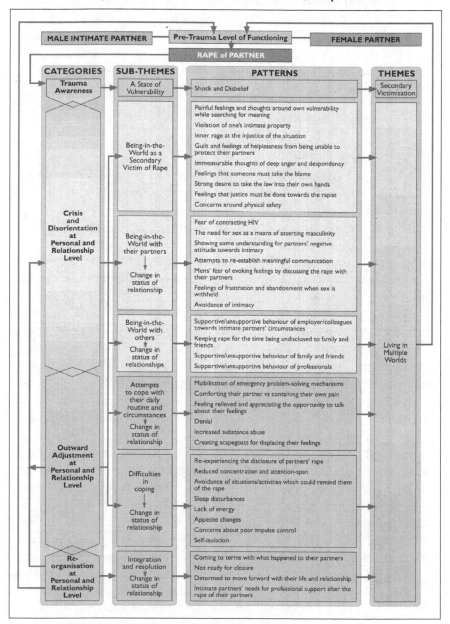

Note: From Nicholas Curwell.

health-related issues, is important. As Remer and Ferguson (1995) commented, the pretrauma phase influences not only the flow of the healing process but also every subsequent phase. All the intimate partners in this study indicated that before the rape they had meaningful lives; a stable, mutually supportive relationship with their partners; and no previous mental illnesses. Five of the nine intimate partners were married, while the remaining four had been in an intimate relationship for more than a year.

Category 1: Trauma Awareness

Theme 1: Being-in-the-World as a Secondary Victim of Rape

In this study, to reconceptualize one's being-in-the-world meant having to incorporate a new self-image as secondary survivor of rape and having to search for meaning in experiences (Morrison et al. 2007; Remer 2001). Although the disclosure of the rape was an overwhelming moment for the intimate partners, their initial levels of understanding about how such an event would affect them, their relationships in the long term, and about what behavior to expect from their partners seemed significantly, though understandably, low.

During the first interviews, most of the partners were tearful and anxious, displaying psychomotor agitation and avoiding eye contact. All were hesitant to talk freely about their experiences, although with the assistance of probing questions, the majority could recall how shocked they were when their partners disclosed their rape to them. Haansbaek (2006) found these types of stress reactions are commonly experienced by intimate partners of female rape victims when they are confronted with the reality of what had happened to their partners. Such reactions, if compounded by a lack of professional support, could pose a risk for the later manifestation of post-traumatic stress (Davis, Taylor, and Bench 1995). As Remer notes, "the toll of the trauma for the primary victim is staggering and for the secondary victim it is mind-boggling" (2001, 1). For the secondary survivor, the rape was also unexpected and they were unprepared for it. The term "secondary trauma" means that those experiencing symptoms were not the direct recipients of the sexual assault trauma (Remer and Ferguson 1995, 407).

Although the symptoms associated with primary and secondary trauma are remarkably similar, there is one fundamental difference: whereas the primary trauma victim experiences symptoms directly associated with some aspect of the traumatic event, the secondary trauma victim experiences symptoms associated with the primary trauma victim (McKenry and Price 2005). A person's reality follows assumptions and expectations held by that person, and his or her life is structured in such a manner so as to create meaning

(Sedler 1987). Being a victim, whether primary or secondary, forces traumatized individuals to realize that their *cognitive baggage,* the assumptions and expectations they have held about themselves and their world, has been severely challenged and may no longer be viable. Moreover, their perceptions are now marked by threat, danger, insecurity, and self-questioning (Janoff-Bullman and Frieze 1983). The rape of their partners, therefore, may threaten the breakdown of their entire conceptual system and force these men to reexamine their assumptions about the world (Magenuka 2006).

Subtheme: Immediate Responses: Shock and Disbelief

The reactions of shock and disbelief are understandably the first reactions all individuals display when dealing with any traumatic experience (Mio and Foster 1991). A common thought was the following: "Why did this happen to me and her?" All found it difficult to find answers. Magwaza (1999) states that when traumatized individuals raise these types of questions, they seemed to be searching for answers about an event for which there could be no reasonable justification. From an initial interview, one intimate partner stated: "After she told me that she was raped, I was so shocked that such an ugly thing could happen to her . . . this is mean, mean . . . how can they do that to her . . . we are such a happy couple . . . I feel so hurt inside."

Category 2: Crisis and Disorientation

Theme 2: Living in Multiple Worlds

Subtheme: Being-in-the-World as a Secondary Victim of Rape

The news of the rape of their partners immediately caused a crisis for these men. Systems theory states if there is a change in one part of the system, there is a change in the whole system (Rawlins, Williams, and Beck 1993). Victims experience a "loss of equilibrium . . . things no longer work the way they used to" (Bard and Sangrey 1979, 14). The following patterns emerged.

Painful feelings and thoughts around their own vulnerability: The study participants were so traumatized and humiliated after learning about their partners' rapes that they experienced a questioning of their self-perceptions. Most described the instant they heard of the rape as a defining moment in their lives, distinguishing between how their lives were before and how they might be in the future. As suggested by the following quote, they felt vulnerable: "The world is screwed, man; I am very angry; they screwed up our lives . . . our lives changed in a second . . . they hurt me too."

Violation of one's intimate property: Mio and Foster (1991) found the perceptions of the intimate partners in their study were that their wives did not possess the "same value" as they did before the rape. In the current study, this view was not evident; rather, some participants experienced their partners' rapes as a sense of loss of their belongings or property; others described it as a violent rather than a sexual attack. A universal feeling among Xhosa intimate partners was that no man has the right to take their property for which they paid *lobola* (bride-price): "The moment that man raped my wife, he took my pride which belongs to me . . . you see, in our culture, we pay *lobola* for our wives, so she is mine, and he cannot do that to me." In Africa, the old custom of *lobola* is still a reality because it creates a solid foundation for the marriage and unity between two families (Petronilla n.d.).

Partners from a Western cultural background also believed the rapist took away what is theirs, but for another reason: men are there to protect their partners, and therefore, they perceive their women as their property, property which they do not share with another man. Their partners are theirs alone. The rape was an act of violence, of theft, more than a sexual crime. The difficulties they experienced in conceptualizing the act were because of the different meanings they attached to the act while searching for answers about what really transpired.

All the intimate partners blamed the government for not doing something about the ongoing violence in South Africa. They perceived the world as cruel and the rape a pointless act of violence. A culture of violence has dominated the South African society for many years. The current levels of criminal and political violence have roots in apartheid and the political struggle against it. Because it is mostly males who are the perpetrators of violence against women who are considered weaker, rape may represent a displacement of anger. It may be equally true that rape is an assertion of power and aggression in an attempt to reassert the rapist's masculinity (Robertson 1998). Rape as a result of xenophobic conflict is a significant, although incidental, finding in this study.

Guilt: Within the first month after the rape, the majority of the intimate partners experienced feelings of guilt for not being there to protect their partners from being raped. They felt that they had abandoned their roles as men (Silverman 1978). It took at least three months to come to the point where they did not feel guilty anymore, because, as time passed, they came to realize there was nothing they could have done to prevent the rape.

Anger: Silverman (1978) reported the husbands and boyfriends in his study openly expressed feelings of anger toward their partners, accusing them of not being careful enough. This sentiment was not expressed by any of the nine participants interviewed for this research; in fact, all of them realized that their partners were raped by people with more power than the women. The moment the intimate partners became aware of the rape, they expressed intense anger and despondency toward themselves for not protecting their partners as well as at the rapist, the police, the justice system, health professionals at the rape centers, and in the case of refugees, at the local Xhosas and the South African government. As one participant described: "I just want to kill him . . . I know I will get crazy if I ever see them, but I am very angry and upset . . . I want to beat him up for what he did to her."

Assigning blame: The participants' narratives revealed a strong sense that "somebody should take the blame" (Smith 2005). Contrary to previous studies (Holmstrom and Burgess 1979; Remer 2001), blaming the raped partner was not a feature in this study. Self-blaming and blaming the rapist, police, or government were more evident. Although the persistent blaming of others and of themselves had a negative impact on their health and relationships, a positive outcome was evident by six months; some intimate partners said in order to move on with their lives and their relationships, they forgave the rapist and no longer regarded all men (and, in particular, not all Xhosas) as bad people.

Fear for safety: Naparstek (2006) believes that most people are oblivious of how much comfort is taken from the belief the world is a predictable place, until it demonstrates its random cruelty in some dramatic way. One of the reasons intimate partners later developed symptoms of post-traumatic stress disorder (PTSD) may stem from their struggle to reconcile the shock of their partners' rape with core beliefs about themselves and the world. Their seemingly secure living environment with their partners took a dramatic twist after the rape.

Jim and Jacobsen (2008) commented that a typical core belief is that the self is basically good, in-control, and invulnerable; moreover, the world is just, benevolent, and meaningful. In this way of thinking, the logic holds that good people who take the necessary precautions will be protected from traumatic life events. A rape of a partner stands in sharp contrast to these beliefs. Participants' narratives reflected a shattered notion of the intimate partners' safe and secure living environment: "I have an intense fear that the same thing can happen to my wife while I am at work . . . so we moved out of the community . . . because of the fear that the same thing might happen again."

Unhappiness about the injustice of the situation: The participants expressed no anger or resentment toward their partners; instead, they described rage toward themselves, the South African government, and the sheer injustice of the situation. Of interest was that the three foreign participants not only voiced their frustration and anger toward the rapist but also toward local Xhosa men (as the perceived perpetrators) and the South African government for not addressing the ongoing violence against women and for not protecting them as refugees.

Rape, as a byproduct of social collapse during wartime, might be used to instill shame and humiliation on the enemy (Carll 2007, 266). Although not in an actual war situation, the refugee intimate partners in the current study equated their partners' rapes to the xenophobic attacks on foreigners that swept through South Africa in 2008. They indicated later that their anger toward the locals had subsided: they saw the rapists as ordinary criminals.

Strong desire to take the law into their own hands: The intimate partners described the rape as meaningless, and for them to regain control, the rapist must be punished. In fact, many were so enraged they had a strong wish to take the law into their own hands and to go and look for the rapists to beat them up. Later, some intimate partners had mixed feelings, ranging from still wishing to go out to look for the rapist, to a desire to avoid seeing the rapist out of fear for their reactions and the consequences, and a desire to suppress memories of the rape.

Need for the rapist to be brought to justice: Participants described their exasperation with the fact that the rapists were still walking free and that they had no trust in the police due to the lack of action on the part of the police. Intimate partners' anger could be related to a strong need for the rapists to receive punishment. According to the just-world hypothesis, individuals need to believe that "people get what they deserve and deserve what they get" (Janoff-Bulman and Wortman 1977, 351). By the end of the study period, the police had apprehended only three perpetrators. At times, some participants expressed ambivalence about their desire for justice because they did not want to see the rapists or expose their partners to traumatic memories of the rape; these desires were interpreted as PTSD-related symptoms of avoidance that are used to protect trauma survivors from painful memories.

Subtheme: Being-in-the-World With Their Partners

Relationships can suffer irrespective of how those who are closest to a rape victim are able to understand the impact of sexual assault and the manner in which these individuals respond to the disclosure of the rape (Astbury 2006). In this study, one intimate partner's relationship was so severely affected by the rape that he had to be referred for marriage counseling at Rape Crisis (a nongovernmental organization). Four of the others were referred for medical treatment to a mental health clinic, while another was admitted to a mental health facility. Although all the participants' relationships were affected negatively, in only one instance was a participant's relationship dissolved because his partner could not cope with her own emotions after the rape.

Both Astbury (2006) and Remer and Ferguson (1995) have found that intimate partners also faced significant adjustments after the rape. Relationship problems can develop as a result of a mismatch between the partner's stages of adjustment or an imbalance in the provision of support. The narratives revealed all the intimate partners' relationships were affected negatively; communication difficulties were commonplace, which left them feeling lonely and rejected. Arguments abounded due to their lack of knowledge about how to support their partners emotionally. The following subthemes allow closer examination of the relationship issues.

Fear of contracting HIV: During the first month, a number of intimate partners revealed an intense fear their partners might have been infected with HIV after the rape and that they might also be infected with HIV. Moreover, they felt uncertain about having sex without a condom after the rape. It was important for them that their partners take their antiviral medication as prescribed. These fears are not unrealistic, as HIV infection is prevalent in South Africa, and some authors argue that rape is a significant driver of the AIDS epidemic (Meel 2005; Usdin et al. 2000).

The need for sex as a means of asserting masculinity: In the initial interview, it emerged that most of the participants avoided sex soon after the rape for various reasons, including not knowing how their partner felt and fear of contracting HIV. All, however, wished to continue engaging in sex as it is important to them as men and that it will help to restore their strained relationships. Condom use increased because of concern about sexually transmitted diseases.

Men's fear of evoking feelings by discussing the rape with their partner: Holmstrom and Burgess (1979) found that 12 of the 15 couples in their study reported communication difficulties after a rape. In the current study, intimate partners reported they did not know how to approach their partners, nor what to say, and feared further arguments or saying the wrong thing. Apprehension about their partners' reactions, unpredictable mood swings, and anger outbursts were compounding factors that made it difficult to discuss their feelings with their partners. Even communication about everyday issues, such as their children, was impaired. They therefore not only avoided conversations about the rape but also barely talked to each other.

Attempts to reestablish meaningful communication: The negative effects on relationships were manifest as strained communication between participants and their partners, described as either "unhealthy" or "unbearable," and led participants to feel lonely and disconnected from each other: "We hardly communicate with each other, and I really miss those precious moments of the past when we were able to share our thoughts with each other . . . if we start talking to each other now it always ends up in a mess . . .

then we will not talk to each other for days." At the end of the six months, most of the participants felt their communication had improved, although it had not fully normalized.

Showing some understanding of partners' negative attitude toward intimacy: Initially, all the participants wished to continue with their normal sexual activities and had trouble understanding that their partners did not want sex. Only some had a reasonable understanding that the rape was an upsetting event for their partners. Furthermore, they felt insecure because they did not know whether their partners would reject their advances.

Feelings of frustration and abandonment when sex is refused: At the fourth-week interview session, all the participants described how the rape had adversely affected their sexual relationships. Only two reported their sexual relationships were back to normal at the session in the sixth month.

Avoidance of intimacy: Although their partners' changes in behaviors were the source of sexual frustration, at the same time, participants also said if they had had better knowledge of what a rape survivor goes through, they may have better understood their partners' avoidance of intimacy. While they hoped matters would improve with time, the avoidance of intimacy worsened for some: "Although I feel sexually frustrated, I do not feel comfortable to ask for sex . . . because she is not the same person I knew . . . this is upsetting and breaks my heart." The avoidance of intimacy was mutual. The intimate partner's ambivalence about sex was also because he feared rejection of the sexual advances. A remarkable finding in the current study is that not one of the participants went to other women for sex.

Davis et al. (1995) wholeheartedly recommended integrated support services should be available for couples because the better informed intimate partners are about the physical and mental health impact of rape on both of them, the better able they would be to cope in their journey from being victims to survivors.

Subtheme: Being-in-the-World With Others
Being with employers and colleagues: Supportive/unsupportive behaviors: Although eight of the intimate partners were permanently employed, only three of them believed they had open relationships with their employers. Disclosure of the rape at work was delayed until an unintended therapeutic benefit of the interviews prompted some of the participants to disclose the event: "It is only you and my boss I trust . . . my boss is now very supportive after I followed your advice to inform him . . . what had happened to me is the reason why I was not myself for the past weeks."

Being-in-the-world with family and friends: Participants initially found it difficult to disclose the rape to others. They feared the reaction of family and friends and being blamed for not protecting their partners. The participants who chose not to disclose also did so to protect both their own feelings and those of their partners.

Keeping the rape from family, friends, neighbors, and the community for the time being: The involvement of social networks is extremely important where recovery from rape is concerned (Emm and McKenry 1988; Van den Berg and Pretorius 1999). Some of the intimate partners in this study were determined to keep the rape undisclosed to family and friends for fear of their reactions, often because they feared being blamed for not protecting their partners. It may be, too, that they simply wanted to protect their partners from exposure to further trauma.

Supportive/unsupportive behavior of family, friends, neighbors, and the community: Although some intimate partners decided not to disclose the rape to family and friends, a few reported that after their friends and neighbors became aware of the rape, their partners became a topic of conversation among them, which was a most upsetting experience. Others expressed that, irrespective of disclosure, not one of their family or friends cared. They had nobody to talk to and withdrew from their social networks. Although intimate partners believed rape is a very private issue, they denied ever pressuring their partners to lie to others about what had happened.

Being with professionals (justice and health care): Supportive/unsupportive behavior: Although some of the intimate partners accompanied their partners to police stations or rape centers, they were unimpressed with the behavior of these professionals for simply ignoring them. These professionals ignored the fact that male intimate partners also have feelings and made them feel disconnected from their partners: "I felt very angry and left out. Everybody at the hospital cared about her and what had happened to her, but nobody asked me how I was feeling . . . nobody told me anything, and yet I am her partner who must live with her." The negative responses toward professionals throughout the study probably reflect the lack of formal, structured counseling services available for the secondary survivors of rape.

Category 3: Outward Adjustment on the
Personal and the Relationship Level

When asked how they managed to deal with the repercussions of the rape, participants indicated they found it staggering to have to cope with their own feelings and the responses of their partners and to have to take over the care of their children and other domestic chores. Some of them were in a state of denial for a substantial period; others resorted to substance abuse to relieve their painful feelings or sought support from the researcher. Some comforted their partners while denying their own pain, created various scapegoats for their own feelings, or vented their anger in a destructive manner. All realized they were in a state of disequilibrium. Their narratives suggest they had failed to restore control over their circumstances and relationships.

Subtheme: Attempts to Cope With
Their Daily Routine and Circumstances
Mobilization of emergency problem-solving mechanisms: Mobilization of emergency problem-solving mechanisms was evident during interview sessions four weeks after the rape: "When I am at work and things get too much for me, I take a walk, just so that I can forget the rape and how I am feeling because I found that if I think too much of it, it affects my work."

Comforting their partners versus containing their own pain: One participant described putting his own needs aside to be there for his partner: "For the first few days after she was raped, I couldn't sleep . . . maybe an hour, two hours, and then I'm awake again. . . . I will never tell her the reason I can't sleep. . . . I will tell her it is because I am worried and concerned about her and want to see if she's okay, whether she needs anything. . . . I can't break down in front of her because I'm supposed to be her strength."

Feeling relieved and appreciating the opportunity to talk about their feelings: Most of the participants reported participating in the study gave them the opportunity to talk about their feelings: "I was so lucky to have met a person who I can talk to . . . if I think of what happened to me, it can also happen to other people, and if there is not a person like you, they will then never have an opportunity to talk to somebody."

Denial: A participant illustrated denial by explaining he would rather put up a front so that others could not see how the rape of his partner had affected him: "If I'm not in this session, I have to tell myself I must be strong . . . don't show my emotions, how I feel about this, what happened to her . . . then I make like nothing happened [crying]. And that's wrong because others doesn't know how I am feeling."

Substance abuse: One participant claimed: "I always use alcohol over weekends, but since the rape, I smoke 20 cigarettes a day and drink heavily to forget the bad experience of the rape because things then can go away when I am drunk." Another participant realized that his drinking was becoming problematic because the behavior resulted in absenteeism from work, which could have serious implications for his future.

Creating scapegoats for displacing their painful feelings: During both the week 4 and week 12 interview sessions, participants described creating scapegoats for displacing their painful feelings: "I am not coping very well . . . and at work or when me and my wife walk in the streets, and somebody just looks at me, I get so agitated that I feel as if I can assault them."

Subtheme: Coping Difficulties on the Personal and Relationship Levels
A significant consequence of the rape is that the partners developed physical, emotional, behavioral, and cognitive symptoms that meet the criteria of PTSD. Smith (2005) interviewed five male partners of adult female rape victims/survivors. Although the outcome of her investigation was based on once-off interviews, the men in her study described similar symptoms of PTSD to those described by the intimate partners in this longitudinal study.

Reexperiencing the disclosure of their partners' rape: Nightmares and flashbacks: One participant described as follows: "When I think of the entrance of my house or come home after work, the moment I see it, I heard how my girlfriend screamed at them to leave her alone." Another claimed, "When I am sleeping, I suddenly wake up after having the most ugly dream of how my girlfriend was screaming and fighting for her life."

Psychological signs of increased arousal (sleep disturbances, irritability, anger outbursts): A participant made the following observation about his response to the rape of his partner: "When people I know asked me why am I so different the past two months, I freak out with anger, pointing fingers at them, and although I feel like smacking them, I rather yell at them to leave me alone."

Avoidance of and withdrawal from situations/activities that could remind them of their partner's rape: The majority of the participants tried to avoid situations and activities that could even remotely remind them of the rape. For example, they avoided reading newspapers and watching television or listening to their favorite radio stations. In fact, to avoid reliving a traumatic event, participants attempted to reduce its impact by diminishing painful emotions associated with memories of the trauma (Everly and Lating 1995).

Concerns about poor impulse control: Intimate partners described themselves as emotionally stable before the rape, yet, for the first three months after their partners' rapes, most of them stated they felt out of control. They had not experienced difficulties in controlling their emotions prior to the rape, but after the rape, they found it difficult to control their emotions, with multiple negative consequences. For example, an intimate partner described how he took out his anger on the cars he worked on and damaged more than one. An inspiring finding was that at six months after the rape, all of the intimate partners expressed that after they started talking to the researcher, they had been looking at their circumstances and relationships from different perspectives. They felt that matters were gradually improving. They sensed that they were starting to heal because they wanted to move on with their lives and relationships.

Self-isolation: Self-isolation is exemplified by a participant who stated that he and his wife decided to keep the rape a secret and started separating themselves from family and friends out of fear that family and friends would find out. Their attempts to isolate themselves, however, had resulted in a lack of support from others.

Category 4: Reorganization on the Personal and Relationship Levels

Returning to their pretrauma level of functioning in this study was identified as the phase of reorganization where the men identified that they were regaining control and starting to incorporate the circumstances of the rape into their lives.

Subtheme: Searching for Integration and Resolution: Accepting or Not Accepting the Rape of Their Partners

Regaining control was not an easy process; movement toward regaining control was halting as participants shifted backward and forward. At the end of the six-month period, seven of the nine participants indicated they had started feeling more in control of themselves. This, in turn, had a positive effect on their relationships. They were determined to return to being the persons they were before the rapes. They had started to accept the rapes of their partners, making it part of their lives, so they could move forward to their prerape functioning at personal and relationship levels.

Not being ready for closure: Some expressed that while they accepted the rape and they felt physically and cognitively better, at a relationship level they were not at the point of being healed completely. Seven of the nine study participants dealt with and largely overcame most of their issues on the personal level. At the relationship level, however, they still grappled with the aftermath of the rape. Their determination to regain control over their lives, in spite of the remaining stumbling blocks that hindered their full recovery, was striking and admirable. The goal of regaining control was not met by all the participants; unfortunately, at the end of the six-month study period, two intimate partners were still not accepting the rapes of their partners and had moved back to the crisis phase.

Expressing their need for professional support: The intimate partners all experienced their participation in this study in a positive manner, for they had, at least, an opportunity to talk to someone about their feelings. They believed their participation assisted them to reach a point of realization that the rape of their partners was a reality in their lives, one with which they had to contend. All participants wished the medical staff at the rape centers and the police could have involved them when their partners were being assisted after the rape. They would have appreciated information about how to deal with their own feelings and what they could expect regarding the behaviors of their partners in order to support them. Other researchers have also concluded that if intimate partners are involved with their partners' treatment from the beginning, they would have some knowledge and insight and gain understanding and the ability to cope with the event (Remer and Ferguson 1995). The current state of affairs is exactly the opposite: there is no involvement, no support, and no compassion.

Conclusion

In this study, the conclusion is that the rape of female victims undoubtedly affects their intimate partners, as secondary victims, both physically and mentally. Secondary survivors suffer far-reaching effects at functional and relationship levels. Progress toward recovery is halting and inconsistent, even for this cohort of nine participants who had the unintended therapeutic benefit of interaction with the researcher during in-depth interviews.

At present, access to medical services and programs in South Africa is nonexistent for intimate partners of rape survivors; the focus is solely on the rape victims or survivors. These participants voiced the appeal on behalf of future intimate partners to be included in couples' therapy because both partners face many challenges during their journeys of healing.

This researcher's voyage with these intimate partners who agreed to be recruited for this study would be in vain if a shift in the ethos of mental health nursing and governmental and nongovernmental organizations regarding postrape care does not occur. As long as health care providers continue to turn a blind eye to the needs of intimate partners, intimate partners will continue to suffer in silence as secondary victims of rape who are denied an opportunity to become secondary survivors.

Implications for Practice
The integrated conceptual model derived from this study could assist researchers and teachers in the health sciences to appreciate the meaning of the lived experiences of male partners of female rape victims. One trusts that it will inspire mental health workers and policymakers to reconsider existing rape care protocols to render integrated care for both intimate partners and their female partners.

Recommendations
In South Africa, there are a few structured postrape care facilities such as the Thutuzela Centers, and there are no policies or standard operating procedures to involve intimate partners in any structured manner. The study

recruits were unanimous in their expression that an urgent need exists for interventions to support both partners in their journeys from being victims to being survivors of rape. Although the research was conducted in Cape Town, South Africa, with the aim of influencing postrape care policy locally, it would seem desirable that the findings and recommendations of this study be applied more widely.

10

Which Conflict?
Which Body? Which Nation?

Prostitution, Gender, and Violence in the Colombian Postconflict Context

José Miguel Nieto Olivar and *Carlos Iván Pacheco Sánchez*

THIS CHAPTER ANALYZES THE WAYS IN WHICH WAR AND ITS AFTERMATH CONSTITUTE symbolic-cultural projects that include gender relations and bodily experiences. Arguments presented here accept the principle that the postconflict period[1] can be defined as a pacified embodiment of war relations and its perspectives and that a continuum of violence exists between times of peace and war (MacKinnon 1993; Olujic 1998). We affirm that during the process of such a prolonged and bloody war as occurred in Colombia, nation-building projects, instead of being imagined (Anderson 1983), are strongly and intensively embodied in individual lives. Employing prostitution as our focal point and examining the experiences of a particular woman, whom we call Lady, we will analyze the complex intersections between violence, gender relations, the routine negotiations of pleasure and autonomy, and the limits of "peace" (Tambiah 2004).

Between January 2000 and September 2002, we worked in a development and human rights nongovernmental organization in Magdalena Medio, located in the conflict-ridden center of Colombia. This region, settled around the middle section of the Magdalena River and its valley, comprises 30 counties in four different states. We carried out our three years of research and work in public health, particularly sexual and reproductive health, in several of these counties but focused most intensely on Puerto Berrío in the State of Antioquia. Hence while the majority of this chapter's empirical data and the narrative center on Puerto Berrío, this material is corroborated by evidentiary examples from other counties in the region.

In Puerto Berrío, as well as in other counties, popular perceptions generally associate prostitution with violence, narcotrafficking, and armed conflict, and frequently include a moral-medical discourse that positions prostitution as a stigmatized activity. These associations directly inform the everyday lives of female prostitutes, as well as the political, legal, and social conditions that permeate the practice of prostitution in Colombia.

The "Heart of Colombia"

> *Corazón de mi patria querida*
> *Tierra viva de pastos y sol*
> [*The heart of my beloved homeland*
> *Lively center of grass and sun*]
> —Excerpt of the hymn of Puerto Berrío

Puerto Berrío is located in the State of Antioquia, with the capital city of Medellín, and derives its most salient political and cultural relationships with the 13 other counties of the state. Geographically situated in the Magdalena River valley, Antioquia's economy is based on extensive cattle ranching, formal and informal trade of consumer goods, the circulation of money produced by narcotrafficking activities, and the presence of both military and paramilitary forces. The commercial pace of Puerto Berrío is intense due to its natural resources, particularly petroleum, mines, and coca, and its proximity to land and fluvial transport. A national highway runs through the center of the city, connecting it to Medellín, as well as to the east and northeast of Colombia, and its river port is one of the most important.

Communist guerrilla activity in the Magdalena Medio region has been strong and intense from the early 1960s, and initially began in opposition to political persecution, multinational economic expansion, and in support of reallocating large tracts of land (*latifundio*). The guerrillas' objective was to seize power from the regional and local spheres and appropriate the central source of political power for themselves. Guerrillas from the Fuerzas Armadas Revolucionarias de Colombia (FARC) and Ejercito de Liberación Nacional (ELN) first became a powerful regional force in the 1980s through their initiatives for organization and education of the peasant and urban masses, as well as significant paramilitary activities, including confrontations with the army, raids on police stations and outposts, and kidnappings of civilians (Álvaro Rodriguez 2009; PNUD 2003).

Just as these guerrilla activities began to intensify, Colombia became a major protagonist in global narcotrafficking activities. This was particularly noticeable in Antioquia and the Magdalena Medio, where Pablo Escobar, the Ochoa family, and other powerful drug lords had their entertainment and cocaine-processing farms. This occurred simultaneously with the national government's implementation of "modernization" projects, including highway construction and improvements, agro-business initiatives, natural resource exploration, and the encouragement of foreign investment.

Financed by wealthy industrialists and foreign investors and operated with the silent collusion of the state and the media, the far right-wing paramilitary group known as the Autodefensas Unidas da Colombia (AUC) grew exponentially between 1985 and 2005. One of the geostrategic focuses of this campaign for political and territorial control was the Magdalena Medio region, which experienced particularly harsh forms of intense violence, cruelty, terror, and the reframing of national history that pervaded the rest of Colombia. In these two decades, nearly all of the cities, important sections of highways and rivers, and some rural areas went under paramilitary control. This was facilitated by the silence and, perhaps, the complicity of the national government and its military (Álvaro Rodriguez 2009; Avilés 2006; Cruz 2007; PNUD 2003).

The FARC grew considerably throughout the 1990s, while intensifying its kidnapping practices, its international investments, and its participation in narcotrafficking, turning into a huge and powerful military force reaching, by 2001, close to 18,000 combatants in the whole country.[2] At the same time it adopted a war strategy similar to the paramilitary methods, perpetrating massacres, intensifying kidnappings, and causing large-scale displacements, while its connections to narcotraffickers grew. During this period, the FARC began to consolidate its control, particularly in the southern part of the country.

In 2002 Álvaro Uribe Velez was elected president after receiving the greatest number of votes in the country's history. His central government proposal was called Seguridad Democratica and was, in essence, a promise of increased security for the middle classes, to be achieved through the strengthening of the armed forces and the intensification of the war against the FARC. A great number of people in Colombia associate his name with the inception and expansion of the paramilitary project. Uribe, once president, instigated a process of *desmovilización* (demobilization) for paramilitary groups that chose that course. Only the AUC opted for *desmovilización*, and Uribe intensified the war effort against the "enemies of the nation," as the national government termed the FARC.

Uribe subsequently implemented the Law of Justice and Reparation, which involved the public recognition of crimes and those implicated in them and the payment of indemnity to victims or their families in conjunction with the reduction of sentences (Avilés 2006). During Uribe's two consecutive presidential terms (2002–2010), the numbers of paramilitary-induced massacres, disappearances, kidnappings, and *desplazamientos* (forced relocation) reduced as the intensity of anti-FARC activities increased and paramilitary leaders gradually lost ground in official media coverage.

The paramilitary war strategy currently in place throughout the country has one of its geostrategic axes in Antioquia.[3] Information available through the media throughout 2007 indicated that the paramilitary was supposedly *desmovilizado* (demobilized), yet in Puerto Berrío there are over 3,000 national troops, an unknown number of active paramilitary, *desmovilizados,* and their followers. The physical and symbolic presence of paramilitaries remains a central element in the city's political and commercial life, as well as for many other cities in the country. Puerto Berrío residents generally agree that the two most popular 2007 mayoral candidates received financial backing from two powerful regional paramilitary leaders, Ernesto Báez, a *desmovilizado,* and Commander Julián Bolívar (El Señor), who was then serving a prison sentence.

The elected mayoral candidate spent part of election day in Puerto Berrío riding around on a motorcycle with Chayanne, a young local paramilitary chief who was murdered soon after the elections. Chayanne attended his last years of primary school in the same school as Lady, one of our principal points of contact throughout our research. Several years before, one of Lady's acquaintances told us that residents of the El Oasis neighborhood witnessed Chayanne engage in the gang rape and torture of a 17-year-old girl from the neighborhood. Chayanne and his fellow perpetrators threw her body, like the bodies of other young women, into a body of water. This violent act, residents explained, occurred *por odiosa* (out of contempt) due to the girl's persistent refusal of the boys' sexual overtures.

Lady's Story

In 2002 Lady was a 16-year-old girl in her last year of high school in Puerto Berrío and had just given birth to little Jeronimo. According to Lady, the child's father was Sergeant Tangarife, a 30-year-old police officer who was married to another woman and refused to acknowledge paternity. Lady, her parents' eldest daughter, lived with her impoverished family in a small house made of wood, tin, and plastic in the highest portion of the El Oasis neighborhood. Lady decided to postpone her last year of high school after Jeronimo was born in order to work to support him. Lady's mother, Marta, occasionally worked cleaning houses; her brothers had left home and rarely provided financial support, and her elderly father was no longer able to work. The family survived with what Marta earned, and Lady found money one way or another to pay for parties, clothes, alcohol, and street snacks. Jeronimo grew malnourished.

One night in 2004 one of the authors received a call from Marta, who told me that Lady had disappeared three days prior while walking with several friends.[4] The next day, Marta called one of the authors again, explaining that Lady was working as a prostitute, which she had done before. Although she was still missing, Marta now knew Lady's working name and that she had accepted a job offer to work in a county two hours away. Yet repeated calls to Lady's mobile phone went unanswered and no one knew anything about her true whereabouts. The mother did not wish to file a report with the police regarding Lady's disappearance.

A few days later, Lady finally called to tell her mother that she was back in Puerto Berrío. Lady confirmed that she had gone to work as a prostitute, and that it had not really been her first time, as she had previously bartered companionship and sex for money and other material goods without necessarily conceptualizing it as prostitution. She described going to work in the other county where she, along with other girls, accepted a proposal from local paramilitaries that consisted of a weekend trip to have sex with soldiers in exchange for a total of 1 million pesos (US$500).[5] They accepted, but once there the situation proved to be much more difficult than she or the others had anticipated due to the large number of men with whom she had to engage in sex and the prohibition to leave before the end of the weekend. Yet this paled in comparison to what ensued when Lady was forced to witness the torture and murder of a colleague, which she graphically recounted:

> We were gathered in a circle, all of us. Then the commander came, said a few words and called that girl, the one I knew from before. It was like a trial. The girl had AIDS and the commander caught wind of it. . . . We could not have AIDS, so that we wouldn't infect them. . . . That's what the commander said, that she was deceiving them, that she had infected soldiers from another county. In front of us she was tortured and killed . . . they hit her, burned her hands and then shot her.

On the night of the murder, a paramilitary acquaintance helped Lady escape to Puerto Berrío. Upon her return, Lady continued to exchange sex for money, although no one in her family or circle of friends said anything explicitly about her behavior. Then one night in 2005 she called me, crying inconsolably and saying that she wanted to stop doing "this." It took me some time to comprehend, without any sort of prejudice, that "this" was different from prostitution itself. She explained:

> I simply cannot get work here. No one wants a fat, ugly, and poor woman such as me, especially now that the work is in the hands of the *desmovilizados*. . . . I can't simply walk away. . . . I have a house, my little sisters don't work, my brothers left [one of them was a paramilitary]. . . . I can't leave my mother with nothing to eat, and if I drop this, certainly it'll be my sister who'll start hooking. Everyday some neighborhood men offer her five hundred pesos [US$0.25] for a blowjob.

Lady had learned that, as the Spanish anthropologist Dolores Juliano (2006) notes, prostitution is the best way for many poor women to negotiate their life circumstances. Prostitution is one of the limited means by which such women can acquire income as well as symbolic achievements such as recognition in the market of desire, education, and working connections. However, prostitution is not extracultural and involves significant stigma. Lady told me that she was abusing alcohol and *soplando perica* (snorting cocaine), as demanded by clients who were *traquetos* (drug traffickers) or *paracos* (paramilitaries). Hence, the "this" that Lady so desperately wanted to escape was not prostitution in itself, but rather her limited set of choices made amid the landscape of Puerto Berrío's modernity, of its promises and betrayals. Lady found herself caught between the promises of democracy, legality, and human rights made by state and nongovernmental organizations, and the practical operations of land-based power, work capacity, automatic happiness, order, and obedience offered by the paramilitaries and narcotraffickers.

In the end, the "this" prompting Lady's desire to escape was the reality of her own life situation as a poor woman looking for money in a context dominated by violent masculinity. Soon after, Lady left with Jeronimo, her parents, and one of her brothers to a small town that bordered Venezuela. The authors never saw her again, but they hear that she is doing better.

War and Violence in Sexualities and Gender Relations

There is an extensive international literature that addresses gender relations, sexuality, and war from a variety of theoretical, methodological, and empirical perspectives (Cahn 2004; MacKinnon 1993; Segal 2008). The consensus in a great deal of this literature seems to hold that rape, mutilation, and kidnappings remain central strategies of war, in which women experience victimization far more than men. Over the course of the past decade, a growing number of feminist and human rights organizations have aimed to render conflict-related violence against women in Colombia visible as a "strategy of war" (Corporación Humanas 2009; Milillo 2006; Mujer y conflicto armado 2002).

Sexual violence in the context of armed conflict remains underreported due to the victims' feelings of shame, their fears of retaliation, and the negligence or complicity of civil servants. In an attempt to address this, the Colombian Constitutional Court has published Edict 092 of 2008 for the "Protection of the fundamental rights of women who were victims of forced displacement (*desplazamiento*) due to armed conflict." The Constitutional Court noted that, "the motivating factor of this decision is the disproportionate impact, in quantitative and qualitative terms, of internal armed conflict and forced migration on Colombian women" (Constitutional Court 2008).

The Constitutional Court (2008) recognizes:

(A) acts of sexual violence perpetrated as a component of violent operations of greater breadth—such as massacres, conquests, looting and destruction of cities, committed against women of all ages in the affected area, by members of armed groups operating outside the scope of the law;

(B) deliberate acts of sexual violence perpetrated not in the context of wider violent actions, but individually and in a premeditated fashion by members of all armed groups that take part in the conflict, which can be translated as part of (i) war strategies meant to generate fear amongst the population, (ii) retaliation against real or alleged supporters of the enemy faction through acts of violence on women or their families or communities, (iii) retaliation against women accused of supporting or informing any of the other groups that have been faced in the past, (iv) the process of obtainment of information through kidnapping and sexual enslavement of the victims, or . . . (vii) of simple ferocity;

(C) sexual violence against women accused of having family or emotional ties (real or alleged) to a member or collaborator of an active armed group, either legal or illegal, as a mean to intimidate the communities or retaliate against them;

(D) The sexual violence against women of all ages, recruited by illegal armed groups, which include in a frequent and systematic fashion: (i) rape, (ii) forced reproductive planning, (iii) sexual enslavement and exploitation, (iv) forced prostitution, (v) sexual abuse, (vi) sexual enslavement by chiefs and commanders, (vii) forced pregnancy, (viii) forced abortion and (ix) contamination with a sexually transmitted disease;

(E) the submission of women of all ages to rape, sexual abuses and harassments, individual or collective, by members of armed groups who operate in the region with the purpose of obtaining their own sexual pleasure;

(F) acts of sexual violence against civilian women that through their public or private behavior have breached social codes of conduct enforced by illegal armed groups in broad extensions of national territory;

(G) acts of sexual violence against women who are members of community, social or political organizations, or who act as leaders or promoters of human rights causes, or against women who compose their families, as a form of retaliation, repression and silencing of their activities by the armed parties;

(H) cases of forced prostitution and sexual slavery of civilian women, perpetrated by members of illegal armed groups; or

(I) threats to commit the aforementioned acts, or similar atrocities.

The Constitutional Court of Colombia highlights the lack of reported and sufficiently systematized data as well as the lack of major studies on violence against women, as opposed to the abundance of speeches, events, and informal reports. From the aforementioned it can be inferred that sexual and gender violence constitutes a weapon of war employed in the Colombian context, where it is executed in various ways and for different purposes. Yet such sexual and gender violence is clearly not a strategy by itself, although it resembles more a weapon whose regular use suggests a strategic component. This leads us to the question of how such violence is strategically employed in the context of the Colombian armed conflict.

Lady's story is not unique to or exclusive of Puerto Berrío, as such narratives can all too frequently be heard in regions under either guerrilla or paramilitary control. We witnessed, for instance, the murder of a girl by her jealous boyfriend, a young local paramilitary who killed her in the central square of the county of San Pablo, in the Magdalena Medio area. He ran her over with his motorcycle and trampled her repeatedly. Shortly thereafter, in the paramilitary-controlled county of La Gloria, several women were burned with acid and later murdered for allegedly engaging in prostitution. On one afternoon we became aware of the violent persecution faced by homosexuals in Barrancabermeja when a boy was picked up by local paramilitaries, had his hair shaved off, was stripped of his clothes, and adorned with a sign that stated his homosexuality in order to publicly humiliate him.

In 2004 the health secretariat of the State of Meta, in the southeast of Colombia, became aware of dozens of men and women who had had their lives threatened by the FARC for being carriers of the HIV virus (Ballvé 2008). According to health workers from various counties of Colombia, paramilitaries and guerrilla fighters demand information regarding HIV-positive individuals from hospitals, labs, and health organizations (Pacheco 2009). Paramilitary troops make a significant effort to quickly identify HIV-positive individuals, which they envision as a component of constructing a "clean" and organized society. Everything that paramilitary troops deem morally negative is persecuted and either controlled or eliminated, including (but certainly not limited to) the consumption and commercialization of drugs, prostitution, homosexuality, thefts, rapes, littering, and the homeless population.

Our data indicate that in several regions the armed groups violently control local sexual economies. On August 5, 2007, the widely read newspaper *El Tiempo* featured a piece denouncing paramilitaries who detained over 80 female sex workers in a *cocalera* (coca growing) region in the south of the country (Lozano, 2007). Vladi, a *desmovilizado* driver for the paramilitaries in Puerto Berrío, explained this process to me, noting:

> We would take 15 to 20 women from Medellín, from here and other counties . . . always the hottest women. . . . And they had to attend to the demands of the troops, for four or five million pesos each [US$2,000–2,500] that the commander paid after the job was done. Sometimes there were between 100 and 200 men. None of those women were obligated, forced, none of them. . . . We asked intermediaries to arrange a number of women and they gathered in a particular date and time and we took them to the farm. This happened here, at El Señor's farm [referring to Commander Julián Bolívar]. They made a lot of money, imagine, "El Señor" paid in cash, one bill on top of the other, and told us to take them home. But that's the thing, isn't it? They had to behave, do their job, not to steal, not to disobey, or any other sort of crap.

Roberto, a local civilian driver, is involved with a local escort business. He received calls from the *caponera* (recruiter) or from one of the *senōres* requesting that he transport a girl from a house to another location. Roberto has never witnessed forced recruitment into prostitution and said that "the girls were making close to two or three million pesos a night [US$1,000–3,000], depending on the party, her body, these kind of things . . . but, of course, they had to satisfy all the wishes of the *senōres*." Vladi, the *desmovilizado* driver, affirms that he has never heard of forced recruitment or the involuntary detention of women under El Señor's orders; however, he did witness or hear reports of murders of female prostitutes who disrespected some commander, infected a soldier with HIV, or stole.

The Colombian conflict has now raged for over 50 years and has changed forms many times, presented itself differently in different regions, and remains very complex in terms of the actors involved. The connection with narcotrafficking is evident, as well as with a vast network of public and private organizations and institutions, which in different ways make themselves participants of the war. The constitution of the FARC as the "enemy of the country," as the country's main problem, justifies not only paramilitary actions but also a number of pro-paramilitary media strategies. One of the most consolidated versions of the war in the media and some public sectors of recent years is, in short, that (a) the war exists because the FARC exists, and (b) that the main drive of the war is the enormous economic profits of narcotrafficking.

However, as we can see, part of the success of the various agents involved in Colombia's bitter conflict lies not only in controlling territory, making more money, and imposing a mayor, but also in insisting, through the media, state numbers, and everyday lives of the population, that their presence brings peace, health, order, and discipline: "modernity" and "development." Moreover, to think of a financial motivation as a final end and to think of the financial as an autonomous field implies a lack of acknowledgment of all that is cultural, symbolic, and political in the field of finances and economics (Sahlins 2003). And if such a perspective is relatively obvious in subjects inscribed in institutional politics, it is not always the case in aspects of the order of everyday life, subjective or corporal, such as gender or sexuality (Das 2007; Rubin 1999; Strathern 1990).

Final Considerations

Lady's powerful story is especially interesting for a number of reasons. On the one hand, it cautions us against equating prostitution with violence or trafficking, and on the other hand, it gives us a concrete experience of a young woman in the context of paramilitary control. Prostitution is always a critical topic when one works in contexts of intense war or poverty, as it is all too easy to lose the specificities and differences of what we see against the anguishing backdrop of violence. It has already been said that the "this" from which Lady wanted to escape was not the exchange, more or less explicit, of sex for money and other commodities. For her, as for many other Colombian women protagonists in this line of work, "this" means the experience of sexual exchange in a context of extreme violence and poverty, and under certain gender policies practically undisputed in debates on democracy, the end of the war, and the country's development (Olivar 2008, 2010).[6]

War, sexuality, and gender relations are permanently in question in the context of Colombia's conflict. For this reason, there is a particular value in symbolic analysis that opens interpretative possibilities through a broader perspective. Through the use of sex as a weapon for war, one creates in bodies and imaginations of the population, differently for men and women, a violent nature of sexuality, a natural violence of relations. Sex, and with it eroticism, pleasure, find their possibilities restricted by a painful experience, and soon the bodies learn fear, displeasure, and disgust.

Hence this way of waging war transforms itself into a powerful, albeit silent, gender pedagogy that lays its greatest emphasis in sexual violence practices through a biopolitics of gender presented as an engine for war and a politico-economic discourse. As described throughout this chapter, discourses that normalize the disciplining of women and an erotica of violence in men are very frequent among the events of a war. This results in a particular construction of naturalized feminine performance that exists in conjunction with the moral norms shared by the general population (*decentes*). Yet this construction carries an even greater strength because it is less visible (Bourdieu 2004), just as it eternalizes and intensifies the absolute asymmetry of certain masculinities on the axis of gender relations. It also supports the normalization of sex as violent and for moral reason as a state prerogative. The limit of violent relations makes the body of a girl, such as Lady, a body easily violated or despised, and allows society—sometimes with pain, sometimes with pleasure—to denigrate prostitutes as symbols of moral degradation.

According to Veena Das (2007), following Wittgenstein, in her study on forms of violence in India, one could imagine that the Colombian war institutes a routine of violence of a vertical order that, by turning into a routine during decades and by penetrating the sphere of intimacy, ends up acquiring an ordinary tone. In other words, in the ordinary of a long war the limits and statutes of life are permanently at stake, because violence that constantly redefines what deserves or not to be treated as human is constant and usual. Consequently, the verticality of war is transferred to the plane of daily relations, and the distinction between times of war and times of peace (Olujic 1998) is easily diluted.

Such is the meaning of biopolitics (Foucault 2008). Such stabilization of the conflict, which in the case of Puerto Berrío it is understood, in

Roberto the local civilian driver's interpretation, as "a peace granted by the *señores*," is subordinate to the acceptance and promotion, through all possible ways, of the *habitus* (Bourdieu 2004) of the group that, through fire and blood, conquered the right to grant. Hence, if to the "modern West" sexual pleasure, affective diversity, and relative gender equity are important aspects for development and justice, in the Colombian war, in its entirety of action (military, political, and through the media), it seems diametrically opposed to these principles.

Bodies in conflict zones stand to lose not only a sense of belonging to a certain territory or group, but also any principle of pleasure, thrust, and autonomy, as they distance themselves radically, in bodily experience, from projects of ordinary solidarities, liberal modernity, and democracy. Investment in the war is big because in the war there exists, as Foucault and Das remind us, the possibility of building upon the bodies of citizens the body of the nation itself, the fundamental limit between what is and is not particularly human, the conditions and limits of the social, sexual, and gender hierarchies.

Notes

1. The postconflict period in Colombia commenced with Law 975 (known as the Justice and Peace Law), which was promulgated by the Álvaro Uribe Velez administration with the intent of giving legal consideration to the *desmovilización* of the paramilitary groups united under the term Autodefensas Unidas de Colombia. Despite the official end of the conflict, these paramilitary groups have been reforming and resurfacing and were named officially and in the media as Emerging Criminal Bands (BACRIM).

2. Valencia (2008) argues that this number was reduced to 11,000 by 2008.

3. It bears mentioning that in 1983 the army headquarters of Decimocuarta Brigada was relocated to Puerto Berrío, a subregion home to major narcotrafficking operations as well as cattle and entertainment farms (El Suan, La Piscina, La Granja, La Guacharaca) belonging to paramilitary leaders and narcotraffickers such as Commander Julián Bolivar.

4. In the context of armed conflict, especially in territories controlled by paramilitary groups, disappearance works as a tool of war, of control, and of fear. Just as in the experience of repressive dictatorships, the threat of being made "to disappear" remains a constant specter.

5. To put this amount into perspective, the monthly minimum wage in Colombia at the time was approximately US$200, and a housekeeper's daily earnings around US$10 per day. A bag of milk in Puerto Berrío cost about US$0.75 and

fashionable jeans, for a woman, ranged between US$50 and US$100. In Colombia, in general terms, the moment of sexual intercourse in sex work is called *rato,* which could be translated as "a time." A *rato,* in the Zone of Tolerance of Puerto Berrío, was worth US$5–10 and in a good weekend a woman made, on average, 10–15 *ratos.* An *amanecida* (an all-nighter) could run US$25–50. A young woman of high "body capital" for local patterns, well connected to hotels and agents, could charge US$100–150 for a *rato* or an *amanecida.*

6. It is for this reason, albeit in a different cultural context, that Tambiah (2004) argues that the political and moral framework of human rights is unprepared to deal with the violence of sexuality in everyday life, let alone in militarized zones.

References

Abu-Lughod, Lila. 2002. Do Muslim women really need saving? Anthropological reflections on cultural relativism and its Others. *American Anthropologist* 104, no. 3:783–90.

Afghanistan, Government of. 1962. *Constitution of Afghanistan.* Kabul: Government of Afghanistan.

Agamben, Giorgio. 1998. *Homo sacer: Sovereign power and bare life.* Trans. Daniel Heller-Roazen. Stanford, CA: Stanford University Press.

Ahmed, Leila. 1992. *Women and gender in Islam.* New Haven, CT: Yale University Press.

Akbar, Ahmed S. 1980. *Pukhtun economy and society.* London: Routledge & Kegan Paul.

Álvaro Rodriguez, Miriam. 2009. De las armas a la desmovilización: el poder paramilitar en Colombia. *Revista Internacional de Sociología* (RIS) 67, no. 52:59–82.

Amnesty International. 1998. Children in South Asia: Securing their rights. Available online at: www.amnesty.org/en/library/asset/ASA04/001/1998/en/d7972c50-e827-11dd-9deb-2b812946e43c/asa040011998fr.pdf (accessed October 12, 2011).

———. 2005. Stop violence against women: How to use international criminal law to campaign for gender-sensitive law reform. Document index: IOR 40/007/2005, May 12. Available online at: www.amnesty.org/en/library/asset/IOR40/007/2005/en/4818edd8-d50c-11dd-8a23-d58a49c0d652/ior400072005en.html (accessed August 30, 2011).

———. 2009. Annual report for Liberia. Available online at: www.amnestyusa.org/annualreport.php?id=ar&yr=2009&c=LBR (accessed June 15, 2011).

Anderson, Benedict. 1983. *Imagined communities: Reflections on the origin and spread of nationalism.* London: Verso.

Arendt, Hannah. 1970. *On violence.* New York: Houghton Mifflin Harcourt.

Artz, Lilian, and Dee Smythe. 2007. The levels of rape and other forms of sexual assault. *South African Crime Quarterly* 22:13–22.

Askin, Kelly. 1999. Sexual violence in decisions and indictments of the Yugoslav and Rwandan tribunals: Current status. *American Journal of International Law* 93:97–123.

———. 2003. Prosecuting wartime rape and other gender-related crimes under international law: Extraordinary advances, enduring obstacles. *Berkeley Journal of International Law* 21:288–349.

Astbury, Jill. 2006. Services for victim/survivors of sexual assault. Identifying needs, interventions and provision of services in Australia. *Australian Centre for the Study of Sexual Assault.* Available online at: http://aifs.gov.au/acssa/pubs/issue/i6.html (accessed July 18, 2008).

Avery, Lisa. 2005. The women and children in conflict protection act: An urgent call for leadership and prevention of intentional victimization of women and children in war. *Loyola Law Review* 51, no. 1:103–38.

Avilés, William. 2006. Paramilitarism and Colombia's low-intensity democracy. *Journal of Latin American Studies* 38:379–408.

Bahgam, S., and W. Mukhatari. 2004. *Study on child marriage in Afghanistan.* Kabul: Medica Mondiale. Available online at: www.medicamondiale.org/file admin/content/07_Infothek/Afghanistan/Afghanistan_Child_marriage_medica_mondiale_study_2004_e.pdf (accessed October 12, 2011).

Ballvé, Teo. 2008. Colombia: AIDS in the time of war. North American Conference on the Americas (NACLA). *Report on the Americas* 41, no. 4:30–34.

Bard, Morton, and Dawn Sangrey. 1979. *The crime victim's book.* New York: Citadel Press.

Barnes, Karen, Peter Albrecht, and Maria Olson. 2007. Addressing gender-based violence in Sierra Leone: Mapping challenges, responses and future entry points. International Alert. Available online at: www.peacewomen.org/assets/file/Resources/NGO/vaw_addressinggender-basedviolenceinsierraleone_2007.pdf (accessed September 1, 2011).

Barnett, Michael. 2002. *Eyewitness to a genocide: The United Nations and Rwanda.* Ithaca, NY: Cornell University Press.

Barry, Michael. 1984. *Le Royaume de l'insolence.* Paris: Flammarion.

Barth, Fredrik. 1981. *Features of person and society in Swat: Collected essays on Pathans.* London: Routledge & Kegan Paul.

Bastick, Megan, Karin Grimm, and Rahel Kunz. 2007. *Sexual violence and armed conflict: Global overview and implications for the security sector.* Geneva: Geneva Center for the Democratic Control of Armed Forces.

BBC News. 2008. Top Afghan policewoman shot dead 28/9/2008 Lt. Col. Malalai Kakar (1967–2008). Available online at: http://news.bbc.co.uk/2/hi/7640263.stm (accessed October 12, 2011).

Bélair, Karine. 2006. Unearthing the customary law foundations of "forced mar-
    riages" during Sierra Leone's civil war: The possible impact of international
    criminal law on customary marriage and women's rights in post-conflict Sierra
    Leone. *Columbia Journal of Gender and Law* 15, no. 3:551–607.
Bledsoe, Caroline.1980. *Women and marriage in Kpelle society.* Stanford, CA: Stan-
    ford University Press.
Bolongaita, Emil. 2005. Controlling corruption in post-conflict countries. *Kroc
    Institute Occasional Paper* 26, no. 2:1–18.
Bourdieu, Pierre. 1979. *La distinction, critique sociale du jugement.* Paris: Editions
    de Minuit.
———. 2004. *Outline of a theory of practice.* Cambridge: Cambridge University
    Press.
Bourne, Randolph. 1916. Trans-National America. *Atlantic Monthly* 118:86–97.
Brownmiller, Susan. 1975. *Against our will: Men, women, and rape.* New York:
    Simon and Schuster.
Bumiller, Kristin. 2008. *In an abusive state: How neoliberalism appropriated the fem-
    inist movement against sexual violence.* Durham, NC: Duke University Press.
Cahn, Naomi. 2004. Beyond retribution and impunity: Responding to war crimes
    of sexual violence. George Washington University Law School Public Law Re-
    search Paper No. 104.
Cammaert, Major-General Patrick (June 19, 2008). Address made at the 5916th
    meeting of the United Nations Security Council regarding Resolution 1820
    on Women and Peace and Security, New York. Available online at: www
    .securitycouncilreport.org/atf/cf/%7B65BFCF9B-6D27-4E9C-8CD3-
    CF6E4FF96FF9%7D/WPS%20SPV5916.pdf (accessed March 7, 2012).
Carll, Elizabeth K. 2007. *Trauma psychology: Issues in violence, disaster, health, and
    illness,* Vol. 1. London: Westport, CT: Praeger.
CIA World Factbook. 2011. *Afghanistan.* Available online at: https://www.cia
    .gov/library/publications/the-world-factbook/geos/af.html (accessed March
    7, 2012).
Charlesworth, Hilary. 2002. International law: A discipline of crisis. *Modern Law
    Review* 65, no. 3:377–92.
Charlesworth, Hilary, and Christine Chinkin. 2000. *The boundaries of interna-
    tional law: A feminist analysis.* Manchester, U.K.: Manchester University Press.
Charlesworth, Hilary, Christine Chinkin, and Shelley Wright. 1991. Feminist ap-
    proaches to international law. *American Journal of International Law* 85:613–45.
Chikwanha, Annie. 2008. The criminal justice system in Sierra Leone. Issue pa-
    per. Human Security Gateway. Available online at: www.humansecuritygate
    way.com/documents/AHSI_SierraLeone_CriminalJusticeReview.pdf (accessed
    June 15, 2011).
Clifford, Cassandra. 2008. *Rape as a weapon of war.* Available online at: http://
    ts-si.org/files/BMJCliffordPaper.pdf (accessed January 25, 2012).
Cockburn, Cynthia. 2007. *From where we stand: War, women's activism and feminist
    analysis.* London: Zed Books.

Cohen, Miriam. 2009. Victims' participation rights within the International Criminal Court: An overview. *Denver Journal of International Law and Policy* 37, no. 3:351–77.

Cohn, Carol. 2008. Mainstreaming gender in UN security policy: A path to political transformation? In *Global governance: Feminist perspectives,* edited by Shirin Rai and Georgina Waylen, 185–206. Basingstoke: Palgrave Macmillan.

Collins, Patricia Hill. 2000. Mammies, matriarchs, and other controlling images. In *Black feminist thought,* 69–96. New York: Routledge.

Comité Internacional de la Cruz Roja (International Committee of the Red Cross). 2009. *Informe Colombia 2009.* Bogotá: CICR.

Constitutional Court of Colombia (multiple years). Available online, in English, at: http://english.corteconstitucional.gov.co/ (accessed February 14, 2012).

Convention Against Torture and Other Cruel, Inhuman or Degrading Treatment or Punishment (CAT). 1984. GA res. 39/46, 1465 UNTS 85.

Convention on the Elimination of All Forms of Discrimination Against Women (CEDAW). 2008. Liberia Country Report. Available online at: http://sim.law. uu.nl/SIM/CaseLaw/uncom.nsf/804bb175b68baaf7c125667foo4cb333/1d2b 974b3bb90850c125763c00425052?OpenDocument (accessed June 1, 2011).

Convention on the Prevention and Punishment of the Crime of Genocide (Genocide Convention). 1948. 78 UNTS 277.

Cooley, John K. 1999. *Unholy wars: Afghanistan, America and international terrorism.* London: Pluto Press.

Coomaraswamy, Radhika. 1994. *Preliminary report submitted by the Special Rapporteur on violence against women, its causes and consequences, in accordance with Commission on Human Rights resolution 1994/45.* UN Document E/CN .4/1995/42, November 22. Available online at: www.unhchr.ch/Huridocda/ Huridoca.nsf/0/75ccfd797b0712d08025670b005c9a7d?Opendocument (accessed August 30, 2011).

Cooper, Belinda. 2009. The limits of international justice. *World Policy Journal* (Fall):91–101.

Corporación Humanas—Centro Regional de Derechos Humanos y Justicia de Género. 2009. *Guía para llevar casos de violencia sexual. Propuestas de argumentación para enjuiciar crímenes de violencia sexual cometidos en el marco del conflicto armado colombiano.* Bogotá: Humanas.

Coulter, Chris. 2005. Female fighters in the Sierra Leone war: Challenging the assumptions? *Feminist Review* 88:54–73.

Coulter, Chris, Marian Persson, and Mats Utas. 2008. *Young female fighters in African Wars: Conflict and its consequences.* Uppsala: Nordic Africa Institute.

Cruz, Edwin. 2007. Los estudios sobre el paramilitarismo en Colombia. *Análisis Político* 60:117–34.

Damgaard, Ciara. 2004. The Special Court for Sierra Leone: Challenging the tradition of impunity for gender-based crimes? *Nordic Journal of International Law* 73:485–503.

Das, Veena. 2007. *Life and words: Violence and the descent into the ordinary.* Berkeley: University of California Press.

Davis, Angela. 2005. *Abolition democracy: Beyond prisons, torture, and empire: Interviews with Angela Y. Davis.* New York: Seven Stories Press.

Davis, Robert C., Brian Taylor, and Steven Bench. 1995. Impact of sexual and nonsexual assault on secondary victims. *Violence and Victims* 10, no. 1:73–84.

Del Ponti, Carla, and Chuck Sudetic. 2009. *Madame prosecutor: Confrontations with humanity's worst criminals and the culture of impunity.* New York: Other Press.

Denoeux, Guilian. 2002. The forgotten swamp: Navigating political Islam. *Middle East Policy* 9, no. 2:56–81.

Dobash, Emerson R., and Russell Dobash. 1979. *Violence against wives: A case against the patriarchy.* New York: Free Press.

Dobbins, James, Seth Jones, Keith Crane, and Beth C. DeGrasse. 2007. *The beginner's guide to nation-building.* Santa Monica: RAND Corporation.

Doezcma, Jo. 2001. Ouch! Western feminists' "wounded attachment" to the "Third World prostitute." *Feminist Review* 67:16–38.

Doherty, Justice Theresa A. 2009. Developments in the prosecution of gender-based crimes: A personal perspective. Colloquium on Sexual Violence as an International Crime. The Grotius Centre, The Hague, Netherlands. June 16–18, 2009.

DuBois, Ellen, Nayereh Tohidi, Maylei Blackwell, V. Spike Peterson, and Leila Rupp. 2005. Transnational feminism: A range of disciplinary perspectives. Los Angeles: UCLA Roundtable, May 18. Available online at: www.international .ucla.edu/news/article.asp?parentid=28482 (accessed February 2, 2008).

Dupree, Louis. 1973. *Afghanistan.* Princeton NJ: Princeton University Press.

Dupree, Nancy Hatch. 1996. Afghan women under the Taliban. In *Fundamentalism reborn? Afghanistan and the Taliban,* edited by William Maley, 145–66. Lahore: Vanguard.

Eaton, Shana. 2004. Sierra Leone: The proving ground for prosecuting rape as a war crime. *Georgetown Journal of International Law* 35, no. 4:873–919.

Eisenstein, Zillah. 2000. Writing bodies on the nation for the globe. In *Women, states and nationalism: At home in the nation?,* edited by Sita Ranchod-Nilsson and Mary-Ann Tétrault, 35–49. London and New York: Routledge.

———. 2007. *Sexual decoys: Gender, race and war in imperial democracy.* Melbourne: Spinifex.

Emm, Deborah, and Patrick C. McKenry. 1988. Coping with victimization: The impact of rape on female survivors, male significant others and parents. *Contemporary Family Therapy* 10, no. 4:272–79.

Engle, Karen. 2005. Feminism and its (dis)contents: Criminalizing wartime rape. *American Journal of International Law* 99:778–816.

Enloe, Cynthia. 2000a. *Maneuvers. The international politics of militarizing women's lives.* Berkeley: University of California Press.

———. 2000b. *Bananas, beaches, and bases: Making feminist sense of international politics.* Berkeley: University of California Press.

————. 2010. *Nimo's war, Emma's war: Making feminist sense of the Iraq war.* Berkeley: University of California Press.

Enloe, Cynthia, and RIS reviewers. 2001. Interview with Professor Cynthia Enloe. *Review of International Studies* 27, no. 4:649–66.

Eriksson Baaz, Maria, and Maria Stern. 2009. Why do soldiers rape? Masculinity, violence, and sexuality in the armed forces in the Congo (DRC). *International Studies Quarterly* 53:495–518.

Ertürk, Yakin. 2008. Statement by UN Special Rapporteur: On violence against women, its causes and consequences. Paper presented at the SIDA Conference on Gender-Based Violence, Hofburg, Vienna, June 8.

Everly, G. S., and J. M. Lating. 1995. *Psychotraumatology: Key papers and core concepts in post-traumatic stress.* New York: Plenum.

Faedi Duramy, Benedetta. 2008. The double weakness of girls: Discrimination and sexual violence in Haiti. *Stanford Journal of International Law* 44, no. 147. Available online at: http://digitalcommons.law.ggu.edu/cgi/viewcontent.cgi?article=1003&context=pubs (accessed January 25, 2012).

Falquet, Jules. 2008. *De gré ou de force. Les femmes dans la mondialisation.* Paris: La Dispute.

Feinman, Ilene Rose. 2000. *Citizenship rites: Feminist soldiers and feminist antimilitarists.* New York: New York University Press.

Figley, Charles R., and Rolf Kleber. 1995. Beyond the victim: Secondary traumatic stress. In *Beyond trauma: Cultural and societal dynamics,* edited by R. Kleber, C. Figley, and B. Gersons, 75–98. New York: Plenum.

Foucault, Michel. 2008. *Em defesa da sociedade.* São Paulo: Martins Fontes.

Frulli, Micaela. 2008. Advancing international criminal law: The Special Court for Sierra Leone recognizes forced marriage as a "new" crime against humanity. *Journal of International Criminal Justice* 6:1033–42.

Frye, Marilyn. 1983. Oppression. In *The politics of reality,* 1–16. Trumansburg, NY: Crossing Press.

————. 1990. The possibility of feminist theory. In *Theoretical perspectives on sexual difference,* edited by Deborah Rhode, 174–83. New Haven, CT: Yale University Press.

Fuller, Graham. 2003. *The future of political Islam.* New York: Palgrave Macmillan.

Fuller, Romi. 2008. Double jeopardy: Being foreign and female increased their vulnerability during xenophobic violence. Available online at: www.pambazuka.org/en/category/comment/48552/print (accessed December 14, 2009).

Gantz, Peter. 2007. The postconflict security gap and the United Nations peace operations system. In *Security, reconstruction and reconciliation: When the wars end,* edited by Muna Ndulo, 247–76. New York: University College of London Press.

Gardam, Judith. 2005. Women and armed conflict: The response of international humanitarian law. In *Listening to the silences: Women and war,* edited by Helen Durham and Tracey Gurd, 109–23. Boston: Martinus Nijhoff.

Gardam, Judith, and Hilary Charlesworth. 2000. Protection of women in armed conflict. *Human Rights Quarterly* 22, no. 1:48–166.

Geneva Centre for the Democratic Control of Armed Forces, International Sector Advisory Team. 2009. MINUSTAH: DDR and police, judicial, and correctional reform in Haiti: Recommendations for change. Available online at: http://issat.dcaf.ch/Home/Community-of-Practice/Resource-Library/Policy-and-Research-Papers/MINUSTAH-DDR-and-Police-Judicial-and-Correctional-Reform-in-Haiti-Recommendations-for-change (accessed March 2, 2012).

Geneva Conventions. 1949. Part III: Status and Treatment of Protected Persons, Article 27. Available online at: www.icrc.org/ihl.nsf/385ec082b509e76c412 56739003e636d/6756482d86146898c125641e004aa3c5 (accessed January 25, 2012).

Geneva Convention (I) for the Amelioration of the Condition of the Wounded and Sick in Armed Forces in the Field, August 12, 1949. Available online at: www.icrc.org/ihl.nsf/INTRO/365?OpenDocument (accessed March 7, 2012).

Geneva Convention (II) for the Amelioration of the Condition of Wounded, Sick and Shipwrecked Members of Armed Forces at Sea, August 12, 1949. Available online at: www.icrc.org/ihl.nsf/INTRO/370?OpenDocument (accessed March 7, 2012).

Geneva Convention (III) Relative to the Treatment of Prisoners of War, August 12, 1949. Available online at: www.icrc.org/ihl.nsf/INTRO/375?OpenDocument (accessed March 7, 2012).

Geneva Convention (IV) Relative to the Protection of Civilian Persons in Time of War, August 12, 1949. Available online at: www.icrc.org/ihl.nsf/INTRO/380 (accessed March 7, 2012).

Geneva Convention, Protocol I additional to the Geneva Conventions. 1977. Available online at: www.icrc.org/ihl.nsf/INTRO/470 (accessed March 7, 2012).

Geneva Convention Protocol II additional to the Geneva Conventions. 1977. Available online at: www.icrc.org/ihl.nsf/INTRO/475?OpenDocument (accessed March 7, 2012).

Geneva Convention (IV) Relative to the Protection of Civilian Persons in Time of War, August 12, 1949. Available online at: www.icrc.org/ihl.nsf/INTRO/380 (accessed March 7, 2012).

German Technical Cooperation/Deutsche Gesellschaft für Technische Zusammenarbeit. 2007. Female genital mutilation in Sierra Leone. Africa Department. Available online at: www.gtz.de/de/dokumente/en-fgm-countries-sierraleone.pdf (accessed September 1, 2011).

Global Rights. 2008. Living with violence: A national report on domestic abuse in Afghanistan. Available online at: www.globalrights.org/site/DocServer/final_DVR_JUNE_16.pdf?docID=9803 (accessed March 2, 2012).

Goldstone, Richard. 2002. Prosecuting rape as a war crime. *Case Western Journal of International Law* 34, no. 3:277–86.

Gottschall, Jonathan. 2004. Explaining wartime rape. *Journal of Sex Research* 41: 129–36.

Greenberg, Marcia E. 2009. A gender assessment for USAID in Liberia. U.S. Agency for International Development. Available online at: www.usaid.gov/ our_work/cross-cutting_programs/wid/pubs/Liberia_Gender_Assessment_ 508.pdf (accessed June 15, 2011).

Grewal, Kiran. 2010. Rape in conflict, rape in peace: Questioning the revolutionary potential of international criminal justice for women's human rights. *Australian Feminist Law Journal* 33:57–80.

Grima, Bénédicte. 1998. *The performance of emotion among Paxtun women.* Karachi: Oxford University Press.

Gruber, Aya. 2009. Rape, feminism, and the war on crime. *Washington Law Review* 84:581–658.

Guarnizo, Luis Eduardo, and Michael Peter Smith. 1998. The locations of transnationalism. In *Transnationalism from below,* edited by Michael Smith and Luis Guarnizo, 3–35. New Brunswick: Transaction.

Haansbaek, Thom. 2006. Male intimate partner to a rape victim: How is he doing? *Journal of Sex Research* 43, no. 1:18–19.

Haiti, Penal Code of. 1835.

Haiti, Republic of. 2011. Republic of Haiti submission to the United Nations Universal Periodic Review: Gender-based violence against Haitian girls and women in internal displacement camps. Twelfth session of the Working Group of the UPR Council. New York: United Nations. Available online at: http://lib.ohchr .org/HRBodies/UPR/Documents/session12/HT/JS2-JointSubmission2-eng .pdf (accessed March 7, 2012).

Halley, Janet. 2008. Rape at Rome: Feminist interventions in the criminalization of sex-related violence in positive international criminal law. *Michigan Journal of International Law* 30, no. 1:1–123.

Handrahan, Lori. 2004. Conflict, gender, ethnicity and post-conflict reconstruction. *Security Dialogue* 35, no. 4:429–45.

Hawthorne, Susan, and Bronwyn Winter, eds. 2002. *September 11, 2001: Feminist perspectives.* Melbourne: Spinifex.

Hélie-Lucas, Marie-Aimée. 1990. Women, nationalism and religion in the Algerian liberation struggle. In *Opening the gates: A century of Arab feminist writing,* edited by Margot Badran and Miriam Cooke, 105–14. London: Virago.

Helms, Elissa. 2003. Women as agents of ethnic reconciliation? Women's NGOs and international intervention in postwar Bosnia-Herzegovina. *Women's Studies International Forum* 26, no. 1:15–33.

Hill, Felicity, Mikele Aboitiz, and Sara Poehlman-Doumbouya. 2003. Nongovernmental organizations' role in the buildup and implementation of Security Council Resolution 1325. *Signs* 28, no. 4:1255–69.

Hogan, Margaret, Kyle Foreman, Mohsen Naghavi, Stephanie Ahn, Mengru Wang, Susanna Makela, Alan Lopez, Rafael Lozano, and Christopher Murray. 2010. Maternal mortality for 181 countries, 1980–2008: A systematic analysis of progress towards Millennium Development Goal 5. *Lancet* 375, no. 9726:1609–23.

Holmstrom, Lynda, and Ann Burgess. 1979. Rape: The husband's and boyfriend's initial reactions. *The Family Coordinator: Jouurnal of Education and Counseling Services* 28, no. 3:321–30.

Human Rights Watch (HRW). 1994. Rape in Haiti: A weapon of terror. July 1. Available online at: www.unhcr.org/refworld/docid/3ae6a7e18.html (accessed September 1, 2011).

———. 2009."We have the promises of the world": Women's rights in Afghanistan. Available online at: www.hrw.org/en/node/86805/section/1 (accessed June 1, 2011).

Huss, Alphonse. 1962. De Quelques problèmes que suscite l'institution et le fonctionnement des juridictions internationales de droit privé. *Netherlands International Law Review* 9, 236–53.

International Criminal Court (ICC). 2000. Elements of Crimes. U.N. Doc. PC-NICC/2000/1/Add.2, note 3. Available online at: www1.umn.edu/humanrts/instree/iccelementsofcrimes.html

———. 2011. The judges. Available online at: www.icc-cpi.int/Menus/ICC/Structure+of+the+Court/Chambers/The+Judges (accessed June 1, 2011).

International Criminal Tribunal for Rwanda (ICTR) Statute. 1994. UN Doc S/RES/955.

International Criminal Tribunal for the Former Yugoslavia (ICTY). 1993. ICTY Statute. UN Doc S/RES/927. Available online at: www1.umn.edu/humanrts/icty/statute.html (accessed March 7, 2012).

———. 2011. Chambers. Available online at: www.icty.org/sections/Aboutthe ICTY/Chambers (accessed June 15, 2011).

Integrated Regional Information Network (IRIN). 2007. Sierra Leone: Women, government launch campaign against sexual violence. IRIN, April 4. Available online at: www.plusnews.org/report.aspx?ReportID=71189 (accessed January 24, 2010).

———. 2009a. Liberia: The new war is rape. IRIN, November 9. Available online at: www.irinnews.org/report.aspx?ReportId=87122 (accessed January 24, 2010).

———. 2009b. Sierra Leone: Sexual violence defies new rape law. IRIN, July 31. Available online at: www.irinnews.org/Report.aspx?ReportId=85511 (accessed January 24, 2010).

———. 2010. Sierra Leone: Impunity in rape cases thrive. IRIN, June 22. Available online at: www.irinnews.org/report.aspx?reportid=89581 (accessed July 18, 2010).

International Rescue Committee. 2009. Level of brutality against women and girls in Congo increasing; UN must do more to protect them. Available online at: www.theirc.org/News/level-brutality-against-women-and-girls-congo-increasing-un-must-do-more-protect-them-irc-press (accessed December 10, 2010).

Inter-Parliamentary Union. Israel: Knesset (Parliament). Available online at: www.ipu.org/parline/reports/2155_E.htm (accessed January 1, 2010).

Iriye, Akira. 2002. *Global community: The role of international organizations in the making of the contemporary world.* Berkeley: University of California Press.

Islamic Republic of Iran. 1979. *Constitution of Iran.* Tehran: Islamic Republic of Iran.

Itano, Nicole. 2007. South Africa begins getting tough on rape. Available online at: www.womensenews.org/article.cfm/dyn/aid/1232 (accessed September 4, 2007).

Jacobson, Celean. 2009. Rape linked to manhood in South Africa. Available online at: http://newsok.com/rape-linked-to-manhood-in-south-africa/article/feed/56238 (accessed January 25, 2012).

Jain, Neha. 2008. Forced marriage as a crime against humanity: Problems of definition and prosecution. *Journal of International Criminal Justice* 6:1013–32.

Janoff-Bulman, Ronnie, and Irene H. Frieze. 1983. A theoretical perspective for understanding reactions to victimization. *Journal of Social Issues* 39, no. 2:1–17.

Janoff-Bulman, Ronnie, and Camille B. Wortman. 1977. Attributions of blame and coping in the real world: Severe accident victims react to their lot. *Journal of Personality and Social Psychology* 35, no. 5:351–63.

Jessup, Philip C. 1956. *Transnational law.* New Haven, CT: Yale University Press.

Jim, Heather S. L., and Paul B. Jacobsen. 2008. Post traumatic stress and post traumatic growth in cancer survivorship: A review. *Cancer Journal* 14, no. 6:414–19.

John-Langba, Johannes. 2008. HIV, sexual violence and exploitation during post-conflict transitions: The case of Sierra Leone. ASCI Research Report no. 19. UNICEF AIDS, Security and Conflict Initiative (ASCI). Available online at: http://asci.researchhub.ssrc.org/working-papers/ASCI%20Research%20Paper%2019-Johannes%20John%20Langba.pdf (accessed June 1, 2011).

Juliano, Dolores. 2006. *Excluidas y marginales.* Madrid: Ediciones Cátedra.

Justesen, Michael, and Dorte Verner. 2007. Factors impacting youth development in Haiti. World Bank Report No.WPS4110, 4.

Kabia, Soccoh. 2010. Follow up to the fourth world conference on women and the twenty-third special session of the General Assembly, titled "Women 2000: Gender equality, development and peace for the twenty-first century." United Nations. 52nd Session of the Commission on the Status of Women.

Kaldor, Mary. 2003. *Global civil society: An answer to war.* Cambridge, U.K.: Polity Press.

———. 2007. *New and old wars: Organized violence in a global era.* Stanford, CA: Stanford University Press.

Kamber, Michael. 2010. The U.N.'s battle against brutality. Available online at: www.nytimes.com/slideshow/2010/10/03/world/africa/Congo-12.html (accessed May 15, 2011).

Kaplan, Caren, and Inderpal Grewal. 1994. Transnational feminist cultural studies: Beyond the Marxism/poststructuralism/feminism Divide. *Positions* 2, no. 2:430–45.

———. 1999. Transnational feminist cultural studies. In *Between woman and nation,* edited by Caren Kaplan, Norma Alarcon, and Minoo Moallem, 348–63. Durham, NC: Duke University Press.

————. 2000. Postcolonial studies and transnational feminist practices. *Jouvert: A Journal of Postcolonial Studies* 5, no. 1. Available online at: http://wsp400 .blogspot.com/2007/10/postcolonial-studies-and-transnational.html (accessed January 25, 2012).

Kapp, Claire. 2008. South Africa failing people displaced by xenophobia riots. *Lancet* 371, no. 9629:1986–87.

Kay Fanm. 2007. Violence envers les femmes et les filles—Bilan de l'année 2006 [Violence against women and girls—Balance of 2006]. February.

Kendall, Sara, and Michelle Staggs. 2005. Silencing sexual violence: Recent developments in the CDF case at the Special Court for Sierra Leone. University of California at Berkeley War Crimes Studies Center. Available online at: www .ocf.berkeley.edu/~changmin/Papers/Silencing_Sexual_Violence.pdf (accessed June 30, 2010).

Keohane, Robert O., and Joseph S. Nye, Jr. 1972. Transnational relations and world politics: An introduction. In *Transnational relations and world politics,* edited by Robert Keohane and Joseph Nye, ix–xxix. Cambridge, MA: Harvard University Press.

Khan, Nighat Said. 2000. The women's movement revisited: Areas of concern for the future. In *Global feminist politics: Identities in a changing world,* edited by Suki Ali, Kelly Coate, and Wangui wa Goro, 5–10. London: Routledge.

Khattak, Saba Gul. 2004. Adversarial discourses, analogous objectives: Afghan women's control. *Cultural Dynamics* 16, nos. 2/3:213–36.

Kieh, George K. 2008. *The first Liberian civil war: The crisis of underdevelopment.* New York: Peter Lang.

Kolbe, Athena, and Royce Hutson. 2006. Human rights abuse and other criminal violations in Port-au-Prince, Haiti: A random survey of households. *Lancet* 368, no. 9538:864–73

Koo, Katrina. 2002. Confronting a disciplinary blindness: Women, war and rape in the international politics of security. *Australian Journal of Political Science* 37:525–36.

Kratochivil, Antonin. 2010. Bakira Hasecic visits a support network in Sarajevo. Available online at: www.independent.co.uk/multimedia/dynamic/00485/ bosnia_Sarajevo_485702s.jpg (accessed June 14, 2011).

Krebs, Ronald. 2006. *Fighting for rights: Military service and the politics of citizenship.* Ithaca, NY, and London: Cornell University Press.

Kumar, Krishna, ed. 2001. *Women and civil war: Impact, organizations, and action.* London: Lynne Rienner.

Laber, Jeri. 1986. Afghanistan's other war. *New York Review of Books,* December 18. Available online at: www.nybooks.com/articles/archives/1986/dec/18/ afghanistans-other-war/ (accessed October 12, 2011).

Liberia Institute of Statistics and Geo-Information Services. 2007. *Core welfare indicators questionnaire in Liberia, 2007.* Monrovia: Liberia Institute of Statistics and Geo-Information Services.

Liberia Institute of Statistics and Geo-Information Services, Ministry of Health and Social Welfare. 2007. *Liberia demographic and health survey.* Monrovia: Liberia Institute of Statistics and Geo-Information Services and Macro International.

Liberia Ministry of Gender and Development. 2009. National gender policy (abridged version). Available online at: www.mogd.gov.lr/mogd/doc/National_ Gender_Policy_FINAL.pdf (accessed June 10, 2011).

Lieven, Anatol, and Maleeha Lodhi. 2011. Bring in the Taliban. *New York Times,* April 22. Available online at: www.nytimes.com/2011/04/23/opinion/23iht-ed lieven23.html (accessed October 12, 2011).

Lozano, Jairo. 2007. El harén que los paras tienen secuestrado en el Putumayo. *El Tiempo,* August 5.

Lugones, Maria. 2007. Heterosexualism and the colonial/modern gender system. *Hypatia* 22, no. 1:186–209.

MacDonald, Alice. 2008. New wars: forgotten warriors: Why have girl fighters been excluded from Western representations of conflict in Sierra Leone? *Africa Development* 33, no. 3:135–45.

MacKinnon, Catherine. 1983. Feminism, Marxism, method and the state: Toward feminist jurisprudence. *Signs: Journal of Women in Culture and Society* 515:635–58.

———. 1993. Crimes of war, crimes of peace. In *On human rights: The Oxford Amnesty lectures,* edited by Stephen Shute and Susan Hurley, 83–109. New York: Basic Books.

———. 1996. From practice to theory, or what is a white woman anyway? In *Radically speaking: Feminism reclaimed,* 45–54. Melbourne: Spinifex.

———. 2002. State of emergency. In *September 11, 2001: Feminist perspectives,* 426–31. Melbourne: Spinifex.

———. 2005. Defining rape internationally: A comment on Akayesu. *Columbia Journal of Transnational Law* 44:940–58.

———. 2006. *Are women human? And other international dialogues.* Cambridge, MA: Harvard University Press.

Magenuka, Nkosazana S. 2006. The personal and embodied experiences of people living with a spinal cord injury in the OR Tambo district municipality in the Eastern Cape. Unpublished thesis, University of South Africa. Available online at: uir.unisa.ac.za/bitstream/handle/10500/2179/thesis.pdf?sequence=1 (accessed January 25, 2012).

Magloire, Daniele. 2002. La violence à l'egard des femmes: Une violation constante des droits de la persone [Violence against women: A constant violation of human rights]. *Chemins Critique* 5, no. 2.

Magwaza, Adelaide S. 1999. Assumptive world of traumatized South African adults. *Journal of Social Psychology* 139, no. 5:622–30.

Malan, Mark. 2008. *Security sector reform in Liberia: Mixed results from humble beginnings.* Carlisle, PA: U.S. Army War College, Strategic Studies Institute.

Mann, Carol. 2005. *Models and realities of Afghan womanhood: A retrospective and prospects.* UNESCO.

————. 2008. A death sentence for women. *The Guardian,* November 7. Available online at: www.guardian.co.uk/commentisfree/2008/nov/07/afghanistan-gender (accessed November 8, 2008).

————. 2009. The law's the problem in Afghanistan. *The Guardian,* December 26. Available online at: www.guardian.co.uk/commentisfree/2009/dec/26/afghanistan-women-customary-law?showallcomments=true#start-of-comments (accessed January 25, 2012).

Marcus, Sharon. 1992. Fighting bodies, fighting words: A theory and politics of rape prevention. In *Feminists theorize the political,* edited by Judith Butler and Joan W. Scott, 385–403. New York and London: Routledge.

Martínez, Aída, and Pablo Rodriguez, eds. 2002. *Placer, dinero y pecado: historia de la prostitución en Colombia.* Bogotá: Aguilar.

Maternowska, M. Catherine. 2006. *Reproducing inequities: Poverty and the politics of population in Haiti.* New Brunswick, NJ: Rutgers University Press.

Mazurana, Dyan, Khristopher Carlson, and Sanam Anderlini. 2004. *From combat to community: Women and girls of Sierra Leone.* Cambridge: Hunt Alternatives Fund.

Mazurana, Dyan, and Susan McKay. 2003. Girls in fighting forces in Northern Uganda, Sierra Leone, and Mozambique: Policy and program recommendations. *Canadian International Development Agency's Child Protection Research Fund.* Available online at: http://unddr.org/docs/Girls_in_Fighting_Forces.pdf (accessed August 30, 2011).

Mazurana, Dyan, Angela Raven-Roberts, and Jane Parpart, eds. 2005. *Gender, conflict and peacekeeping.* Lanham, MD: Rowman & Littlefield.

McKay, Susan. 2004. Reconstructing fragile lives: Girls' social reintegration in northern Uganda and Sierra Leone. *Gender and Development* 12, no. 3:19–30.

McKenry, Patric C., and Sharon J. Price. 2005. *Families and change: Coping with stressful events and transitions.* 2nd ed. Thousand Oaks, CA: Sage.

Meel, Banwari L. 2005. Incidence of HIV infection at the time of incident reporting, in victims of sexual assault, between 2000 and 2004 in Transkei, Eastern Cape, South Africa. *African Health Sciences* 5, no. 3. Available online at: www.pubmedcentral.nih.gov/articlerender.fcgi?artid=1831937 (accessed May 5, 2007).

Meintjes, Sheila, Meredeth Turshen, and Anu Pillay, eds. 2002. *The aftermath: Women and post-conflict transformation.* London: Zed Books.

Merry, Sally Engle. 2006. *Human rights and gender violence: Translating international law into local justice.* Chicago: University of Chicago Press.

Mertus, Julie. 2003. The impact of intervention on local human rights culture: A Kosovo case study. In *Just intervention,* edited by Anthony Lang, 155–73. Washington, DC: Georgetown University Press.

Mezey, Gillian. 1994. Rape in war. *Journal of Forensic Psychiatry* 5, no. 3:583–97.

Milillo, Diana. 2006. Rape as a tactic of war: Social and psychological perspectives. *Journal of Women and Social Work* 21, no. 2:196–205.

Mio, Jeffery S., and John D. Foster. 1991. The effects of rape upon victims and families: Implications for a comprehensive family therapy. *American Journal of Family Therapy* 19, no. 2:147–59.

Moghadam, Valentine M. 2005. *Globalizing women: Transnational feminist networks.* Baltimore: Johns Hopkins University Press.

———, ed. 1994. *Gender and national identity.* London: Zed Books.

Mohanty, Chandra Talpade. 2003. "Under Western Eyes" revisited: Feminist solidarity through anticapitalist struggles. In *Feminism without borders,* edited by Chandra Talpade Mohanty, 221–52. Durham, NC, and London: Duke University Press.

Mookherjee, Nayanika. 2008. Gendered embodiments: Mapping the body-politic of the raped woman and the nation in Bangladesh. *Feminist Review* 88:37–53.

Moore, Brenda L. 1996. From underrepresentation to overrepresentation: African American women. In *It's our military, too!: Women and the U.S. military,* edited by Judith Hicks Stiehm,115–35. Philadelphia, PA: Temple University Press.

Morgan, Robin, ed. 1984. *Sisterhood is global.* New York: Feminist Press at City University of New York.

Morrison, Zoë, Antonia Quadara, and Carol Boyd. 2007. Ripple effects of sexual assault. *Australian Institute of Family Studies,* 7. Available online at: http://aifs .gov.au/acssa/pubs/issue/i7.html (accessed July 18, 2008).

Muddell, Kelli. 2007. Capturing women's experiences of conflict: Transitional justice in Sierra Leone. *Michigan State Journal of International Law* 15, no. 1:85–100.

Mujer y conflicto armado, mesa de trabajo. 2002. *Informe sobre violencia sociopolítica contra mujeres, jóvenes y niñas en Colombia.* Bogotá: Tercer informe.

Naparstek, Belleruth. 2006. *Invisible heroes: Survivors of trauma and how they heal.* Beccles, Suffolk: William Clowes.

Narayan, Uma. 1997. *Dislocating cultures: identities, traditions, and third-world feminism.* New York: Routledge.

Ndulo, Muna, ed. 2007. *Security, reconstruction and reconciliation: When the wars end.* New York: University College of London Press.

Nordic Africa Institute. 2009. *Sexual exploitation and abuse by peacekeeping operations in contemporary Africa: Policy notes.* Uppsala: Nordic Africa Institute.

Nowrojee, Binaifer. 2005. Making the invisible war crime visible: Post-conflict justice for Sierra Leone's rape victims. *Harvard Human Rights Journal* 18:85–105.

Nussbaum, Martha. 2000. *Sex and social justice.* Oxford: Oxford University Press.

Nyers, Peter. 2006. Human hospitality/animal animosity: Canadian responses to refugee crises at the millennium. In *Rethinking refugees: Beyond states of emergency,* 69–95. New York: Routledge.

Nylind, Linda. 2006. Photograph: A rape victim in MSF's Centre Seruka in Bujumbura, Burundi. Available online at: www.msf.org.uk/burundi_handover_ 20090619.news (accessed January 25, 2012).

Olivar, José Miguel. 2008. A angústia dos corpos indóceis: prostituição e conflito armado na Colômbia contemporânea. *Cadernos PAGU* 31:365–97.

————. 2010. Guerras, trânsitos e apropriações: políticas da prostituição de rua a partir das experiências de quatro mulheres militantes em Porto Alegre, Brasil. PhD dissertation on Social Anthropology. Universidade Federal do Rio Grande do Sul. Porto Alegre: PPGAS/UFRGS.

Olujic, Mariab. 1998. Embodiment of terror: Gendered violence in peacetime and wartime in Croatia and Bosnia-Herzegovina. *Medical Anthropology Quarterly* 12, no. 1:31–50.

Omanyondo, Marie-Claire, O. 2005. Sexual gender-based violence and health facility needs assessment (Lofa, Nimba, Grand Gedeh and Grand Bassa Counties) Liberia. World Health Organization. Available online at: www.who.int/hac/crises/lbr/ Liberia_RESULTS_AND_DISCUSSION13.pdf (accessed September 1, 2011).

Oosterveld, Valerie. 2009. The Special Court for Sierra Leone's consideration of gender-based violence: Contributing to transitional justice? *Human Rights Review* 10:73–98.

Organization for Economic Cooperation and Development (OECD). 2010. Fact sheet: Women in Parliament. Available online at: www.oecd.org/dataoecd.org/ data/oecd/45/63/3796630.pdf (accessed January 2, 2010).

Ortega, Mariana. 2006. Being lovingly, knowingly ignorant: White feminism and women of color. *Hypatia* 21, no. 3:56–74.

Orzek, Ann M. 1983. Sexual assault: The female victim, her male partner, and their relationship. *Personnel and Guidance Journal* 62, no. 3:143–46.

Pacheco, Carlos Iván. 2009. War and the right to health in Colombia: A case study of the Department of Nariño. *Social Medicine* 4, no. 3:155–65.

Papanek, Hanna. 1982. Purdah in Pakistan: Seclusion and modern occupations for women. In *Separate worlds: Studies of purdah in South Asia,* edited by Hanna Papanek and Gail Minault, 190–216. Columbus, MO: South Asia Books.

Park, Augustine. 2006. "Other inhumane acts": Forced marriage, girl soldiers and the Special Court for Sierra Leone. *Social and Legal Studies* 15, no. 3:315–37.

Pateman, Carole. 1988. *The sexual contract.* Cambridge, U.K.: Polity Press.

Peace Women. Campaign for Good Governance. 2004. Silent victims, young girls at risk: An evaluation of post-war rape and the response to rape in the provinces of Sierra Leone. Available online at: www.peacewomen.org/ (accessed March 1, 2010).

Peace Women. United Nations Security Council Resolution 1325 on Women, Peace and Security. Available online at: www.peacewomen.org/un/sc/1325.html (accessed January 10, 2010).

Peach, Lucinda Joy. 1996. Gender ideology in the ethics of women in combat. In *It's our military, too!: Women and the U.S. military,* edited by Judith Hicks Stiehm, 156–94. Philadelphia, PA: Temple University Press.

Petersen, Spike, ed. 1992. *Gendered state: Feminist (re)visions of international relations theory.* Boulder: Lynne Rienner.

Peterson, V. Spike, and Laura Parisi. 1998. Are women human? It's not an academic question. In *Human rights fifty years on: A reappraisal,* edited by Tony Evans, 132–60. Manchester, U.K.: Manchester University Press.

Petronilla, Samuriwo. (n.d.). The gender twist: The business of lobola. *Jesuit Communications.* Available online at: www.jescom.co.zw/index.php?option=com_content &task=view&id=76&Itemid=69 (accessed March 7, 2012).

Physicians for Human Rights. 2002. War related sexual violence in Sierra Leone: A population-based assessment. Available online at: http://physiciansfor humanrights.org/library/documents/reports/sexual-violence-sierra-leone.pdf (accessed June 1, 2011).

Piah, Jerolinmick. 2009. *The relevance of gender statistics in policymaking in Liberia.* Global Forum on Gender Statistics, ESA/STAT/AC.168/7. Available online at: http://unstats.un.org/unsd/demographic/meetings/wshops/Ghana_Jan2009/ Doc7.pdf (accessed May 10, 2011).

Porter, Elisabeth. 2007. *Peacebuilding: Women in international perspective.* London: Routledge.

Porter, Patrick. 2009. *Military orientalism: Eastern war through Western eyes.* New York: Columbia University Press.

Power, Samantha. 2002. *A problem from hell: America and the age of genocide.* New York: Basic Books.

Programa de las Naciones Unidas para el Desarrollo (PNUD). 2003. *Informe nacional de desarrollo humano Colombia.* Bogotá: Programa de las Naciones Unidas para el Desarrollo.

Prosecutor v. Akayesu. 1998. Case No. ICTR-96-4-T. Judgment. Sept. 2. Sentencing Decision. Oct. 2. Available online at: www.un.org/ictr/english/judgements/ akayesu.html (accessed March 7, 2012).

Prosecutor v. Kunarac. 2001. Case IT-96-23. Judgment. February 22. Available online at: www.unhcr.org/refworld/docid/3ae6b7560.html (accessed March 7, 2012).

Puri, Jyoti. 2008. Gay sexualities and complicities: Rethinking the global gay. In *Gender and globalization in Asia and the Pacific: Method, practice, theory,* edited by Kathy Ferguson and Monique Mironesco, 59–79. Honolulu: University of Hawaii Press.

Purvis, Andew. 2006. Ten questions for Carla del Ponte. *Time,* August 13. Available online at: www.time.com/time/magazine/article/0,9171,1226057,00.html (accessed January 10, 2011).

Rashid, Ahmed. 2000. *Taliban: Militant Islam, oil, and fundamentalism in Central Asia.* New Haven, CT: Yale University Press.

———. 2008. *Descent into chaos: The United States and the failure of nation building in Pakistan, Afghanistan, and Central Asia.* London: Viking.

Rawlins, Ruth P., Sophronia R. Williams, Cornelia K. Beck. 1993. *Mental health-psychiatric nursing: Holistic life-cycle approach.* 3rd ed. St Louis, MO: Mosby.

Razack, Sherene. 2008. *Casting out: The eviction of Muslims from Western law and politics.* Toronto: University of Toronto Press.

Rehn, Elizabeth, and Ellen Johnson Sirleaf. 2002. *Women, war, peace: The independent experts' assessment on the impact of armed conflict on women and women's role in peace-building.* UN Women: Progress of the World's Women, Vol. 1.

Available online at: www.unifem.org/materials/item_detail.php?ProductID=17 (accessed June 1, 2011).

Remer, Rory. 2001. *Secondary victims of trauma: Secondary survivors.* Available online at: www.uky.edu/~rremer/secondarysur/SOCIASEC.doc (accessed February 12, 2007).

Remer, Rory, and Robert A. Ferguson. 1995. Becoming a secondary survivor of sexual assault. *Journal of Counselling and Development* 73, no. 4:407–13.

Republic of Rwanda Ministry of Gender and Family Promotion. 2004. *Violence against women.* Available online at: www.grandslacs.net/doc/4005.pdf (accessed November 6, 2008).

Revolutionary Association of the Women of Afghanistan (RAWA). Last modified March 7, 2010. Emancipation of Afghan women not attainable as long as the occupation, Taliban and "National Front" criminals are not sacked! Available online at: www.rawa.org/rawa/2010/03/07/emancipation-of-afghan-women-not-attainable-as-long-as-the-occupation-taliban-and-national-front-criminals-are-not-sacked.html (accessed April 1, 2010).

Richie, Beth. 2000. A black feminist reflection on the anti-violence movement. *Signs: Journal of Women in Culture and Society* 25:1133–37.

Rimalt, Noya. 2007. Women in the sphere of masculinity: The double-edged sword of women's integration in the military. *Duke Journal of Gender Law and Policy* 14:1097–110.

Robertson, Mary. 1998. *An overview of rape in South Africa.* Available online at: www.csvr.org.za/wits/articles/artrapem.htm (accessed March 7, 2012).

Rome Statute of the International Criminal Court. 1998. July 17, 2187 U.N.T.S. 3.

Rotberg, Robert. 2004. *When states fail: Causes and consequences.* Princeton, NJ: Princeton University Press.

Rothenberg, Bess. 2003. "We don't have time for social change": Cultural compromise and the battered woman syndrome. *Gender and Society* 17, no. 5:771–87.

Roy, Oliver. 1985. *L'Afghanistan, Islam et modernité politique.* Paris: Seuil.

———. 2002. *L'Islam mondialisé.* Paris: Seuil.

Rubin, Gayle. 1999. Thinking sex: Notes for a radical theory of the politics of sexuality. In *Culture, sexuality, and society: A reader,* edited by Richard Parker and Peter Aggleton, 143–78. New York: Routledge.

Sahlins, Marshal. 2003. *Cultura e razão prática.* Rio de Janeiro: Zahar.

Sasson-Levy, Orna, and Sarit Amram-Katz. 2007. Gender integration in Israeli officer training: Degendering and regendering the military. *Signs: Journal of Women in Culture and Society* 33, no. 1:105–24.

Save the Children. 2011a. *Afghanistan: Children in crisis.* Available online at: www.savethechildren.org/atf/cf/%7B9def2ebe-10ae-432c-9bd0-df91d2eba74a%7D/afghanistan_children.pdf (accessed March 7, 2012).

———. 2011b. *Champions for children: State of the world's mothers.* Westport, CT: Save the Children.

Scharf, Michael P., and Suzanne Mattler. 2005. Forced marriage: Exploring the viability of the Special Court for Sierra Leone's new crime against humanity.

In *African Perspectives on International Criminal Justice,* edited by Evelyn An-
kumah, Edward Kwakwa, and Africa Legal Aid, 77–102. The Hague, Accra,
Pretoria: Africa Legal Aid Special Book Series.

Schmitt, Frederika, and Patricia Yancey Martin. 1999. Unobtrusive mobilization by
an institutionalized rape crisis center: "All we do comes from victims." *Gender
and Society* 13, no. 3:364–84.

Schwartz, S., K. Pratt, L. Fletcher, A. Mander, and J. Penso. 1994. Rape as a weapon
of war in the former Yugoslavia. *Hastings Women's Law Journal* 5:69–88.

Sedler, Florence. 1987. Life transition theory: The resolution of uncertainty. *Nursing and Health* 10, no. 8:437–51.

Segal, Lynne. 2008. Gender, war and militarism: making and questioning the links.
Feminist Review 88:21–35.

Seifert, Ruth. 1994. War and rape: A preliminary analysis. In *Mass rape: The war
against women in Bosnia-Herzegovina,* edited by Alexandra Stiglmayer, 54–72.
Lincoln: University of Nebraska Press.

Sharma, Aradhana, and Akhil Gupta. 1991. *The anthropology of the state: A reader.*
Oxford: Blackwell.

Sierra Leone, Government of. 2009. *Sierra Leone demographic and health survey.*
Calverton, MD and Freetown, Sierra Leone: Statistics Sierra Leone and ICF
Macro. Available online at: www.measuredhs.com/pubs/pdf/FR225/FR225.
pdf (accessed September 1, 2011).

Silverman, Daniel C. 1978. Sharing the crisis of rape: Counseling the mates and
families of victims. *American Journal of Orthopsychiatry* 48, no. 1:166–73.

Skaine, Rosemarie. 1999. *Women at war: Gender issues of Americans in combat.* Jef-
ferson, NC: McFarland.

Smith, Marilyn E. 2005. Female sexual assault: The impact on the male significant
other. *Issues in Mental Health Nursing* 26, no. 2:149–67.

Snyder, C. S., Wesley J. Gabbard, J. Dean May, and Nihada Zulcic. 2006. On the
battleground of women's bodies: Mass rape in Bosnia-Herzegovina. *Affilia:
Journal of Women and Social Work* 21, no. 2:184–95.

SOFA. 2007. Rapport Bilan IV [Report Balance IV]. January.

Soh, Sarah. 2009. *The comfort women: Sexual violence and postcolonial memory in
Korea and Japan.* Chicago: University of Chicago Press.

Spees, Pam. 2003. Women's advocacy in the creation of the International Criminal Court: Changing the landscapes of justice and power. *Signs: A Journal of
Women in Culture and Society* 28, no. 4:1233–54.

Speziale, Helen J., and Dona Rinaldi Carpenter. 2003. *Qualitative research in nursing. Advancing the humanistic imperative.* 3rd ed. Philadelphia: Lippincott Williams & Wilkins.

Spivak, Gayatri Chakravorty. 1988. Can the subaltern speak? In *Marxism and the
interpretation of culture,* edited by Cary Nelson and Lawrence Grossberg, 271–
313. Urbana: University of Illinois Press.

———. 1993. *Outside in the teaching machine.* New York: Routledge.

———. 2004. Righting wrongs. *South Atlantic Quarterly* 103, nos. 2/3:523–81.

Sriram, Chandra L. 2006. Wrong-sizing international justice? The hybrid tribunal in Sierra Leone. *Fordham International Law Journal* 29:472–506.

Staggs Kelsall, Michelle, and Shanee Stepakoff. 2007. "When we wanted to talk about rape": Silencing sexual violence at the Special Court for Sierra Leone. *International Journal of Transitional Justice* 1:355–74.

Statistics Sierra Leone and ICF Macro. 2009. *Sierra Leone demographic and health survey 2008.* Calverton: Statistics Sierra Leone and ICF Macro.

Stiehm, Judith. 1996. *It's our military, too!: Women and the U.S. military.* Philadelphia: Temple University Press.

Stiehm, Judith Hicks. 1982. The protected, the protector, the defender. *Women's Studies Forum* 5, nos. 3/4:367–76.

Strathern, Marilyn. 1990. *The gender of the gift: Problems with women and problems with society in Melanesia.* Berkeley: University of California Press.

Sweetman, Caroline, ed. 2005. *Gender, peacebuilding and reconstruction.* Oxford: Oxfam.

Swiss, Shana, Peggy Jennings, Gladys Aryee, Grace Brown, Ruth Jappah-Samukai, Mary Kamara, Rosana Schaak, and Rojatu Turay-Kanneh. 1998. Violence against women during the Liberian civil conflict. *Journal of the American Medical Association* 279, no. 8:625–29.

Table de Concertation Nationale sur les violences specifiques faites aux femmes et leur prise en charge [Table of National Cooperation on specific forms of violence against women and relevant measures]. 2005. Report of the Commission for the Collection of Data, 8. November.

Tambiah, Yasmin. 2004. Sexuality and women's rights in armed conflict in Sri Lanka. *Reproductive Health Matters* 12, no. 23:78–87.

Teitel, Rudi G. 2000. *Transitional justice.* Oxford: Oxford University Press.

Tomcyzk, Basia, Howard Goldberg, Curtis Blanton, Rose Gakuba, Geetor Saydee, Priya Marwah, and Elisabeth Rowley. 2007. Women's reproductive health in Liberia: The Lofa County reproductive health survey January–February. UN Population Fund.

Tripp, Aili Mari. 2008. Challenges in transnational feminist mobilization. In *Global feminism: Transnational women's activism, organizing, and human rights,* edited by Myra Ferree and Aili Tripp, 296–312. New York: New York University Press.

Tripp, Aili, Isabel Casimiro, Joy Kwesiga, and Alice Mungwa. 2009. *African women's movements: Changing political landscapes.* New York: Cambridge University Press.

Tryggestad, Torunn L. 2009. Trick or treat? The UN and implementation of Security Council Resolution 1325 on Women, Peace and Security. *Global Governance* 15:539–57.

Tyrrell, Ian. 2007. *Transnational nation: United States history in global perspective since 1789.* Basingstoke, U.K.: Palgrave Macmillan.

United Nations. 1948. Convention on the prevention and punishment of the crime of genocide. UN Document A/RES/260 A (III).

———. 1979. Convention on the elimination of all forms of discrimination against women. December 18.

———. 1993. General Assembly resolution adopting the Declaration on the Elimination of Violence Against Women. UN Document A/RES/48/104.

———. 1994. Preliminary report of the Special Rapporteur on violence against women to the Commission on Human Rights. UN Document E/CN.4/1995/42.

———. 1998. Rome Statute of the International Criminal Court. UN Document A/CONF.183/9.

———. 1999. Report of the international criminal tribunal for the prosecution of persons responsible for genocide and other serious violations of international humanitarian law committed in the territory of Rwanda and Rwandan citizens responsible for genocide and other such violations committed in the territory of neighboring states between 1 January and 31 December 1994. UN Document A/54/315 S/1999.

———. 2000. Security Council Resolution 1325. October 31. UN Document S/RES/1325.

———. 2008a. Security Council Resolution 1820. June 19. UN Document S/RES/1820.

———. 2008b. Parliamentary hearings at the United Nations, New York. 20–21 November. Background document: Session II. Available online at: www.ipu.org/splz-e/unga08/s2.pdf (accessed March 7, 2012).

United Nations Assistance Mission in Afghanistan (UNAMA). 2009a. Arbitrary detention in Afghanistan: A call for action, vol. I: Overview and recommendations. Available online at: www.unhrc.org/refworld/docid/49d07f272.html (accessed October 12, 2011).

———. 2009b. Silence is violence. Available online at: http://unama.unmissions.org/Portals/UNAMA/Press%20Releases/VAW%20Rpt%20FINAL%207%2July%2009.pdf (accessed October 12, 2011).

United Nations Children's Fund (UNICEF). 2009. Percentage of women 15–49 who have been cut. Available online at: www.childinfo.org/fgmc_prevalence.php (accessed September 1, 2011).

United Nations Department of Economic and Social Affairs. 2003. *Women, peace and security at a glance.* New York: United Nations Department of Public Information.

United Nations Development Program (UNDP). 2010a. Newsroom: Sierra Leone forum condemns violence against young girls. Available online at: http://content.undp.org/go/newsroom/2010/march/forum-condemns-violence-against-young-girls.en;jsessionid=a36KJ98TQLy9?categoryID=1796994&lang=en (accessed January 25, 2012).

————. 2010b. *Afghanistan.* Available online at: http://hdrstats.undp.org/en/countries/profiles/AFg.html (accessed October 12, 2011).

United Nations Division for the Advancement of Women. Beijing+5 process and beyond. Available online at: www.un.org/womenwatch/daw/followup/beijing+5.htm (accessed January 10, 2010).

United Nations Economic and Social Council. 1998. Contemporary forms of slavery: Systematic rape, sexual slavery and slavery-like practices during armed conflict. Available online at: www.unhchr.ch/Huridocda/HuRidoca.nsf/0/3d25270b5fa3ea998025665f0032f220?opendocument (accessed October 12, 2011).

————. 2000. Report of the Special Rapporteur on violence against women on the mission to Haiti. UN Doc. No. E/CN4./2000/68/Add.3, January 27.

————. United Nations Economic and Social Council. 2001. *Integration of the human rights of women and the gender perspective: Violence against women.* E/CN.4/2002/83/Add.2, February 11. Available online at: www.unhchr.ch/Huridocda/Huridoca.nsf/0/b8dedfadc369a158c1256b81005a84f9/$FILE/G0210732.pdf (accessed February 23, 2012).

United Nations General Assembly. 2006. Children and armed conflict. Report of the Secretary General. UN Doc. No. A/61/529-S/2006/826. October 26.

————. 2007. Implementation of General Assembly Resolution 60/251 of March 2006 entitled "Human rights council. Human Rights Council 4th Session, A/HRC/4/96. Available online at: www.unhcr.org/refworld/pdfid/46231edc2.pdf (accessed September 1, 2011).

United Nations International Research and Training Institute for the Advancement of Women (INSTRAW). 2009. *Women, peace and security in Liberia: Supporting the implementation of Resolution 1325 in Liberia.* A UN-INSTRAW Background Paper. Santa Domingo: Institute for the Advancement of Women.

United Nations Population Division. 2008. *World marriage data.* Available online at: www.un.org/esa/population/publications/WMD2008/Main.html (accessed September 1, 2011).

United Nations Population Fund (UNFPA). 2005. *Gender-based violence in Sierra Leone: A case study.* New York: United Nations Population Fund.

United Nations Secretary-General. 2000. Report of the Secretary-General on the establishment of a Special Court for Sierra Leone. UN Document S/2000/915. October 4. Available online at: http://daccess-ods.un.orgTMP/7263913.7506485.html (accessed March 2, 2012).

————. 2004. *The rule of law and transitional justice in conflict and post-conflict societies: Report of the Secretary-General,* UN Document S/2004/616, 23 August 2004.

United Nations Security Council. 2006. Resolution 1702 of August 15, 2006, S/RES/1702.

————. 2009. Report of the Security Council mission to Haiti. April 3, S/2009/175.

United States Department of State. 2007. Country reports on human rights practices: Rwanda. Available online at: www.state.gov/j/drl/rls/hrrpt/2006/81364.htm (accessed March 7, 2012).

———. 2010a. 2009 Human Rights Report: Liberia. Bureau of Democracy, Human Rights and Labor. Available online at: www.state.gov/j/drl/rls/hrrpt/2009/af/135961.htm (accessed February 23, 2012).

———. 2010b. 2009 Human Rights Report: Sierra Leone. Bureau of Democracy, Human Rights and Labor. Available online at: www.state.gov/g/drl/rls/hrrpt/2009/af/135975.htm (accessed September 1, 2011).

United States General Accounting Office. 1987. Testimony. Combat exclusion laws for women in the military. November 19. Available online at: http://gao.gov/d39t12/134619.pdf (accessed March 23, 2009).

Usdin, Shereen, Nicola Christofides, Lebo Malepe, and Aadielah Maker. 2000. Advocating for implementation of the new Domestic Violence Act in South Africa. *Sexual Health Exchange* 4:10–11.

Valencia, León. 2008. Commentary: FARC fighting two wars. *Reuters,* September 9. Available online at: www.reuters.com/article/idUSDIS95174420080909 (accessed May 14, 2010).

Van den Berg, Dorette, and Ronel Pretorius. 1999. The impact of stranger rape on the significant other. *Acta Criminologica* 13, no. 3:92–104.

Vertovec, Steven. 1999. Conceiving and researching transnationalism. *Ethnic and Racial Studies* 22, no. 2:447–62.

Vogelman, Lloyd. 1990. Violent crime: Rape. Available online at: www.csvr.org.za/wits/papers/paprapel.htm (accessed June 3, 2007).

Wagner, J. 2005. The systematic use of rape as a tool of war in Darfur: A blueprint for international war crimes prosecutions. *Georgetown Journal of International Law* 37:193–243.

Ward, Jeanne, and Mendy Marsh. 2006. Sexual violence against women and girls in war and its aftermath: Realities, responses and required resources. United Nations Population Fund. Available online at: www.unfpa.org/emergencies/symposium06/docs/finalbrusselsbriefingpaper.pdf (accessed March 1, 2012).

Weinstein, Laurie, and Christie White, eds. 1997. *Wives and warriors: Women and the military in the United States and Canada.* New York: Bergin & Garvey.

West, Carolyn. 2002. Battered, black, and blue: An overview of violence in the lives of black women. *Women and Therapy* 25, nos. 3/4:5–27.

Wichterich, Christa. 2000. *The globalized woman: Reports from a future of inequality.* Trans. Patrick Camiller. London: Zed/Melbourne: Spinifex.

Wies, Jennifer. 2006. The changing relationship of women helping women: Patterns and trends in domestic violence advocacy. Dissertation, Department of Anthropology, University of Kentucky.

Winter, Bronwyn. 2002. If women really mattered . . . In *September 11, 2001: Feminist Perspectives,* edited by Susan Hawthorne and Bronwyn Winter, 450–80. Melbourne: Spinifex.

———. 2006. Religion, culture and women's human rights: Some general political and theoretical considerations. *Women's Studies International Forum* 29, no. 4 (Special issue on Islam, gender and human rights in Asia and the Pacific):381–93.

———. 2012. Politicizing the personal: questioning the public/private divide. In *A cultural history of women in the modern age,* edited by Liz Conor, Vol. 6 of "A Cultural History of Women," edited by Linda Kalof. Oxford: Berg.

Women and Children Legal Research Foundation. 2008. Women's access to justice—Problems and challenges. Available online at: www.wclrf.org/English/eng_pages/sitemap.htm (accessed October 12, 2011).

Womenaid International and the Institute for Afghan Studies. 2000. Emergence of Taliban. Available online at: www.womenaid.org/humanrights/shadows/taliban.htm (accessed October 12, 2011).

Wood, S. K. 2004. A woman scorned for the "least condemned" war crime: Precedent and problems with prosecuting rape as a serious war crime in the International Criminal Tribunal for Rwanda. *Columbia Journal of Gender and Law* 13:274–327.

World Bank. 2006. Haiti—Social resilience and state fragility in Haiti, a country social analysis. Report No. 36069-HT, April 27.

World Bank, Republic of Haiti. 2006. Enhanced heavily indebted poor countries initiative. Preliminary document, Report No. 36917, August 15.

World Health Organization (WHO). 2002. *World report on violence and health.* Geneva: WHO. Available online at: www.who.int/violence_injury_prevention/violence/world_report/en/ (accessed January 25, 2012).

World Health Organization, Joint United Nations Program on HIV/AIDS and United Nations International Children's Fund. 2008. *Epidemiological factsheet on HIV and AIDS: Core data on epidemiology and response.* Freetown, Sierra Leone. Available online at: http://apps.who.int/globalatlas/predefinedReports/EFS2008/full/EFS2008_SL.pdf (accessed February 4, 2010).

Yoshida, Takashi. 2009. *The making of the "rape of Nanking": History and memory in Japan, China, and the United States.* Oxford: Oxford University Press.

Young, Iris Marion. 2003. The logic of masculinist protection: Reflections on the current security state. *Signs: Journal of Women in Culture and Society* 29, no. 1:1–27

Yuval-Davis, Nira.1997. *Gender and nation.* London: Sage.

Ziegler, Sara, and Gregory Gunderson. 2005. *Moving beyond G.I. Jane: Women and the U.S. military.* Lanham, MD: University Press of America.

Zuckerman, Elaine, and Marcia Greenberg. 2004. The gender dimensions of post-conflict reconstruction: An analytical framework for policymakers. *Gender and Development* 12, no. 3:70–82.

Contributors

Susan Dewey is an assistant professor at the University of Wyoming. Her research focuses on the intersections between feminized labor, violence against women, and public policy. She is author or lead editor of six books as well as over two dozen articles and book chapters and is currently working with women market traders in Fiji in addition to her research with sex workers, social service providers, and law enforcement officials in the Denver, Colorado, area. Her most recent book, published with the University of California Press, is *Neon Wasteland: On Love, Motherhood, and Sex Work in a Rust Belt Town.*

Benedetta Faedi Duramy is an associate professor of law at Golden Gate University School of Law in San Francisco where she teaches classes in international human rights as well as gender and children's issues in international law. The author of several book chapters and articles, she completed her doctoral program at Stanford Law School where she has been the recipient of numerous awards for her extensive research and scholarship on gender-based violence, with a special focus on Haiti. She formerly was a researcher for the Child Protection Unit of the United Nations Stabilization Mission in Haiti and worked in private practice in London.

Avory Faucette is a queer feminist legal activist, writer, and current director of operations at the National Center for Transgender Equality. Avory focuses on topics in the areas of queer issues, feminism, and international human rights while maintaining blogs at Radically Queer, Girl w/Pen, and

Gender Across Borders. Avory is published in the *Journal of Gender, Race, and Justice* and will be featured in the upcoming anthology, *Queering Sexual Violence*. Avory is particularly interested in intersecting identities and those at the margins of gender and sexuality and holds a law degree from the University of Iowa.

Kiran Grewal is a lecturer in human rights at the University of Sydney, Australia. Her areas of research expertise are sexual violence and the intersections of race, gender, and national identity. Also a qualified lawyer, Kiran has worked as a solicitor in Australia, an assistant legal advisor at the International Secretariat of Amnesty International, and as a trial monitor at the Special Court for Sierra Leone. Her current research is focused on the relationship between international legal interventions in postconflict societies and local women's rights activism in Sierra Leone, Kosovo, and Nepal.

Carol Mann, a social anthropologist and historian, specializes in the study of gender and armed conflict. She is a Paris-based research associate at SOAS (School of Oriental and African Studies, University of London), started the first seminar in France on gender and armed conflict, at the Sorbonne (Paris I), and has taught this in different locations, including Kabul and Kisangani (DRC). She is the author of many articles and book chapters, especially on Afghanistan; and several studies, the latest being *Femmes en guerre 1914–1945* (Pygmalion, Paris) and *Femmes afghanes en guerre* (Le Croquant, Paris), both published 2010. She directs FEMAID and Women in War, both charitable associations registered in France working on gender issues in conflict zones.

Peace A. Medie is a PhD candidate in the graduate school of public and international affairs at the University of Pittsburgh and a dissertation fellow in the African and African Diaspora Studies program at Boston College. Her dissertation, titled "Police Behavior in Post-Conflict States: Explaining Variation in Responses to Domestic Violence, Human Trafficking and Rape," studies the factors that lead police officers in Liberia to forward most cases of some violent crimes against women to court but allow others to be resolved in the private sphere. It probes the roles of international actors and local nongovernmental organizations in policy implementation.

José Miguel Nieto Olivar holds a PhD in social anthropology from the Universidade Federal do Rio Grande do Sul in Porto Alegre, Brazil. He is currently a postdoctoral researcher at the Gender Study Center at Universidad Estadual de Campinas (PAGU/UNICAMP), as well as a researcher at the Society, Health and Culture Research Center (CHSRC) in Colombia.

Carlos Iván Pacheco Sánchez is a medical doctor who specializes in epidemiology. He is also a PhD candidate in sociology and a research associate at the Society, Health and Culture Research Center (CHSRC) in Colombia, and at the COPOLIS interuniversity group in Spain. His research focuses on public health and sociology, with an emphasis on studies of sexuality, gender, sexual and reproductive health, HIV/AIDS, sexual rights, reproductive rights, and gender-based violence.

Laura Sparling is a feminist educator and activist based in Toronto, Canada. She completed a master's degree in international affairs in 2009 and is now working toward a degree in education at the University of Toronto. Much of her academic work has focused on international issues concerning women, including feminist critiques of refugee law, human trafficking policies, and transitional justice processes. She has recently returned to Canada after a year of working in Chiapas, Mexico, where she cooperated with a women's rights organization while also working as a researcher for a University of Minnesota–based research project of local rights-based organizations.

Tonia St. Germain is associate professor and director of gender studies at Eastern Oregon University. She writes and teaches on law and gender, sexual and gender-based violence, and human rights. She holds a law degree from Antioch School of Law and served as public policy director for the New York Coalition Against Sexual Assault. She received research fellowships from Five College Women's Studies Research Center and Legal Studies at University of Massachusetts at Amherst.

Evalina van Wijk is a lecturer in mental health nursing at the Western Cape College of Nursing, Cape Town, South Africa. As a trauma counselor, she works with trauma and rape survivors and their families. Her research focuses on the experiences and needs of male intimate partners of female rape survivors. Currently she is involved with violence prevention programs for mothers and children age 6 to 14 years and started a support group for female rape victims and their male intimate partners in Cape Town. The aim is to start more support groups in other areas in the Western Cape for rape survivors and their intimate partners—of any gender. These will be run by other voluntary counselors she has trained.

Bronwyn Winter works in the Department of French Studies at the University of Sydney, where her teaching ranges from postcolonial studies to European and French intellectual, political, and social history, from international and global studies to comparative literature. She is contributing coeditor of *September 11, 2001: Feminist Perspectives* (Spinifex 2002), and author of *Hijab and the Republic: Uncovering the French Headscarf Debate* (Syracuse University Press 2008). Her most recent articles venture far from France to cover post-9/11ism in the Philippines, and she is currently working on her next book, *9/11 Emergency: Did September 11, 2001 Change the World for Women?*

Index

Also available from Kumarian Press

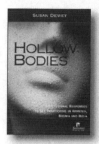

Hollow Bodies: Institutional Responses to Sex Trafficking in Armenia, Bosnia and India
Susan Dewey

"As a multisited ethnography that asks us to rethink an important policy issue, *Hollow Bodies* is applied anthropology at its best . . . Dewey has filled an important gap in our knowledge about discourses on trafficking at the local and global level." —*American Ethnologist*

"*Hollow Bodies* is a very, very good book. Susan Dewey's ethnographic cases of international and local officials, as some try to thwart traffickers while others become unwittingly complicit in trafficking, is so revealing. This is feminist investigating at its best."

—Cynthia Enloc, author of *Globalization and Militarism: Feminists Make the Link*

Reluctant Bedfellows: Feminism, Activism and Prostitution in the Philippines
Meredith Ralsto, Edna Keeble

"The book is commendable for its insightful portrayal of the authors' pains—but more so gains—as they put to action the ideologies of transnational feminism and transversal politics."

—*International Feminist Journal of Politics*

"I'm hard pressed to name another book of its kind that explores so passionately the question of ethics and morality in regard to transnational feminist action and the problems that drive a wedge between women of differing citizenship, privilege and culture . . . critical and compassionate." —*Bitch Magazine*

War's Offensive on Women: The Humanitarian Challenge in Bosnia, Kosovo, and Afghanistan
Julie A. Mertus

"Julie Mertus uses women's own voices and richly detailed case studies to show us precisely how so many humanitarian aid operations manage to ignore the experiences and needs of women in war zones. Mertus goes beyond the problems, and maps out pragmatic solutions."

—Cynthia Enloe, author of *Globalization and Militarism: Feminists Make the Link*

"Demonstrates a well-structured balance among an introductory overview of gender and humanitarian action, case studies, the changing legal framework of humanitarian and refugee law, and priorities for policy making." —*Signs*, Vol. 28, No. 4

Visit Kumarian Press at **www.kpbooks.com** or call **toll-free 800.232.0223** for a complete catalog.

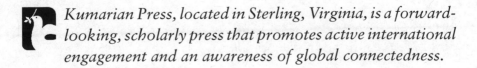
Kumarian Press, located in Sterling, Virginia, is a forward-looking, scholarly press that promotes active international engagement and an awareness of global connectedness.